Keto Instant Pot®

130+ Healthy Low-Carb Recipes
for Your Electric Pressure Cooker or Slow Cooker

 &

Maria Emmerich

Victory Belt Publishing

First Published in 2019 by Victory Belt Publishing Inc.

Copyright © 2019 Maria Emmerich

ISBN-13: 978-1628603-28-6

The author is not a licensed practitioner, physician, or medical professional and offers no medical diagnoses, treatments, suggestions, or counseling. The information presented herein has not been evaluated by the U.S. Food and Drug Administration, and it is not intended to diagnose, treat, cure, or prevent any disease. Full medical clearance from a licensed physician should be obtained before beginning or modifying any diet, exercise, or lifestyle program, and physicians should be informed of all nutritional changes.

The author/owner claims no responsibility to any person or entity for any liability, loss, or damage caused or alleged to be caused directly or indirectly as a result of the use, application, or interpretation of the information presented herein.

Instant Pot is a registered trademark of Instant Brands Inc. All other trademarks are the property of their respective owners. Victory Belt Publishing is not associated with any product or vendor mentioned in this book.

Front and back cover photos by Hayley Mason and Bill Staley

Recipe photos by Maria Emmerich

Cover design by Charisse Reyes

Interior design by Yordan Terziev and Boryana Yordanova

Printed in Canada

TC 0118

I want to dedicate this book to you—yes, you. Your support
has made this all possible. Thank you, thank you, thank you
from Maria, Craig, Micah, and Kai!

table of contents

"Food can be the most powerful form of medicine or the slowest form of poison."

—Ann Wigmore

introduction

You wouldn't put diesel fuel in a gasoline engine and expect it to run, but that's what many people are guilty of doing to their bodies on a daily basis. They fuel their bodies with processed, prepackaged foods that make those bodies stop running efficiently, as proven by evolutionary science. I was once guilty of this practice also.

I grew up with a passion for sports as well as food; my body shape revealed my two loves. I was athletic yet fat. Weight loss was difficult for me—until I found the right foods, and then it became easy. Overweight and frustrated, I decided to ditch the fake foods and throw out the government's recommendations to eat more whole grains. Instead, I included more fat and protein in my diet, especially for breakfast. (Skim milk in your cereal doesn't count as protein!) After decades of being told by marketing geniuses that "fat-free" was the way to lose weight, eating fat had become scary for me. Once I started adding fat to my diet, though, I slept more deeply, and in that first week I felt calmer and better than I ever had.

I soon learned the secrets of the hormone insulin and the lesser-known hormone leptin. By evolving toward a very low-glycemic, high-fat (not high-protein) diet, I resensitized my biochemistry to these essential hormones, which turn off severe food cravings. Best of all, my made-over diet required a lot less self-deprivation. The nutrient-rich, relatively high-fat approach that I have developed, which replaces starchy foods and sugar with healthier ingredients like almond flour and coconut flour, is what finally gave me total peace with food—something I had never imagined possible. The weight came off easily, and I lost even more than my original goal.

Before my revelation about the biochemistry of food and our weight, I was so proud of my "perfect" diet of whole grains, fruits, and fat-free desserts, but I was puzzled as to why I still had uncontrollable food cravings. By adopting a high–healthy fat, grain-free, starch-free diet and finding the right supplements to correct my biochemical imbalances, I finally found peace in my body. I didn't feel deprived or compelled to overeat.

The "secret" is to control insulin and leptin. Any diet that stops blood sugar and insulin spikes also allows the cells of the body to regain sensitivity to leptin, the noteworthy anti-aging and weight- and hunger-regulating hormone. The hardest part is to overcome the fear of fat, because it is almost impossible to obtain this effect without significant amounts of fat in your diet. High protein alone doesn't work, because excess protein also turns to sugar in the body. Low-fat, high-protein diets fail to prevent blood sugar spikes and do not allow leptin levels to increase. Ron Rosedale, MD, author of *The Rosedale Diet* and a pioneering scientist on leptin, states, "If you don't get enough fat, you will likely eat too much protein, which then turns to sugar."

I am writing this book for everyone who has been frustrated with the way they feel and for parents who want to start feeding their families real food—and possibly resolve some health-related issues along the way. Nutrition is a huge part of how we feel and function every day. I love feeling energetic and confident, and I want you to feel that way, too. I was miserable when I constantly deprived myself and felt guilty whenever I ate. I want everyone to find peace and enjoyment in real food, which can turn into holistic peace in everyday life.

how food changed my life

I am passionate about helping people heal their bodies through food because mainstream medicine has failed me and my family numerous times. I struggled with my weight and eating habits throughout adolescence and into adulthood. As an overweight sixteen-year-old, I lacked energy and didn't know why. After a visit to my doctor, I walked away with a prescription for an antidepressant; it wasn't the answer I was looking for.

That same week, my dog was losing patches of her hair. The veterinarian asked, "What are you feeding her?" It was like a light bulb turned on in my head. I went home and immediately changed my diet, too. I started limiting carbohydrates and focusing on nutrient-rich foods. Seeing results, I decided to pursue a degree in nutrition and physiology.

At seventeen, I met my future husband, Craig. After we married, I really just wanted to be a mom. Because I had polycystic ovary syndrome (PCOS), which can cause infertility, we looked into adoption. Just as we were making headway and getting excited about the possibility of becoming parents, Craig, an electrical engineer, lost his job.

We lost every penny. We lost our house, our cars, everything. We would go on dates to the library and vacation at my parents' cabin. That's when I started writing. What started as a cathartic stress-reliever quickly turned into something more. A friend read what I had written and told me, "You need to start a blog. Write down your recipes, put them in a cookbook, and raise money for your adoption."

A year and a half later, we adopted two boys from Ethiopia: Kai was four months old, and Micah was eighteen months. But it would be months before we could bring them home to Wisconsin.

About four months after we adopted the boys, Craig suffered another job loss. We kept it a secret for a while; it was such a scary time for us, and Craig didn't want to feel like he was failing his family. But because I was able to build a nutrition consulting

business and publish a number of bestselling books, and because I have the support of so many loyal readers, my boys now have the best stay-at-home dad ever! I thought motherhood was my calling, but as it turns out, being a mother is only one part of my story.

We have had some tough times, but Craig and I remain strong together. I am so grateful for each day.

Life for our family may seem easy now, but believe me, we still have difficulties. We are dealing with one of those trying times as I write this book. Four years ago, Craig developed chronic pain. When I say "chronic," I mean severe pain that kept him from living life with us. We blamed it on a slipped disc from an old football injury. The pain progressively got so bad that there were days he didn't want to get out of bed. His mood deteriorated, and he seemed to give up on life. He walked with an extreme hunchback, and his weight was down to 133 pounds. In the summer of 2017, I said, "Sweetie, you are only in your forties. You need to figure this out! You do not deserve to live like this!"

I described Craig's situation to a dear friend, and he told me that Craig likely had Lyme disease. I told my friend that Craig's doctor had tested him for Lyme three years earlier, and the test came back negative. My friend explained that the traditional Lyme test has a 90 percent false negative rate and urged us both to get a very expensive IGeneX test, which is believed to be more accurate. Sure enough, Craig's test came back positive (thankfully, mine did not), and we began the intense journey of healing from Lyme, which often causes people to get worse before they get better.

It was during this period of healing for Craig that I wrote this book. I often write during intense difficulties in my life because I need something to focus on. I sometimes wonder if I am given these trials because they push me to help others. I'm crying as I write this . . . I would not wish Lyme disease on my worst enemy!

As Craig focused on getting better, I started doing all the things he could no longer do, which meant that my multitasking nature went into overdrive. I felt like I had one too many balls in the air and was about to drop one at any time.

Eating keto was the only thing that helped minimize Craig's inflammation, so making healthy meals for him was a priority. While keeping up with the growing number of phone consults with my nutrition clients and creating keto courses to help educate others, I still made time to cook delicious keto meals. It was my Instant Pot and slow cooker that I relied on to accomplish this task day after day. These time-saving appliances made it possible for me to put healthy meals on the table without taking focus away from my life's work.

Keto isn't a diet for my family; it is a lifestyle. We love food, and we will always love food. But even more, we love the way we feel eating this way! That is why I spend so much time and money creating new recipes for you, my readers. I want you to be able to commit to the keto lifestyle 100 percent. Sure, planning and preparing meals takes time, but we all have to prioritize our time. When you feel and look amazing, you will not regret the time you put into it!

This book contains many of the recipes that I prepared while Craig was healing and I was continuing to grow my business. I've also adapted some of my all-time fan favorite recipes, such as protein noodle lasagna, shrimp scampi, flourless chocolate tortes, and ginger ale, for the Instant Pot! It was no small feat, but I enjoy a challenge.

Whatever your reason for seeking new keto recipes for your Instant Pot (or your slow cooker), I hope you find inspiration in these pages!

"A woman is like a tea bag;
you never know how
strong it is until you put it
in hot water."

—Eleanor Roosevelt

to pressure-cook or slow-cook?

I wrote this book for anyone seeking a wholesome, healthy solution to the question of what's for dinner, and who doesn't have hours to spend in the kitchen. The Instant Pot is the perfect solution: it cooks meals in lightning speed. The Instant Pot and other electric pressure cookers use super-hot steam to create a high-pressure environment, which cooks food in a fraction of the time it would take on the stovetop or in the oven, and certainly in a slow cooker.

Yet I realize that not all of you may have already purchased a pressure cooker. You may have reservations about using a pressure cooker, or you may be emotionally attached to your slow cooker; its "set it and leave it" style of cooking makes it a good solution for busy cooks, but it's not exactly fast. And, unlike a pressure cooker, you need to plan ahead when using a slow cooker.

If you are in love with your slow cooker and are on the fence about buying an Instant Pot, no worries—you can make the recipes in this book using your slow cooker. Because I want this book to work for everyone, almost every recipe includes instructions for using an Instant Pot *or* a slow cooker. But for those times when life gets hectic and you forget to plan eight hours ahead, you might want to consider buying an Instant Pot. An Instant Pot makes delicious meals in minutes versus hours in a slow cooker.

choosing an Instant Pot

An Instant Pot is a special brand of electric pressure cooker that takes the scariness out of pressure cooking. The cool thing about an Instant Pot is that it does more than just pressure-cook food; you can also use it to steam, sauté, slow-cook, and more. You can make everything from eggs to stews, meatloaf, and even cheesecake!

If you are going to purchase an Instant Pot, my suggestion is to get the largest model you can afford, preferably an 8-quart Instant Pot. With a bigger Instant Pot, you can make a large batch of a dish so that you have lots of leftovers—to me, the leftovers always taste better anyway. If you have a 6-quart Instant Pot, that's not a problem; the majority of the recipes in this book can be made in a 6-quart Instant Pot.

I also suggest getting an Instant Pot with a wide variety of functions. The available functions depend on the model of Instant Pot you purchase. Most models have a Sauté mode, a Pressure Cook

HELPFUL TIP: Get an 8-quart Instant Pot if you love making big batches of broth, want leftovers for easy meals, and want to make large cheesecakes.

(or Manual) mode, and a Slow Cook mode. Even though the majority of the recipes this book use the Sauté setting and/or the Pressure Cook/Manual setting, you will not be disappointed if you have an Instant Pot with multiple cooking functions for other recipes you want to try.

Whether you're using an Instant Pot or a slow cooker, I always suggest reading the manual that comes with your appliance before undertaking any recipe. This is especially important when you are first learning to use an electric pressure cooker; its safe use involves a few more steps than a slow cooker.

Instant Pot tips

I'll highlight some key steps in using an Instant Pot in this section, but note that these tips are not a replacement for reading the manual that comes with your appliance.

filling and sealing your Instant Pot

When using the Pressure Cook or Manual mode, the inner pot should not be filled more than two-thirds full.

Before beginning to pressure-cook, make sure that the steam release handle is in the Sealing position.

using the Instant Pot modes

There are many cooking options available on most Instant Pot models, including "Rice" and "Yogurt." I'll discuss the three most commonly used modes below.

Sauté · **Sauté (Brown)**
The most common temperature options for this setting are "Less," "Normal," and "More." In some models, the equivalent temperature options are "Low," "Medium," and "High" or simply "Low" and "High." Unless otherwise stated, I always use the "Normal" or "Medium" setting for the Sauté mode. If the only choice on your Instant Pot is "Low" or "High," use "High."

Please note that when using the Sauté mode, you should never have the lid on the pressure cooker.

Pressure Cook (or Manual)

`Manual`

The most common temperature options for this setting are "Less," "Normal," and "More." There are exceptions: In the Instant Pot MAX series, the equivalent temperature options are "Low," "High," and "MAX." In the LUX series, this mode is called "Manual," and to adjust the mode, you increase or decrease the pressure-cooking time.

Unless otherwise stated, I always use the middle setting for the Pressure Cook mode: "Normal" or "High," depending on the model.

Please note that whether the mode is called Pressure Cook or Manual, it is the same concept. With this knowledge, you can follow my recipes no matter what brand of multicooker or electric pressure cooker you have. Just pressure-cook for the time allotted in the directions.

Slow Cook

`Slow Cook`

The most common temperature options for this setting are "Less," "Normal," and "More." Unless otherwise stated, I always use the "Normal" setting for the Slow Cook mode. (If your Instant Pot model uses different terms for the temperature options, such as "Low," "Med," and "High," simply choose the middle, or medium, level.)

In this book, I use the Slow Cook mode to reheat food (see page 17). But you can, of course, use the Slow Cook mode to make slow-cooked meals in your Instant Pot, in lieu of using a traditional slow cooker. When you use your Instant Pot on the Slow Cook mode, the default time is 4 hours, and the temperature runs about medium-high, which is somewhere between a traditional slow cooker's low and high settings. One reason you may want to use the Slow Cook mode to cook a recipe is to have more time to serve dinner. On a busy evening, it is nice that family members can open the Instant Pot and eat warm, delicious, slow-cooked food as needed.

Cancel

`Cancel`

You use the Cancel button on the Instant Pot when you need to switch to another mode or when you need to stop the cooking altogether. When you press Cancel, the Instant Pot goes into standby mode.

releasing the pressure

When the food is done, you need to release the pressure from the cooker before you can safely open it. You have two options for doing so: natural release or quick release. I use both methods, depending on the recipe.

Note that the cooking times listed in the recipes in this book do not include time to release the pressure. Please make sure to factor this extra time into your planning.

natural release

With the natural release option, you let the Instant Pot cool down naturally until the float valve drops down. This can take anywhere from 10 to 40 minutes, depending on the amount of food in the cooker.

quick release

To quickly release the pressure, you turn the steam release handle to the Venting position. This lets steam out and causes the float valve to drop down. Be mindful: The escaping steam is extremely hot and can cause scalding. Please read the manual that came with your Instant Pot for more detailed safety instructions on using this method of releasing the pressure.

opening the lid

Once the internal pressure has been fully released and the cooker has cooled, you may open the lid. Before you open the lid, the float valve should be in the down position. If the float valve is still in the up position or you find that it's difficult to turn the lid, the Instant Pot is still pressurized. Never force open the lid.

diagnosing Instant Pot fails

Several recipe testers helped me perfect the recipes in this book. If a recipe didn't taste fantastic, I didn't include it. If you try one of these recipes and yours doesn't turn out as expected, here are some common problems that can occur when you are cooking with an Instant Pot:

The seal was broken.

This is why I keep multiple sealing rings in a drawer (see page 18). If you do not seal your Instant Pot properly, food will not pressure-cook, or it will take longer to cook. You may notice a loud sound or hear air leaking out of the pot if the seal isn't properly in place. The sealing rings also can fail after frequent use.

You used a larger or smaller piece of protein than the recipe calls for.

For example, one of my testers used boneless chicken thighs instead of the larger boneless chicken breasts specified in the ingredient list for the Easy Reuben Chicken recipe on page 232. She said it was delicious but overcooked. If you decide to use a different size, cut, or type of protein, make sure to adjust the cooking time accordingly.

Condensation leaked in.

Water can ruin recipes, especially cheesecakes. Skipping a step such as placing a paper towel over a dish can cause it to curdle or cause a sauce like the one in the Alfredo Veggies recipe on page 80 to become too watery.

You substituted coconut flour for almond flour.

Coconut flour is completely different from almond flour. The recipes are tested exactly as written, so if you change an ingredient, I can't promise the best result. That said, here is a handy chart for baking with coconut flour:

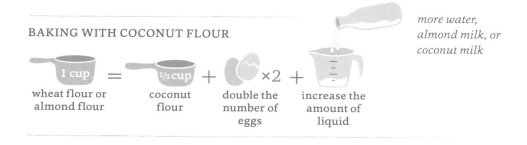

BAKING WITH COCONUT FLOUR

1 cup wheat flour or almond flour = 1/3 cup coconut flour + double the number of eggs ×2 + increase the amount of liquid

more water, almond milk, or coconut milk

reheating leftovers in an Instant Pot

You can use an Instant Pot not just to cook, but also to reheat leftovers. Specific reheating instructions are included with the recipes in this book. Below are my general reheating tips using the most common Instant Pot cooking modes.

  ## Slow Cook

This mode works great for reheating soups and drinks such as hot chocolate (page 312).

 Time: The timing is flexible; anything more than 5 minutes works. I like reheating soups using the Slow Cook setting because I can turn it on to reheat, and my family can scoop out some soup whenever they want to eat it. Select Less to heat foods gently, make sure the venting is set to either the right or the left, and then select Slow Cook.

BEST RECIPES TO REHEAT ON SLOW COOK MODE:

Soup recipes (pages 88–143)

Stuffed mushrooms (pages 68 and 72)

Sauté

This mode works nicely for recipes that you want to recrisp on the outside, such as Melt-in-Your-Mouth Pork Belly (page 192). Make sure to add a tablespoon of fat to the pot before adding leftovers for reheating.

 Time: On average, 2 to 3 minutes per side of a piece of meat will be just enough time to heat it through and recrisp the outside.

BEST RECIPES TO REHEAT ON SAUTÉ MODE:

BBQ Shrimp 272

Pesto Fish Packets 274

 ## Keep Warm

I like this mode for any recipe that is made in a casserole dish. You place the leftovers in a 1-quart casserole dish and use a foil sling (see page 19) to lower the dish into the Instant Pot. Cover the pot with a glass lid and press the "Keep Warm" button. Periodically check to see if contents such as cheese are melted.

Time: The timing is flexible here, too; anything more than 5 minutes works. I like this setting because I can turn it on to reheat, and we can eat whenever we are ready.

BEST RECIPES TO REHEAT ON KEEP WARM MODE:

Crustless Quiche Lorraine 48

Pizza Dip

Crab Rangoon Dip 60

Asian Orange Short Ribs 170

Santa Fe Meatloaf 146

White Fish Poached in Garlic Cream Sauce 278

my top Instant Pot accessories

The following accessories will make cooking with an Instant Pot easier! The costs are approximate.

1. Extra Stainless-Steel Inner Cooking Pot

The Instant Pot comes with one inner cooking pot. I like to have a few extras because I often store leftovers right in the pot, which means fewer dirty dishes to clean. Too often I would get frustrated that I didn't have a clean inner pot when I wanted to test a recipe. So I bought a few more, and I was super happy that I did! Be sure to buy inner pots that fit your Instant Pot.

Cost: $30

2. Extra Sealing Rings

If you use your Instant Pot a lot, which I think you will after making my recipes, you will want to buy a few extra rings to ensure a proper seal.

Cost: $10

It's helpful to have different rings for savory, sweet, and seafood dishes. Flavors transfer easily, and using different rings for different types of foods helps ensure that your cheesecake won't have a fishy taste! You can even buy different colors of rings and designate one color for seafood, one for savory foods, and one for sweet recipes.

3. Glass Lid

If you love slow cooking like I do, then you will want a glass lid for the Slow Cook setting on your Instant Pot (as I suggest using in the reheating instructions on page 17). You can see what's cooking (or reheating) inside the pot.

Cost: $10

4. Silicone Lid

A silicone lid is great if you are a minimalist like me. All you do is secure the silicone lid over the inner cooking pot and store the leftovers in the fridge; there's no need to transfer the food to another container, and one less dish to wash!

Cost: $10

5. Gripper Clips

I invested in gripper clips after getting burned too many times while trying to lift hot food out of the Instant Pot. These are totally worth the money in my eyes!

Cost: $9

6. Foil Sling

A foil sling allows you to easily lift a cake pan or casserole dish out of an Instant Pot or slow cooker. You can also use it to gently lower a pan or dish into the cooking pot. To make a foil sling, take a 2½-foot square piece of foil and fold up one long edge in 2-inch increments. Keep folding until you have a 2½-foot by 2-inch piece of foil. Set the foil sling on a trivet in the Instant Pot with the long edges hanging out and then set the pan on top of the sling.

Cost: <$1

NOTE: Keep the foil sling for future recipes that require you to lift out a pan or dish, such as Crustless Quiche Lorraine (page 48), which is made in a 1-quart casserole dish, and Cinnamon Roll Cheesecake (page 292), which is made in a 7-inch springform pan.

7. 4-Ounce Ramekins or Mason Jars

You do not want to miss out on my Crème Brûlée (page 284), Deconstructed Tiramisu (page 290), and Upside-Down Maple Bacon Mini Cheesecakes (page 306), and you can't make any of those recipes if you don't have the right-sized ramekins on hand! Ramekins of this size are also handy for making baked eggs (page 52) and mini meatloaves (pages 152 and 158). Mason jars can also be used for this purpose.

Cost: $12

8. 1-Quart Casserole Dish

A 1-quart casserole dish is great for making a variety of keto recipes in your Instant Pot, such as Protein Noodle Lasagnas (page 172) and Alfredo Veggies (page 80).

Cost: $15

9. 6-Cup Bundt Pan

I didn't use to have a Bundt pan that fit into my 8-quart Instant Pot. However, when I was creating a couple of the delicious recipes for this book—the Glazed Pumpkin Bundt Cake (page 302) and the Maple-Glazed Zucchini Bundt Cake (page 308)—I found that a 6-cup Bundt pan fits perfectly.

Cost: $11

10. Steamer Basket

I use my Instant Pot steamer basket for cooking fish and for the Mashed Cauliflower recipe on page 330. The steamer basket has a perfectly designed little handle that helps you lift the basket from the pot when your dish is finished (and keeps you from burning your hand). Some models are sold with an extra sealing ring, which is always nice to have.

Cost: $15

11. **Stackable Steamer Pans**

I love using stackable steamer pans to reheat leftovers in my Instant Pot. They're awesome for heating two different dishes at one time. For example, I'll place Swedish Meatballs (page 156) in one pan and Sesame Broccoli (page 78) in the other. Then I'll seal the lid, press Manual (the equivalent of Pressure Cook on other models), set the timer for 5 minutes, and . . . ta-da! Dinner is ready in an Instant (Pot)!

Cost: $15

12. **7-Inch Springform Pan**

A springform pan is great for making cheesecakes: a 7-inch pan fits perfectly in a 6-quart or an 8-quart Instant Pot.

Cost: $7–12

BONUS *Instant Pot accessory:*

Egg Steamer Rack

This accessory is a bonus because I like to keep things simple. I've made hard-boiled eggs in my Instant Pot without a special egg steamer rack; however, if you like gadgets, an egg rack is a great way to prevent eggs from rolling around and breaking.

Cost: $10

using a slow cooker

A slow cooker enables you to cook foods slowly all day or over time, without needing to hover over the stove. You can literally walk away, especially if you own the type of slow cooker with a built-in timer that you can set to shut off the cooker after a set amount of time. Its gentle long-cooking works perfectly to tenderize inexpensive cuts of meat, making it a good choice for a family on a budget.

Most slow cookers have only two or three settings, and while excellent at slow cooking, their function is much more limited than those of the newest generation of electric pressure cookers, such as the Instant Pot.

That said, I still sometimes pull out my slow cooker and use it to prepare "set-it-and-forget-it" recipes, especially on weekends when I'm in less of a rush. I typically use the low setting when preparing recipes in a traditional slow cooker.

Slow cookers vary in size from less than 0.5 quart to 10 quarts. A 6-quart slow cooker will work for nearly all the recipes in this book, because you can almost always make a recipe that calls for a smaller slow cooker, such as a 4-quart size, in a larger slow cooker (but, obviously, this does not work in reverse!). Occasionally, a recipe will call for an 8-quart slow cooker. All of these recipes can be halved if needed to be prepared in a smaller slow cooker.

slow cooker tips

1. I often prep ingredients and fill my slow cooker the night before while my kids help clean up after dinner; before the boys were old enough to assist, my husband, Craig, helped while we chatted about the day. For example, if a recipe calls for browning or searing meat, dicing an onion, or mincing garlic, I do all that work the night before. Then I put the prepped ingredients in the insert of the slow cooker and set it in the fridge. This helps minimize stress the next day because I don't need to worry about what we are going to eat that night!

2. I also prep any fixings, toppings, or garnishes needed to complete a meal the night before, such as slicing lime wedges, cleaning fresh herbs, or cleaning lettuce leaves for wraps. That makes the next night's dinner easy as pie!

3. It is best to cook grass-fed cuts of meat on the slow cooker's low setting. The lower the heat, the less "gamey" the meat will taste.

4. Cauliflower "rice" is a great accompaniment to many slow cooker meals. Prepare it the night before by pulsing cauliflower in a food processor until you have rice-sized pieces. All you have to do is stir-fry the cauli-rice in a little butter just before serving your slow cooker meal over it.

5. Store Low-Carb Loaf Bread (page 326) and other keto bread options in the freezer for easy additions to slow cooker meals. I always have keto bread and buns in my freezer. If you do not have any bread prepared, you can always wrap foods in lettuce!

planning for success

We all know that preparing food at home is important for many reasons. For one, you are in control of the ingredients to make your meals as healthy as possible. You can choose sauces and seasoning mixes without hydrogenated oils, high-fructose corn syrup, artificial colors, gluten, artificial sweeteners, or added sugar.

But making food at home can be daunting. As a working mom of two boys, healthy eating is a priority for me. I get asked all the time, "How do you it all? How do you run a thriving nutrition business, home-school your children, work out, and still find time to get delicious keto meals on the table?"

I plan ahead! This way, I can enjoy life. I was even paddle boarding in Maui and watching for humpback whales while typing notes on my iPhone about these tips. No lie—I was multitasking!

Plan, Plan, Plan = *Success*

"Always start out with a larger pot than what you think you need."

—Julia Child

top 10 meal-prep tips

Here are my best meal-prep tips for success on a ketogenic diet. Before you nail down this meal-prep habit, I suggest that you set an alarm on your phone every evening to remind yourself to do a few simple prep tasks. And if you forget to prep, no worries: the Instant Pot and slow cooker directions are at your fingertips!

 *1.* Make a list of the recipes you want to try, then read through the recipes in their entirety to be sure that you understand the steps involved and that you have enough time to make them.

 *2.* Make a grocery list and shop for ingredients! Be sure to include freezer bags and labels on your list.

 *3.* Lay out the ingredients for the recipes you want to prepare.

 *4.* Label each bag with the name of the dish, the date, and any further directions needed.

 *5.* Clean, chop, and prep the ingredients: for example, dice onions and bell peppers and roast or mince garlic.

 *6.* Place meats and other proteins in the freezer bags, add the veggies, and then top with other ingredients, like sauces.

 *7.* Press out any air, seal the bags, and lay them flat.

 *8.* Freeze and relax!

 *9.* The night before you want to make a meal, simply remove the prepped ingredients from the freezer to thaw. Even if you forget to defrost the ingredients, you can still cook the recipe from frozen. Simply add five minutes to the pressure cooking time or two hours on low if using a slow cooker. Again, rejoice that you don't have a huge mess to clean up!

10. Better yet, double each recipe, and you'll have two weeks' worth of meals to enjoy!

top 5 "starter" recipes

If you're looking for some basic (and all-time favorite!) recipes to get started with, here are some of my go-tos. I make these all the time. The last four on the list, while great on their own, are also perfect for use in other recipes and as the base for many different meals.

Reuben Soup
88

Five-Ingredient Pork Roast
196

Roast Chicken
222

Healing Bone Broth
320

Hard-Boiled Eggs
331

top 10 freezer recipes

I love to prepare meals with my kids. It's a great way to teach them a life skill while enjoying time with them. The boys help me prep the ingredients, and then we put the prepped ingredients in containers, label them, and freeze them, as outlined on the preceding page. When it's time to make the meal, all I have to do is pop the frozen ingredients into my slow cooker and cook on low while I work all day. Or, if I forgot to plan ahead, I pop the ingredients into my Instant Pot and add five extra minutes to the pressure-cooking time listed in the recipe. Here are my favorite freezer-meal recipes:

Santa Fe Meatloaf
146

Swedish Meatballs
156

Corned Beef & Cabbage
164

Barbacoa
178

Sweet 'n' Sour Pork
194

Sesame Chicken
226

Chicken Asparagus Rolls
234

Chicken with Mushroom Cream Sauce
240

Chicken Cordon Bleu
248

Italian Salmon
258

recipes that reheat in minutes!

What is a busy person supposed to eat when work runs long and there's nothing prepared? Well, here are my favorite recipes to refrigerate for up to five days and reheat quickly. Many of these dishes freeze well, too!

 88
Reuben Soup

 96
Pumpkin Chili

 128
Egg Roll Soup

 136
Broccoli Cheddar Soup

 146
Santa Fe Meatloaf

 150
Lamb Vindaloo

 160
BBQ Short Ribs

 164
Corned Beef & Cabbage

 174
Korean Rib Wraps

 180
Chili Cheese Dog Casserole

 224
Buffalo Chicken Lettuce Wraps

 244
Chicken & Bacon Lasagna Roll-Ups

 332
Mama Maria's Marinara Sauce

keto ingredients

The key to any healthy diet is eating real, whole foods. When following a ketogenic diet, you'll want to seek out certain keto-friendly ingredients and avoid others.

fats

On a keto diet, you need lots of healthy fat to burn as fuel. As important as it is to seek out healthy fats, it's just as critical to avoid unhealthy fats.

Healthy Fats

Fats with high amounts of saturated fatty acids (SFAs)—such as coconut oil, MCT oil, butter, ghee, lard, and tallow—are best. They are stable and anti-inflammatory, protect against oxidation, and have many other important health benefits. Organic and grass-fed sources are always best.

On the opposite page is a chart of the best oils and fats to use, with their SFA and polyunsaturated fatty acid (PUFA) contents.

If you're not dairy-sensitive, the following are great healthy, keto-friendly dairy fats to include in your diet in addition to those oils and fats listed in the chart:

- Butter: 50% SFA, 3.4% PUFA
- Ghee: 48% SFA, 4% PUFA
- Heavy cream: 62% SFA, 4% PUFA
- Cream cheese: 56% SFA, 4% PUFA
- Cheddar cheese: 64% SFA, 3% PUFA
- Sour cream: 58% SFA, 4% PUFA
- Crème fraîche: 64% SFA, 3% PUFA

Note: You may be able to tolerate ghee even if you're dairy-sensitive because the milk proteins have been removed.

WHAT IS MCT OIL?

MCT stands for "medium-chain triglycerides," which are chains of fatty acids. MCTs occur naturally in coconut oil, palm oil, and dairy, and they're particularly helpful on a keto diet because the body uses them quickly. Any MCTs not immediately used by the body are converted to ketones.

MCT oil is extracted from coconut or palm oil and contains concentrated levels of MCTs, so it's great for adding ketones to your diet. When MCT oil appears in a recipe in this book, it's always my first choice, but to make the recipes as accessible as possible, I've provided alternative oil choices as well.

Fat	SFA	PUFA	Notes
Almond oil	8.2%	17%	• Has a mild, neutral flavor • Works great in sweet dishes and Thai dishes • Use for nonheat applications, such as salad dressings • Can also be used on the skin
Avocado oil	11%	10%	• Has a mild, neutral flavor • Works great in savory and sweet dishes • Can be heated
Beef tallow	49.8%	3.1%	• Has a mild beef flavor • Works great in savory dishes • Can be heated
Cocoa butter	60%	3%	• Has a mild cocoa flavor • Works great in sweet and savory dishes • Can be heated
Coconut oil	92%	1.9%	• Has a strong coconut flavor • Works great in sweet dishes and Thai dishes • Can be heated • Can also be used on the skin
Duck fat	25%	13%	• Has a rich duck flavor • Works great for frying savory foods • Can be heated
Extra-virgin olive oil*	14%	9.9%	• Has a strong olive flavor • Works great in Italian dressings • Use for nonheat applications, such as salad dressings
Hazelnut oil	10%	14%	• Has a mild hazelnut flavor • Works great in sweet dishes and Thai dishes • Use for nonheat applications, such as salad dressings
High oleic sunflower oil	8%	9%	• Has a mild sunflower seed flavor • Works great in sweet dishes and Thai dishes • Use for nonheat applications, such as salad dressings
Lard	41%	12%	• Has a mild flavor • Works great for frying sweet or savory foods • Can be heated
Macadamia nut oil	15%	10%	• Has a mild nutty flavor • Works great in salad dressings • Use for nonheat applications, such as salad dressings
MCT oil**	97%	less than 1%	• Has a neutral flavor • Works great in savory dishes and baked goods • Can be heated to no higher than 320°F
Palm kernel oil***	82%	2%	• Has a neutral flavor • Works great in baked goods • Can be heated

*Extra-virgin olive oil is great for cold applications, such as salad dressings, but should not be used for cooking; heat causes the oil to oxidize, which is harmful to your health.

**MCT oil can be found at most health food stores. If you have trouble finding it, you can use avocado oil, macadamia nut oil, or extra-virgin olive oil instead, keeping in mind that avocado oil is the most neutral-flavored of the three.

***Be sure to purchase sustainably sourced and processed palm kernel oil. There are ecological concerns associated with some palm oils.

Unhealthy Fats

You should avoid two kinds of fat on a ketogenic diet: trans fats and polyunsaturated fatty acids (PUFAs).

Trans fats are the most inflammatory fats; in fact, in terms of health, they are among the worst substances that we can consume. Many studies have shown that eating foods containing trans fats increases the risk of heart disease and cancer.

Here is a list of trans fats to avoid at all costs:

- Hydrogenated or partially hydrogenated oils (check ingredient labels)
- Margarine
- Vegetable shortening

You should limit your consumption of PUFAs because they are prone to oxidation. Many cooking oils are high in PUFAs. Here is a list of the most common ones:

Fat	PUFA
Grapeseed oil	70.6%
Sunflower oil	68%
Flax oil	66%
Safflower oil	65%
Soybean oil	58%
Corn oil	54.6%
Walnut oil	53.9%
Cottonseed oil	52.4%
Vegetable oil	51.4%
Sesame oil	42%
Peanut oil	33.4%
Canola oil	19%

PURCHASING KETO-FRIENDLY INGREDIENTS

You can purchase keto-friendly fats and other pantry products in most grocery stores. They're also available on my website, MariaMindBodyHealth.com/store.

To save money, I recommend buying ingredients in bulk—including perishables like meat and fresh veggies. You can freeze them (a chest freezer is a great investment!) and thaw them when you need them.

Remember, choosing the best-quality organic foods is always best.

proteins

 It's always best to choose grass-fed or pasture-raised meats and wild-caught seafood. Not only do they have more nutrients, but they also haven't been exposed to added hormones, antibiotics, or other potential toxins. For help choosing sustainably sourced seafood, check out the Monterey Bay Aquarium Seafood Watch app and website, seafoodwatch.org.

Farmed Meats

- Beef
- Goat
- Lamb
- Pork

Game Meats

- Bear
- Boar
- Buffalo
- Elk
- Rabbit
- Venison

Poultry

- Chicken
- Duck
- Game hen
- Goose
- Ostrich
- Partridge
- Pheasant
- Quail
- Squab
- Turkey

Eggs

- Chicken eggs
- Duck eggs
- Goose eggs
- Ostrich eggs
- Quail eggs

Fish

- Catfish
- Cod
- Haddock
- Halibut
- Herring
- Mackerel
- Mahi mahi
- Sablefish
- Salmon
- Sardines
- Snapper
- Swordfish
- Tilapia
- Trout
- Tuna
- Walleye

Seafood/Shellfish

- Clams
- Crab
- Lobster
- Mussels
- Oysters
- Prawns
- Scallops
- Shrimp
- Snails

The charts on the next two pages list the calories, macronutrients, and fiber contents of common cuts of meat and types of seafood. You can read more about choosing quality eggs on pages 32 and 33.

NUTRITIONAL INFO (in grams, per 4 ounces)

Beef	CALORIES	FAT	PROTEIN	CARBS	FIBER	% FAT	% PROTEIN	% CARBS
Rib-eye steak	310	25.0	20.0	0.0	0.0	73%	26%	0%
Rib roast	373	28.0	27.0	0.0	0.0	69%	30%	0%
Beef back ribs	310	26.0	19.0	0.0	0.0	75%	25%	0%
Porterhouse steak	280	22.0	21.0	0.0	0.0	70%	30%	0%
T-bone steak	170	12.2	15.8	0.0	0.0	64%	36%	0%
Top loin steak	270	20.0	21.0	0.0	0.0	67%	31%	0%
Tenderloin roast	180	8.0	25.0	0.0	0.0	40%	56%	0%
Tenderloin steak	122	3.0	22.2	0.0	0.0	60%	40%	0%
Tri-tip roast	340	29.0	18.0	0.0	0.0	77%	21%	0%
Tri-tip steak	200	11.0	23.0	0.0	0.0	50%	46%	0%
Top sirloin steak	240	16.0	22.0	0.0	0.0	60%	37%	0%
Top round steak	180	9.0	25.0	0.0	0.0	45%	56%	0%
Bottom round roast	220	14.0	23.0	0.0	0.0	57%	42%	0%
Bottom round steak	220	14.0	23.0	0.0	0.0	57%	42%	0%
Eye round roast	253	13.4	32.0	0.0	0.0	48%	51%	0%
Eye round steak	182	9.0	25.0	0.0	0.0	45%	55%	0%
Round tip roast	199	12.0	22.9	0.0	0.0	54%	46%	0%
Round tip steak	150	6.0	23.5	0.0	0.0	36%	63%	0%
Sirloin tip center roast	190	7.0	31.0	0.0	0.0	33%	65%	0%
Sirloin tip center steak	190	7.0	31.0	0.0	0.0	33%	65%	0%
Sirloin tip side steak	190	6.0	34.0	0.0	0.0	28%	72%	0%
Skirt steak	255	16.5	27.0	0.0	0.0	58%	42%	0%
Flank steak	200	8.0	32.0	0.0	0.0	36%	64%	0%
Shank cross cut	215	6.7	38.7	0.0	0.0	28%	72%	0%
Brisket flat cut	245	14.7	28.0	0.0	0.0	54%	46%	0%
Chuck 7 bone pot roast	240	14.0	28.0	0.0	0.0	53%	47%	0%
Chuck boneless pot roast	240	14.0	28.0	0.0	0.0	53%	47%	0%
Chuck steak boneless	160	8.0	22.0	0.0	0.0	45%	55%	0%
Chuck eye steak	250	18.0	21.0	0.0	0.0	65%	34%	0%
Shoulder top blade steak	204	13.0	22.0	0.0	0.0	57%	43%	0%
Shoulder top blade flat iron	204	13.0	22.0	0.0	0.0	57%	43%	0%
Shoulder pot roast	185	7.0	30.7	0.0	0.0	34%	66%	0%
Shoulder steak	204	12.0	24.0	0.0	0.0	53%	47%	0%
Shoulder center ranch steak	152	8.0	24.0	0.0	0.0	40%	60%	0%
Shoulder petite tender	150	7.0	22.0	0.0	0.0	42%	59%	0%
Shoulder petite tender medallions	150	7.0	22.0	0.0	0.0	42%	59%	0%
Boneless short ribs	440	41.0	16.0	0.0	0.0	84%	15%	0%

NUTRITIONAL INFO (in grams, per 4 ounces)

Pork	CALORIES	FAT	PROTEIN	CARBS	FIBER	% FAT	% PROTEIN	% CARBS
Chop	241	12.0	33.0	0.0	0.0	45%	55%	0%
Loin	265	15.5	30.8	0.0	0.0	53%	46%	0%
Hocks	285	24.0	17.0	0.0	0.0	76%	24%	0%
Leg ham	305	20.0	30.4	0.0	0.0	59%	40%	0%
Rump	280	16.2	32.8	0.0	0.0	52%	47%	0%
Tenderloin	158	4.0	30.0	0.0	0.0	23%	76%	0%
Middle ribs (country style)	245	16.0	25.0	0.0	0.0	59%	41%	0%
Loin back ribs (baby back ribs)	315	27.0	18.0	0.0	0.0	77%	23%	0%
Belly	588	60.0	10.4	0.0	0.0	92%	7%	0%
Shoulder	285	23.0	19.0	0.0	0.0	73%	27%	0%
Butt	240	18.0	19.0	0.0	0.0	68%	32%	0%
Bacon	600	47.2	41.8	0.0	0.0	71%	28%	0%

NUTRITIONAL INFO (in grams, per 4 ounces)

Poultry	CALORIES	FAT	PROTEIN	CARBS	FIBER	% FAT	% PROTEIN	% CARBS
Chicken breast, skinless	138	4.0	25.0	0.0	0.0	26%	72%	0%
Chicken breast, skin-on	200	8.4	31.0	0.0	0.0	38%	62%	0%
Chicken leg, skinless	210	9.5	30.7	0.0	0.0	41%	58%	0%
Chicken leg, skin-on	255	15.2	29.4	0.0	0.0	54%	46%	0%
Chicken thigh, skinless	165	10.0	19.0	0.0	0.0	55%	46%	0%
Chicken thigh, skin-on	275	17.6	28.3	0.0	0.0	58%	41%	0%
Chicken wings	320	22.0	30.4	0.0	0.0	62%	38%	0%
Chicken drumstick	178	9.9	22.0	0.0	0.0	50%	49%	0%
Game hen	220	16.0	19.0	0.0	0.0	65%	35%	0%
Pheasant	200	10.5	25.7	0.0	0.0	47%	51%	0%
Turkey	175	9.9	21.0	0.0	0.0	51%	48%	0%
Goose	340	24.9	28.5	0.0	0.0	66%	34%	0%
Duck	228	13.9	26.3	0.0	0.0	55%	46%	0%

NUTRITIONAL INFO (in grams, per 4 ounces)

Fish	CALORIES	FAT	PROTEIN	CARBS	FIBER	% FAT	% PROTEIN	% CARBS
Tuna (yellowfin)	150	1.5	34.0	0.0	0.0	9%	91%	0%
Tuna (canned)	123	0.8	27.5	1.5	0.0	6%	89%	5%
Salmon	206	9.0	31.0	0.0	0.0	39%	60%	0%
Anchovies	256	15.9	28.0	0.0	0.0	56%	44%	0%
Sardines	139	7.5	18.0	0.0	0.0	49%	52%	0%
Barramundi	110	2.0	23.0	0.0	0.0	16%	84%	0%
Trout	190	8.6	28.0	0.0	0.0	41%	59%	0%
Walleye	156	7.5	22.0	0.0	0.0	43%	56%	0%
Cod	113	1.0	26.0	0.0	0.0	8%	92%	0%
Sea bass	135	3.0	27.0	0.0	0.0	20%	80%	0%
Halibut	155	3.5	30.7	0.0	0.0	20%	79%	0%
Mackerel	290	20.3	27.0	0.0	0.0	63%	37%	0%
Arctic Char	208	10.0	29.0	0.0	0.0	43%	56%	0%

NUTRITIONAL INFO (in grams, per 4 ounces)

Seafood/Shellfish	CALORIES	FAT	PROTEIN	CARBS	FIBER	% FAT	% PROTEIN	% CARBS
Scallops	97	1.0	19.0	3.0	0.0	9%	78%	12%
Mussels	97	2.8	13.5	4.5	0.0	26%	56%	19%
Clams	82	1.1	15.0	3.0	0.0	12%	73%	15%
Shrimp	135	2.0	25.8	1.7	0.0	18%	78%	4%
Oysters	58	1.9	6.5	3.1	0.0	29%	33%	38%
Crab	107	2.0	22.0	0.0	0.0	17%	82%	0%
Lobster	116	1.8	25.0	0.0	0.0	14%	86%	0%
Caviar	260	12.0	31.0	8.0	0.0	42%	48%	12%

Finding the Best-Quality Eggs

Eggs are an amazingly nutritious food, especially the yolks, which are full of choline, healthy fats, and a ton of flavor. And high-quality eggs—those from healthy, happy, humanely raised hens—are even more nourishing and tastier. So which eggs are the best quality?

Brown or white eggs

There's absolutely no difference in quality between brown and white eggs; the only thing that determines the color of an egg is the breed of the hen. Do not choose eggs based on color.

Egg grades

Eggs can be grade AA, A, or B. There is little to no difference in the taste, though, and no difference in nutritional value. Grade AA eggs have the thickest, firmest whites and high, round yolks. This grade of egg is virtually free of defects and is best for frying, poaching, or other methods where presentation is important. Grade A eggs are the same quality as grade AA, but the whites are categorized as "reasonably" firm. Most grade B eggs are sold to restaurants, bakeries, and other food institutions and are used to make liquid, frozen, and dried egg products.

Vegetarian fed

All this label means is that the hens have been fed a diet based on corn (which is usually genetically modified). To ensure that the hens consume a strictly vegetarian diet, they are kept in cages. But chickens are natural omnivores; they evolved to eat insects, worms, and grubs as well as grass and grains. They weren't meant to be vegetarians!

Certified organic

This label means that the hens are kept in barns rather than cages. They are required to have access to the sun, but that doesn't necessarily mean they can go outside; there may be a small window in the barn for sunlight. The hens are fed an organic vegetarian diet that is free of antibiotics and pesticides. This label is regulated with inspections.

Free-range or cage-free

This sounds like a good choice, right? Well, all these terms really mean is that the hens are not caged. There is no requirement to let the hens outside; there are no mandatory inspections to regulate this claim; and there are no guidelines for what the birds should be fed.

Omega-3 enriched

This label indicates that the hens' feed has extra omega-3 fatty acids added to it in the form of flaxseed. But eggs already are a good source of omega-3s, so there's no need to seek out eggs bearing this label.

Since most of the terms used on egg labels don't help us figure out which eggs are healthiest, here are some guidelines to follow when egg shopping:

- Be conscious of antibiotic and hormone use. While the USDA prohibits the use of hormones for egg production, and the use of therapeutic antibiotics is illegal unless hens are ill, these rules aren't always enforced. The only way to ensure that the hens were not given antibiotics is to purchase certified organic eggs.

- To guarantee that you eat truly free-range eggs, purchase eggs from pastured hens. Pastured hens can eat their natural diet of greens, seeds, worms, and bugs, and studies show that eggs from pastured hens may contain more omega-3 fatty acids, vitamins, and minerals than eggs from other hens.

- Smaller eggs tend to have thicker shells than large eggs and therefore are less likely to become contaminated by bacteria.

- Be cautious of unregulated labels. Terms like "natural" and "cage-free" are frequently used, but these claims may not necessarily be valid. Claims on eggs with the USDA shield have been verified by the United States Department of Agriculture, so always look for the shield when purchasing eggs from a store.

EGG REPLACER

The only keto egg replacer that I recommend for people who cannot tolerate eggs is unflavored gelatin. In place of one egg, use 1 tablespoon of gelatin mixed with 3 tablespoons of water. I don't recommend chia or flax seeds because of their estrogenic properties as well as their high total carb count.

nuts and seeds

Small portions of nuts and seeds are fine on a keto diet, but they can take some people with metabolic syndrome out of ketosis. If you are extremely metabolically damaged and your goal is to lose weight, I suggest limiting your consumption of ketogenic dishes that use almond flour, nuts, or seeds; use those recipes in moderation, not every day. There are so many recipes to choose from that you will never feel deprived! Nuts are also constipating, so if you suffer from lack of stool elimination, I suggest limiting or cutting out nuts altogether, along with dairy.

veggies

Fresh vegetables are packed with nutrients and are an important part of a ketogenic diet, but it's important to choose nonstarchy vegetables, which are lower in carbs than starchy vegetables, to ensure that you stay in ketosis. The following are some of the nonstarchy vegetables that I use most:

- Arugula
- Asparagus
- Bok choy
- Broccoli
- Cabbage
- Cauliflower
- Celery
- Collard greens
- Endive
- Garlic
- Kale
- Kelp
- Lettuce: Boston, radicchio, red leaf, romaine
- Mushrooms
- Onions: green, red, white, yellow
- Peppers: bell peppers, chilies, jalapeños
- Seaweed
- Swiss chard
- Watercress

herbs and spices

Fresh herbs are the most nutritious plants you can consume. For example, everyone thinks spinach is an amazingly nutritious food, but fresh oregano has eight times the amount of antioxidants! Sure, you don't eat a cup of oregano, but it goes to show that a little bit of an herb provides a huge benefit. Here are some of my favorite herbs and spices:

- Anise
- Annatto
- Basil
- Bay leaf
- Black pepper
- Caraway seed
- Cardamom
- Cayenne pepper
- Celery seed
- Chervil
- Chili powder
- Chives
- Cilantro
- Cinnamon
- Cloves
- Coriander
- Cumin
- Curry powder
- Dill
- Fenugreek
- Galangal
- Ginger powder
- Lemongrass
- Licorice
- Mace
- Marjoram
- Mint
- Mustard seed
- Oregano
- Paprika
- Parsley
- Peppermint
- Rosemary
- Saffron
- Sage
- Spearmint
- Star anise
- Tarragon
- Thyme
- Turmeric powder
- Vanilla beans

fruits

We tend to think of fruit as a health food, but in reality, most fruits are full of carbs and sugar. In fact, studies show that the produce we consume today is lower in nutrients and much higher in sugar than it was in Paleolithic times.

In general, you should avoid high-sugar fruits like bananas, grapes, and mangoes on a ketogenic diet. But that doesn't mean you have to avoid all fruits! I once made a keto fruit salad of cucumbers, olives, eggplant, and capers, all covered in a Greek vinaigrette (see page 260 for my dressing recipe). So yes, fruits are certainly allowed. Just seek out those that are low in sugar, including the following.

- Avocados
- Cucumbers
- Eggplant
- Lemons
- Limes
- Olives
- Seasonal wild berries (in moderation)
- Tomatoes

beverages

It probably goes without saying that you should avoid sodas and fruit juices—they're full of sugar that will raise your blood glucose and kick you out of ketosis. But that doesn't mean you're limited to drinking water! You can consume all of these beverages on a ketogenic diet.

- Green tea
- Mineral water
- Organic decaf caffè Americano (espresso mixed with water)
- Unsweetened almond milk
- Unsweetened cashew milk
- Unsweetened coconut milk
- Unsweetened hemp milk

When it comes to plain water, reverse osmosis is best.

baking products

Yes, you can have baked goods on keto! See pages 37 and 38 for recommended sweeteners.

- Baking powder and/or soda
- Blanched almond flour
- Cocoa butter
- Coconut flour
- Egg white protein powder (check carbs and added ingredients—I recommend Jay Robb brand)
- Guar gum (a thickener)
- Maca powder
- Unsweetened baking chocolate
- Unsweetened cocoa powder
- Xanthan gum (a thickener)

sauces and flavor enhancers

- Coconut aminos or organic wheat-free tamari (note that tamari is more potent, so you don't need to use as much)

- Fish sauce

- Hot sauce

- Pure vanilla extract and other flavored extracts

- Vinegars: apple cider, balsamic, coconut, rice, red wine, white wine

canned and jarred foods

It is always better to buy fresh ingredients, but here are some keto-friendly foods that are also great canned or jarred:

- Banana peppers
- Capers
- Coconut milk (full-fat)
- Fermented pickles*
- Fermented sauerkraut*
- Marinara sauce (check for oils and added sugars)**
- Olives (choose jarred over canned)
- Paleo mayo (made with avocado oil)

- Pickled eggs
- Pickled herring
- Pizza sauce (check for oils and added sugars)**
- Salmon
- Sardines
- Tomato paste**
- Tomato sauce**
- Tuna

*Not only is fermenting a great way to preserve food, but it also creates beneficial gut bacteria and helpful digestive enzymes. Fermented sauerkraut is particularly rich in B vitamins.

**When it comes to tomato products, make sure you buy jarred, never canned. The linings of cans often contain BPA, a chemical that's associated with several health problems and may affect children's development. Tomatoes' high acidity can cause more BPA to leach into the food.

other convenience items

- Boxed beef, chicken, and/or vegetable broth
- EPIC bars (made from grass-fed meat—but check for added sugars)

- Mikey's English Muffins
- Nori wraps
- Pure Wraps

natural sweeteners

In my recipes, I always use natural sweeteners. Just as sugarcane and honey are found in nature, so are erythritol and the stevia herb.

However, I prefer not to use sweeteners such as honey, maple syrup, and agave in my recipes because, even though they're natural, they raise blood sugar, which not only causes inflammation but also will take you out of ketosis.

Fructose is particularly problematic. More than glucose, it promotes a chemical reaction called *glycation,* which results in advanced glycation end products (AGEs). AGEs form a sort of crust around cells that has been linked with a wide range of diseases, from diabetes and heart disease to asthma, polycystic ovary syndrome, and Alzheimer's. Fructose also contributes to nonalcoholic fatty liver disease. For these reasons, I avoid sweeteners that are high in fructose: table sugar, high-fructose corn syrup, honey, agave, and fruit.

The following is a list of the natural sweeteners that I do recommend, all of which have little effect on blood sugar.

Erythritol
Erythritol is a sugar alcohol that is found naturally in some fruits and fermented foods. It is generally available in granulated form, though sometimes you can find it powdered. If you purchase a granulated product, such as Sukrin or Wholesome! All-Natural Zero, I recommend grinding it to a powder before using it.

Swerve and other blended sweeteners
These products combine two zero-calorie natural sweeteners, erythritol (see above) and oligosaccharides, which are found in many plants. They do not affect blood sugar and measure cup for cup like table sugar. I use the powdered form of Swerve (the one labeled "confectioners") because it dissolves particularly well. I also recommend Pyure (erythritol and stevia), Norbu (erythritol and monk fruit), Natvia (erythritol and stevia), Lakanto (erythritol and monk fruit), and Zsweet (erythritol and stevia).

Stevia
Stevia is available as a powder or a liquid. Because it is so concentrated, many companies add bulking agents like maltodextrin to the powdered form so that it's easier to bake with. Stay away from those products. Look for products that contain only stevia or stevia combined with another natural, keto-friendly sweetener.

Stevia glycerite
This is a thick liquid form of stevia that is similar in consistency to honey. Do not confuse it with liquid stevia, which is much more concentrated. Stevia glycerite is about twice as sweet as sugar, making it a bit less sweet than liquid or powdered stevia. I prefer stevia glycerite because, unlike powdered and liquid stevia, it has no bitter aftertaste. Stevia glycerite is great for cooking because it maintains its flavor when heated. However, it doesn't caramelize or create bulk, so most baking recipes call for combining it with another sweetener.

Monk fruit

Also known as lo han kuo, monk fruit comes in pure liquid and powdered forms. Because it is 300 times sweeter than sugar, the powdered form is typically bulked up with another sweetener so that it measures cup for cup like sugar. Check the ingredients for things like maltodextrin and only buy brands that add keto-friendly sweeteners, such as erythritol.

Xylitol

Xylitol is a naturally occurring low-calorie sweetener found in fruits and vegetables. It has a minimal effect on blood sugar and insulin. Xylitol has been known to kick some people out of ketosis, so if you're using it in baking or cooking, monitor your ketones closely and stop using it if you find that you're no longer in ketosis.

Yacón syrup

This thick syrup is pressed from the yacón root and tastes a bit like molasses. I use yacón syrup sparingly—a tablespoon here and there to improve the texture and flavor of sauces—both because it is very expensive and because it has some fructose in it.

Blending Sweeteners for the Tastiest Keto Treats

I don't write recipes like this because it causes a lot of confusion for people who are new to keto, but to make the best-tasting desserts, I like to blend three different natural sweeteners. For example, if a recipe calls for 1 cup of confectioners'-style Swerve, I use:

| 1 cup Swerve | 1 tsp stevia glycerite | 10 to 15 drops of liquid monk fruit |

So if you think that desserts made with Swerve have too much of an aftertaste or a cooling effect on your mouth, I highly recommend that you try making baked goods and keto ice cream with this combination of sweeteners.

Adding a pinch of salt also increases the sweetness of a dish because salt is a flavor enhancer.

Using Sweeteners in the Recipes in This Book

If you're trying keto for the first time, the recipes in this book should have just the right amount of sweetness. But as you continue with a ketogenic lifestyle, you may find that foods naturally begin to taste sweeter, and you may want to reduce the amount of sweetener used in the recipes.

Whenever a recipe requires a powdered sweetener, my go-to choice is the powdered (confectioners) form of Swerve because it gives a smoother finished product and better overall result. That said, you can always pulverize a granular form of erythritol, such as Wholesome! All-Natural Zero, in a blender or clean coffee grinder to get a powdered texture.

If a recipe calls for a specific sweetener or form of sweetener (such as powdered or liquid), do not substitute any other sweetener; these recipes rely on these particular sweeteners. For example, in recipes where the sweetener has to melt, some products won't work—so it's important to use exactly what's called for.

If a sweetener in an ingredient list is followed by "or equivalent," such as "¼ cup Swerve confectioners'-style sweetener or equivalent amount of liquid or powdered sweetener," you are free to use any keto-friendly sweetener, liquid or powdered. For example, you could use liquid stevia, stevia glycerite, monk fruit, Zsweet, or xylitol.

If you prefer to use a keto-friendly sweetener other than Swerve, here are the conversion ratios:

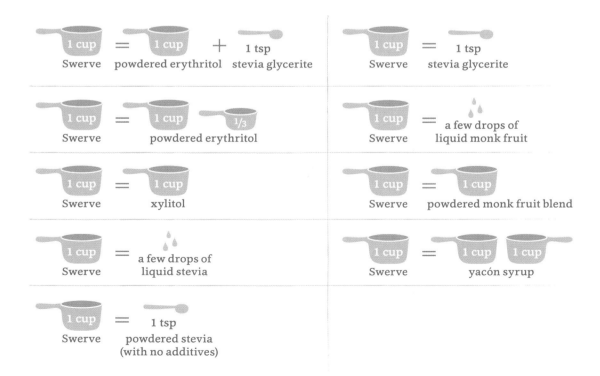

using the recipes in this book

This book's 130-plus recipes include some handy features to help you along on your keto journey. The main instructions for each recipe are for the Instant Pot; slow cooker directions are listed at the bottom, marked with this icon:

icons

I've marked the recipes with a number of icons, as applicable. First, there are icons highlighting those recipes that are free of dairy, eggs, and/or nuts, which are problematic for some people:

If a recipe as written isn't free of a particular allergen but a substitution or omission will make it free of that allergen, you will see the word OPTION below the icon, like this:

I have also noted which recipes are vegetarian for those of you who follow a vegetarian keto lifestyle or frequently seek out meat-free meals. Look for this icon:

At the back of the book, I've included handy charts showing which recipes fall into each of these categories; see pages 334 to 336.

The main instructions for each recipe are for the Instant Pot; slow cooker directions are listed at the bottom, marked with this icon:

nutritional information

I've also included nutritional information for each recipe, listing the total calories along with the fat, protein, carbohydrate, and fiber counts in grams, as shown below. You will find this information helpful as you fine-tune your personal targets for these macronutrients. Optional ingredients and garnishes are not included in these calculations.

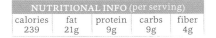

NUTRITIONAL INFO (per serving)				
calories	fat	protein	carbs	fiber
239	21g	9g	9g	4g

breakfast

pumpkin coffee cake

yield: one 7-inch round cake (8 servings) *prep time:* 10 minutes *cook time:* 30 minutes

This cake is so rich and creamy that it reminds me of pumpkin cheesecake, yet it is much easier and more affordable to make than a cheesecake because it contains less almond flour, fewer eggs, and no butter (unless you opt to use butter in the topping).

STREUSEL TOPPING:

¼ cup blanched almond flour

¼ cup Swerve confectioners'-style sweetener or equivalent amount of powdered sweetener (see page 39)

2 tablespoons coconut oil or unsalted butter, softened

½ teaspoon ground cinnamon

CAKE:

2 cups blanched almond flour

¾ cup Swerve confectioners'-style sweetener or equivalent amount of powdered sweetener (see page 39)

½ teaspoon fine sea salt

1 cup pumpkin puree

2 large eggs, beaten

2 teaspoons pumpkin pie spice

2 teaspoons vanilla extract

GLAZE:

3 tablespoons unsweetened almond milk, plus a little more if needed

½ cup Swerve confectioners'-style sweetener or equivalent amount of powdered sweetener (see page 39)

1. Set a trivet in a 6-quart Instant Pot and pour in 1 cup of cold water. Grease the sides of a 7-inch round cake pan and line the bottom with greased parchment paper.

2. Make the streusel topping: In a small bowl, mix together the topping ingredients with a fork.

3. Make the cake batter: In a medium-sized bowl, mix together the cake ingredients until thoroughly combined.

4. Scoop half of the batter into the prepared cake pan, then sprinkle half of the streusel topping on top. Repeat with the remaining batter and topping.

5. Use a foil sling (see page 19) to lower the cake pan onto the trivet in the Instant Pot. Tuck in the sides of the sling.

6. Seal the lid, press Pressure Cook or Manual, and set the timer for 30 minutes. Once finished, let the pressure release naturally. When the pressure has fully released, lift the cake pan out of the Instant Pot using the foil sling.

7. Meanwhile, make the glaze: Whisk together the almond milk and sweetener in a small bowl, until slightly runny in consistency. If the glaze is too thick, add a little more milk.

8. Allow the cake to cool in the pan for 10 minutes, then invert onto a plate and peel off the parchment paper. Then invert again onto a serving platter. Spoon the glaze over the top of the cake.

Grease a 4-quart slow cooker. Cut a sheet of parchment paper to fit the bottom and grease it well. Complete Steps 2 through 4, scooping the batter directly into the prepared slow cooker. Cover and cook on low for 3 to 4 hours, until a toothpick inserted in the center comes out clean. Complete Steps 7 and 8 to make the glaze and serve the cake.

STORE in an airtight container in the fridge for up to a week or in the freezer for up to a month.

NUTRITIONAL INFO (per serving)				
calories	fat	protein	carbs	fiber
239	21g	9g	9g	4g

blueberry cereal

option

yield: 4 servings *prep time:* 5 minutes *cook time:* 2 minutes

2 tablespoons Swerve confectioners'-style sweetener or equivalent amount of liquid or powdered sweetener (see page 39)

⅓ cup crushed roasted almonds, pecans, or walnuts

¼ cup blanched almond flour

¼ cup vanilla-flavored egg white protein powder

¼ cup (½ stick) unsalted butter (or coconut oil for dairy-free), softened

1 teaspoon blueberry extract

1 teaspoon ground cinnamon

Unsweetened vanilla-flavored almond milk, for serving (optional)

1. Place all of the ingredients in a 3-quart or larger Instant Pot. Stir well to combine.

2. Seal the lid, press Pressure Cook or Manual, and set the timer for 2 minutes. (The pressure ball may not rise much, but it needs only enough heat to create a crispy cereal after cooling.) Once finished, let the pressure release naturally.

3. Stir well, then pour the cereal onto a sheet of parchment paper to cool. It will be crispy when completely cool. Serve the cereal in bowls. Pour almond milk over the cereal, if desired.

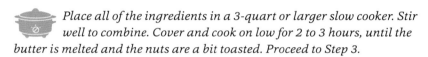 *Place all of the ingredients in a 3-quart or larger slow cooker. Stir well to combine. Cover and cook on low for 2 to 3 hours, until the butter is melted and the nuts are a bit toasted. Proceed to Step 3.*

STORE in an airtight container in the fridge for up to a week or in the freezer for up to a month.

NOTE: If you use coconut oil instead of butter, this cereal is "shelf stable" and doesn't need to be refrigerated—perfect for outings and trips!

NUTRITIONAL INFO (per serving)				
calories	fat	protein	carbs	fiber
283	25g	10g	7g	4g

crustless quiche lorraine

yield: 4 servings   *prep time:* 5 minutes   *cook time:* 37 minutes

4 strips bacon, chopped

2 cups sliced button or cremini mushrooms

½ cup diced onions

8 large eggs

1½ cups shredded Gruyère or Swiss cheese (about 6 ounces)

1 cup unsweetened almond milk

¼ cup sliced green onions, plus more for garnish if desired

½ teaspoon fine sea salt

¼ teaspoon ground black pepper

2 tablespoons coconut flour

1. Place the bacon in a 6-quart Instant Pot. Press Sauté and cook, stirring often, until crisp, about 4 minutes. Remove with a slotted spoon and place on a paper towel–lined plate to drain, leaving the drippings in the pot.

2. Sauté the mushrooms and diced onions in the bacon drippings for 3 minutes, or until the onions are soft. Press Cancel to stop the Sauté. Remove from the pot and set aside in a large bowl. Wipe the Instant Pot clean.

3. Set a trivet in the Instant Pot and pour in 1 cup of cold water.

4. In a medium-sized bowl, whisk together the eggs, cheese, almond milk, green onions, salt, and pepper. Pour the egg mixture into the bowl with the mushrooms and onions and stir to combine. Mix in the coconut flour. Pour the quiche mixture into a greased 1-quart round casserole dish. Top with the cooked bacon.

5. Use a foil sling (see page 19) to lower the casserole dish onto the trivet in the Instant Pot. Tuck in the sides of the sling.

6. Seal the lid, press Pressure Cook or Manual, and set the timer for 30 minutes. Once finished, let the pressure release naturally. Lift the casserole dish out of the Instant Pot using the foil sling.

7. Allow the quiche to cool for 15 to 30 minutes before serving, then cut into 4 pieces. Garnish with more sliced green onions, if desired.

 *Line the bottom and sides of a 4-quart slow cooker with parchment paper, leaving some overhanging. Grease the paper well. In a medium-sized skillet over medium heat, cook the bacon until crisp. Remove the bacon, leaving the drippings in the skillet, and set on a paper towel–lined plate to drain. In the same skillet, sauté the mushrooms and onions in the bacon drippings over medium-high heat until the onions are soft. Remove from the skillet and set aside in a large bowl. Proceed to Step 4, but pour the quiche mixture directly into the lined slow cooker. Cover and cook on low for 4 to 5 hours, until a knife inserted in the center of the quiche comes out clean. Use the parchment paper to lift the quiche out of the slow cooker, then complete Step 7.*

STORE in an airtight container in the fridge for up to a week or in the freezer for up to a month. To reheat, place in a 350°F oven for 5 minutes, or until heated through.

NUTRITIONAL INFO (per serving)				
calories	fat	protein	carbs	fiber
434	30g	31g	7g	2g

granola

yield: 12 servings *prep time:* 5 minutes *cook time:* 2 minutes

2 cups chopped raw pecans

½ cup chopped raw walnuts

½ cup slivered almonds

1 cup sunflower seeds

½ cup sesame seeds

1¾ cups vanilla-flavored egg white protein powder

1¼ cups (2½ sticks) unsalted butter or coconut oil, softened

½ cup Swerve confectioners'-style sweetener or equivalent amount of liquid or powdered sweetener (see page 39)

1 teaspoon ground cinnamon

½ teaspoon fine sea salt

Unsweetened vanilla-flavored almond milk, for serving (optional)

1. Place all of the ingredients in a 3-quart or larger Instant Pot. Stir well to combine.

2. Seal the lid, press Pressure Cook or Manual, and set the timer for 2 minutes. (The pressure ball may not rise much, but it needs only enough heat to create a crispy granola after cooling.) Once finished, let the pressure release naturally.

3. Stir well and pour the granola onto a sheet of parchment paper to cool. It will become crispy when completely cool.

4. Serve the granola in bowls. Pour almond milk over the granola, if desired.

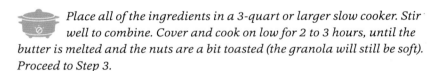

Place all of the ingredients in a 3-quart or larger slow cooker. Stir well to combine. Cover and cook on low for 2 to 3 hours, until the butter is melted and the nuts are a bit toasted (the granola will still be soft). Proceed to Step 3.

STORE in an airtight container in the fridge for up to a week or in the freezer for up to a month.

NOTE: If you use coconut oil rather than butter, this granola is "shelf stable" and doesn't need to be refrigerated—perfect for outings and trips!

NUTRITIONAL INFO (per serving)				
calories	fat	protein	carbs	fiber
492	44g	17g	9g	5g

easy baked eggs

option *yield:* 2 servings *prep time:* 5 minutes *cook time:* 5 minutes

4 large eggs, beaten

4 slices ham, diced (omit for vegetarian)

½ cup shredded cheddar cheese (about 2 ounces)

½ cup heavy cream

½ teaspoon fine sea salt

Pinch of ground black pepper

Fresh herbs of choice, for garnish (optional)

1. Grease two 4-ounce ramekins. In a large bowl, whisk the eggs, ham (if using), cheese, cream, salt, and pepper until well combined. Divide the egg mixture equally between the ramekins.

2. Set a trivet in a 6-quart Instant Pot and pour in 1 cup of cold water. Use a foil sling (see page 19) to lower the ramekins onto the trivet. Tuck in the sides of the sling.

3. Seal the lid, press Pressure Cook or Manual, and set the timer for 5 minutes. Once finished, turn the valve to venting for a quick release. Lift the ramekins out of the Instant Pot using the foil sling.

4. Serve garnished with fresh herbs, if desired.

Complete Step 1, then place the ramekins in a 6-quart slow cooker. Add enough hot water to the slow cooker to come about halfway up the sides of the ramekins; this ensures even baking and a creamy texture. Cover and cook on high for 2 hours, or until the eggs are just set and still a little jiggly in the middle. Proceed to Step 4.

STORE in an airtight container in the fridge for up to 3 days. To reheat, place in a preheated 350°F oven for 5 minutes, or until heated through.

NUTRITIONAL INFO (per serving)				
calories	fat	protein	carbs	fiber
592	51g	33g	3g	0.2g

pumpkin pie breakfast pudding

option option

yield: 4 servings   *prep time:* 5 minutes   *cook time:* 5 minutes

1 cup pumpkin puree

4 ounces cream cheese (½ cup)
(or Kite Hill brand cream cheese
style spread for dairy-free),
softened

¼ cup heavy cream (or
unsweetened almond milk for
dairy-free)

½ cup Swerve confectioners'-style
sweetener or equivalent amount
of liquid or powdered sweetener
(see page 39)

2 large eggs

1 teaspoon ground cinnamon

1 teaspoon pumpkin pie spice

Chopped raw walnuts, for garnish
(optional; omit for nut-free)

1. Place all of the ingredients except the walnuts in a food processor and purée until smooth. Divide the puree among four 4-ounce ramekins or mason jars.

2. Set a trivet in a 6-quart Instant Pot and pour in 1 cup of cold water. Use a foil sling (see page 19) to lower the ramekins onto the trivet.

3. Seal the lid, press Pressure Cook or Manual, and set the timer for 5 minutes. Once finished, turn the valve to venting for a quick release. Lift the ramekins out of the Instant Pot using the foil sling.

4. Serve warm or chilled. Garnish with chopped walnuts, if desired.

Complete Step 1. Pour 1 cup of hot water into an 8-quart slow cooker. Place the ramekins in the slow cooker. Cover and cook on low for 3 hours, or until the pudding has thickened and coats the back of a spoon. Proceed to Step 4.

STORE in an airtight container in the fridge for up to 5 days.

NUTRITIONAL INFO (per serving)				
calories	fat	protein	carbs	fiber
202	17g	6g	5g	1g

appetizers & sides

buffalo wings with blue cheese dressing

 yield: 16 servings *prep time:* 5 minutes *cook time:* 10 minutes

3 pounds chicken wingettes

Fine sea salt and ground black pepper

SAUCE:

3 cups Buffalo wing sauce

2 tablespoons unsalted butter or coconut oil, melted

1 teaspoon hot sauce

BLUE CHEESE DRESSING:

2½ ounces blue cheese, crumbled

3 tablespoons beef broth, homemade (page 320) or store-bought

3 tablespoons sour cream

2 tablespoons mayonnaise

2 teaspoons white wine vinegar

⅛ teaspoon garlic powder

Fine sea salt and ground black pepper, to taste

Celery sticks, for serving

1. Pat the chicken wings dry and season well with salt and pepper.

2. Set a trivet in a 6-quart Instant Pot and pour in ½ cup of cold water. Set the wings on the trivet. Seal the lid, press Pressure Cook or Manual, and set the timer for 5 minutes. Once finished, let the pressure release naturally.

3. Meanwhile, place an oven rack one notch above the center position and preheat the oven to broil. Lay a sheet of parchment paper on a rimmed baking sheet.

4. Make the sauce: Place the wing sauce, butter, and hot sauce in a large bowl and mix together. Remove the chicken wings from the Instant Pot and add to the sauce; toss to coat the wings with the sauce.

5. Place the coated wings on the lined baking sheet and broil for 5 minutes, or until crispy on the edges.

6. Meanwhile, make the dressing: Place all of the dressing ingredients in a medium-sized bowl and stir well to combine.

7. Serve the wings with the blue cheese dressing and celery sticks.

Complete Step 1. Place the wing sauce, butter, and hot sauce in a 6-quart slow cooker and stir to combine. Add the chicken wings, stirring to coat with the sauce. Cover and cook on low for 3 to 4 hours, until the juices run clear when the thickest part of a wing is cut to the bone (or the internal temperature reaches 165°F). Complete Step 3, then proceed to Step 5.

STORE in an airtight container in the fridge for up to 5 days or in the freezer for up to a month. To reheat, place in a preheated 400°F oven for 5 minutes, or until heated through.

NUTRITIONAL INFO (per serving)				
calories	fat	protein	carbs	fiber
213	15g	15g	6g	3g

crab rangoon dip

 yield: 4 servings *prep time:* 5 minutes *cook time:* 30 minutes

2 (8-ounce) packages cream cheese, softened

4 green onions, chopped

2 tablespoons peeled and grated fresh ginger

1½ teaspoons coconut aminos

½ teaspoon lemon juice

2 tablespoons Swerve confectioners'-style sweetener or equivalent amount of liquid or powdered sweetener (see page 39)

½ teaspoon garlic powder

2 cups fresh lump crab meat, or 3 (6-ounce) cans lump crab meat

Sliced green onions, for garnish

Pork rinds and/or sliced bell peppers (any color), for serving

1. Place the cream cheese, green onions, ginger, coconut aminos, lemon juice, sweetener, and garlic powder in a food processor and blend until smooth. Gently stir in the crab meat.

2. Set a trivet in a 6-quart Instant Pot and pour in ½ cup of cold water. Grease a 1-quart round casserole dish, then spread the dip mixture in an even layer in the dish. Use a foil sling (see page 19) to lower the casserole dish onto the trivet in the Instant Pot. Tuck in the sides of the sling.

3. Seal the lid, press Pressure Cook or Manual, and set the timer for 30 minutes. Once finished, let the pressure release naturally. Lift the casserole dish out of the Instant Pot using the foil sling.

4. Garnish with sliced green onions. Serve with pork rinds and/or bell pepper strips.

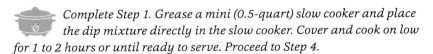 *Complete Step 1. Grease a mini (0.5-quart) slow cooker and place the dip mixture directly in the slow cooker. Cover and cook on low for 1 to 2 hours or until ready to serve. Proceed to Step 4.*

STORE in an airtight container in the fridge for up to 5 days. To reheat, place in a preheated 350°F oven for 5 minutes, or until warmed to your liking.

NUTRITIONAL INFO (per serving)				
calories	fat	protein	carbs	fiber
491	40g	24g	5g	1g

pizza hit breadsticks

 yield: 6 servings   *prep time:* 15 minutes   *cook time:* 30 minutes

SEASONING:

¼ cup grated Parmesan cheese (about ¾ ounce)

3 tablespoons garlic powder

1 tablespoon onion powder

1 tablespoon dried oregano leaves

BREADSTICKS:

1¼ cups whole-milk ricotta cheese (10 ounces), homemade (page 322) or store-bought

½ cup coconut flour

1 teaspoon baking powder

5 large eggs

½ teaspoon fine sea salt

Pizza Dip (page 64) or marinara sauce, homemade (page 332) or store-bought, for serving

1. Set a trivet in a 6-quart Instant Pot and pour in ½ cup of cold water. Line a 7-inch round cake pan or springform pan with parchment paper, then grease the parchment.

2. Make the seasoning: Put the Parmesan cheese, garlic powder, onion powder, and oregano in a small bowl and stir well to combine.

3. Make the breadsticks: Place the ricotta, coconut flour, baking powder, eggs, salt, and ¼ cup of the seasoning in a large bowl and mix using a hand mixer until very smooth. Scoop the dough into the prepared pan and smooth the top. Sprinkle with the remaining seasoning.

4. Use a foil sling (see page 19) to lower the pan onto the trivet in the Instant Pot. Tuck in the sides of the sling.

5. Seal the lid, press Pressure Cook or Manual, and set the timer for 30 minutes. Once finished, let the pressure release naturally. Lift the pan out of the Instant Pot using the foil sling.

6. Let the bread rest for 10 minutes, then invert onto a plate and peel off the parchment. Then invert again onto a cutting board. Once cool, cut the bread into 1-inch-wide sticks. Serve with Pizza Dip or marinara.

Line a 6-quart slow cooker with parchment paper, leaving some overhanging, then grease the parchment. Complete Steps 2 and 3, scooping the dough into the lined slow cooker. Cover and cook on low for 5 to 7 hours, until the bread is baked through. Lift the bread out of the slow cooker using the parchment. Proceed to Step 6.

STORE in an airtight container in the fridge for up to a week or in the freezer for up to a month. To reheat, place on a baking sheet in a preheated 350°F oven for 4 minutes, or until warmed to your liking.

NUTRITIONAL INFO (per serving)				
calories	fat	protein	carbs	fiber
214	13g	12g	10g	4g

pizza dip

 yield: 4 servings *prep time:* 5 minutes *cook time:* 30 minutes

¾ cup whole-milk ricotta cheese (6 ounces), homemade (page 322) or store-bought

¾ cup marinara sauce, homemade (page 332) or store-bought, or pizza sauce

1 clove garlic, minced

6 ounces Italian cheeses, finely grated (¾ cup)

TOPPING OPTIONS:

Sliced cooked sausage

Sliced pepperoni

Sliced bell peppers

Sliced black olives

Sliced mushrooms

Sliced onions

Pizza Hit Breadsticks (page 62) or pork rinds, for serving (use pork rinds for egg-free)

1. Set a trivet in a 6-quart Instant Pot and pour in ½ cup of cold water. Grease a 1-quart round casserole dish. Spread the ricotta in an even layer in the greased dish.

2. In a medium-sized bowl, stir together the marinara and garlic. Pour the sauce over the ricotta and spread evenly. Layer the shredded cheese over the sauce, then layer your favorite pizza toppings on top.

3. Use a foil sling (see page 19) to lower the casserole dish onto the trivet in the Instant Pot. Tuck in the sides of the sling.

4. Seal the lid, press Pressure Cook or Manual, and set the timer for 30 minutes. Once finished, let the pressure release naturally. Lift the casserole dish out of the Instant Pot using the foil sling.

5. Serve with breadsticks or pork rinds.

Grease a mini (0.5-quart) slow cooker. Spread the ricotta in an even layer directly in the slow cooker. Complete Step 2. Cover and cook on low for 2 to 4 hours, until the cheeses are melted. Proceed to Step 5.

STORE in an airtight container in the fridge for up to 5 days. To reheat, place in a preheated 350°F oven for 5 minutes, or until heated through.

NUTRITIONAL INFO (per serving)				
calories	fat	protein	carbs	fiber
262	21g	17g	4g	1g

tender mexican spice wings

  yield: 10 servings *prep time:* 5 minutes *cook time:* 10 minutes

30 chicken wingettes or drumettes

3 tablespoons melted coconut oil or bacon fat

TACO SEASONING:

1 tablespoon chili powder

½ tablespoon ground cumin

1 teaspoon fine sea salt

½ teaspoon garlic powder

½ teaspoon onion powder

½ teaspoon paprika

FOR SERVING:

Guacamole

Lime wedges

1. Pat the chicken dry and place in a large bowl. Pour the melted coconut oil over the chicken and toss to coat.

2. Make the taco seasoning: Place the ingredients in a small bowl and stir to combine. Sprinkle on all sides of the wings.

3. Set a trivet in a 6-quart Instant Pot and pour in ½ cup of cold water. Place the chicken on the trivet. Seal the lid, press Pressure Cook or Manual, and set the timer for 5 minutes. Once finished, let the pressure release naturally.

4. Meanwhile, place an oven rack one notch above the center position and preheat the oven to broil. Place a piece of parchment paper on a rimmed baking sheet.

5. Place the chicken on the lined baking sheet and broil for 5 minutes, or until crispy on the edges. Serve with guacamole and lime wedges.

Complete Steps 1 and 2. Place the seasoned chicken in a 4-quart or larger slow cooker. Cover and cook on low for 3 to 4 hours, until the juices run clear when the thickest part of a piece of chicken is cut to the bone (or the internal temperature reaches 165°F). Proceed to Step 4.

STORE in an airtight container in the fridge for up to 5 days or in the freezer for up to a month. To reheat, place in a preheated 400°F oven for 5 minutes, or until heated through.

NUTRITIONAL INFO (per serving)				
calories	fat	protein	carbs	fiber
164	14g	10g	2g	1g

crab-stuffed mushrooms

 yield: 6 servings *prep time:* 5 minutes *cook time:* 6 minutes

18 medium-sized button mushrooms

¼ cup plus 2 tablespoons grated Parmesan cheese (about 1 ounce)

3 tablespoons mayonnaise

3 tablespoons sour cream

1 teaspoon minced garlic

1 (6½-ounce) can lump crab meat, rinsed and drained well, or 1 cup fresh crab meat

Dash or two of hot sauce, to taste

Ground black pepper, to taste

Sliced green onions, for garnish

1. Wash the mushrooms and remove the stems. Set the caps aside on a paper towel to dry. Discard the stems.

2. Put the Parmesan cheese, mayonnaise, sour cream, and garlic in a small bowl and stir to combine. Fold in the crab meat. Add the hot sauce and pepper and stir gently. Spoon a heaping teaspoon of the crab filling into each mushroom cap.

3. Set a trivet in a 6-quart Instant Pot and pour in ½ cup of cold water. Arrange the mushroom caps, filling side up, in a 1-quart round casserole dish. Use a foil sling (see page 19) to lower the casserole dish onto the trivet. Tuck in the sides of the sling.

4. Seal the lid, press Pressure Cook or Manual, and set the timer for 6 minutes. Once finished, turn the valve to venting for a quick release. Lift the casserole dish out of the Instant Pot using the foil sling.

5. Garnish with sliced green onions. Best served warm.

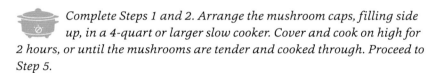 *Complete Steps 1 and 2. Arrange the mushroom caps, filling side up, in a 4-quart or larger slow cooker. Cover and cook on high for 2 hours, or until the mushrooms are tender and cooked through. Proceed to Step 5.*

STORE in an airtight container in the fridge for up to a week or in the freezer for up to a month. To reheat, place in a preheated 350°F oven for 5 minutes, or until heated through.

NUTRITIONAL INFO (per serving)				
calories	fat	protein	carbs	fiber
113	8g	8g	2g	1g

mexican meatballs

 yield: 4 servings   *prep time:* 5 minutes   *cook time:* 14 minutes

1 tablespoon coconut oil

¼ cup chopped onions

2 cloves garlic, minced

1 teaspoon fine sea salt

2 pounds ground beef

3 cups salsa, divided

1 large egg

½ teaspoon ground cumin

Shredded cheddar cheese, for garnish (omit for dairy-free)

Guacamole, for serving (optional)

1. Place the coconut oil in a 6-quart or larger Instant Pot and press Sauté. Once melted, add the onions and garlic, season with the salt, and sauté until the onions are translucent, about 4 minutes. Transfer the onion mixture to a small bowl and set aside to cool. Press Cancel to stop the Sauté.

2. Put the ground beef, 1 cup of the salsa, the egg, and cumin in a large bowl. When the onion mixture is no longer hot to the touch, add it to the bowl with the meat and work everything together with your hands. (To check for seasoning, see the Tip below.)

3. Shape the meat mixture into eight 2-inch balls and place the meatballs in the Instant Pot, leaving a little space between them. Pour the remaining 2 cups of salsa around the meatballs.

4. Seal the lid, press Pressure Cook or Manual, and set the timer for 10 minutes. Once finished, let the pressure release naturally.

5. To serve, transfer the sauce and meatballs to a large serving platter. Garnish with shredded cheddar cheese and serve with guacamole, if desired.

Complete Steps 1 and 2 using a small skillet over medium heat to sauté the onions and garlic. Shape the meat mixture into eight 2-inch balls and place the meatballs in a 6-quart or larger slow cooker. Cover and cook on low for 6 to 8 hours, until the meatballs are cooked through and firm to the touch. Drain any fat from the slow cooker. Pour in the remaining 2 cups of salsa, cover, and cook on low for 30 more minutes. Proceed to Step 5.

STORE in an airtight container in the fridge for up to a week or in the freezer for up to a month. To reheat, place in a preheated 350°F oven for 5 minutes, or until heated through.

TIP: To check the seasoning of the meatball mixture, cook a smidgen of the mixture in a small skillet and taste it. It should taste amazing! If it doesn't, it likely needs more salt. Adjust the seasoning, then proceed with the recipe.

NUTRITIONAL INFO (per serving)				
calories	fat	protein	carbs	fiber
676	51g	41g	8g	1g

gyro mushrooms

 yield: 4 servings *prep time:* 5 minutes *cook time:* 12 minutes

20 large button mushrooms

2 tablespoons unsalted butter or coconut oil

¼ cup diced red onions

½ pound ground lamb or pork

2 cloves garlic, minced

1 teaspoon fine sea salt

½ teaspoon ground black pepper

½ teaspoon paprika

4 ounces feta cheese, crumbled

1 teaspoon Greek seasoning

Dried oregano leaves, for garnish

Cherry tomatoes, quartered, for serving

Greek olives, for serving

1. Wash the mushrooms. Cut off the stems and finely chop them. Set the caps aside on a paper towel to dry.

2. Place the butter, onions, and chopped mushroom stems in a 6-quart Instant Pot. Press Sauté and cook for 3 minutes, or until the onions begin to soften. Add the lamb, garlic, salt, pepper, and paprika and cook, crumbling the meat with a spatula, until the lamb is lightly browned and cooked through, about 3 minutes. Press Cancel to stop the Sauté.

3. Transfer the lamb mixture to a medium-sized bowl. Add the feta cheese and Greek seasoning. Stir to combine the ingredients, then stuff 1 tablespoon of the filling mixture into each mushroom cap.

4. Wipe the Instant Pot clean. Set a trivet in the Instant Pot and pour in ½ cup of cold water. Arrange the mushroom caps, filling side up, in a 1-quart round casserole dish. Use a foil sling (see page 19) to lower the casserole dish onto the trivet. Tuck in the sides of the sling.

5. Seal the lid, press Pressure Cook or Manual, and set the timer for 6 minutes. Once finished, turn the valve to venting for a quick release. Lift the casserole dish out of the Instant Pot using the foil sling.

6. Garnish with oregano and serve with cherry tomatoes and Greek olives. Best served warm.

Complete Steps 1 through 3 using a skillet over medium heat to sauté the vegetables and meat. Place the mushroom caps, filling side up, directly in a 6-quart slow cooker. Cover and cook on high for 2 hours. Proceed to Step 6.

STORE in an airtight container in the fridge for up to a week or in the freezer for up to a month. To reheat, place in a preheated 350°F oven for 5 minutes, or until heated through.

NUTRITIONAL INFO (per serving)				
calories	fat	protein	carbs	fiber
315	25g	19g	7g	2g

ham & cauliflower au gratin

 yield: 6 servings   *prep time:* 12 minutes   *cook time:* 5 minutes

6 ounces cream cheese (¾ cup), softened

¼ cup chicken broth, homemade (page 320) or store-bought

2 tablespoons grated Parmesan cheese

½ teaspoon fine sea salt

¼ teaspoon ground black pepper

1 medium head cauliflower, cut into bite-sized pieces

3 cups diced ham

¼ cup thinly sliced green onions

¾ cup shredded provolone cheese (about 3 ounces)

1. Place the softened cream cheese in a large bowl and whisk to loosen. (If you don't use a whisk to loosen the cream cheese, you will end up with clumps.) Slowly pour in the broth while whisking to combine. Mix in the Parmesan cheese, salt, and pepper.

2. Add the cauliflower, ham, and green onions to the bowl and stir well to combine. Scoop the mixture into a 1-quart round casserole dish.

3. Set a trivet in a 6-quart Instant Pot and pour in ½ cup of cold water. Use a foil sling (see page 19) to lower the casserole dish onto the trivet. Tuck in the sides of the sling.

4. Seal the lid, press Pressure Cook or Manual, and set the timer for 5 minutes. Once finished, turn the valve to venting for a quick release. Lift the casserole dish out of the Instant Pot using the foil sling.

5. Top with the provolone cheese. Loosely cover the pot and allow the cheese to melt, about 8 minutes. Best served warm.

Complete Steps 1 and 2, scooping the mixture directly into a 6-quart slow cooker. Cover and cook on high for 1 to 2 hours or on low for 4 to 5 hours, until the cauliflower is tender. Proceed to Step 5.

STORE in an airtight container in the fridge for up to a week or in the freezer for up to a month. To reheat, place in a preheated 350°F oven for 5 minutes, or until heated through.

NUTRITIONAL INFO (per serving)				
calories	fat	protein	carbs	fiber
308	17g	29g	8g	2g

french onion casserole

yield: 8 servings *prep time:* 5 minutes *cook time:* 13 minutes

3 large sweet onions, thinly sliced

1½ cups beef broth, homemade (page 320) or store-bought

3 tablespoons unsalted butter

1 teaspoon coconut aminos, or ¼ teaspoon wheat-free tamari

1 teaspoon fresh thyme leaves

½ teaspoon fine sea salt

GARLIC TOASTS:

3 (¾-inch-thick) slices Low-Carb Loaf Bread (page 326)

3 tablespoons unsalted butter, softened

1 clove garlic, smashed to a paste, or 1 teaspoon garlic puree

2 cups shredded Swiss or extra-sharp cheddar cheese (about 8 ounces), divided

1. Place the onions, broth, butter, coconut aminos, thyme, and salt in a 6-quart Instant Pot. Seal the lid, press Pressure Cook or Manual, and set the timer for 5 minutes. Once finished, turn the valve to venting for a quick release.

2. Meanwhile, prepare the toasts: Preheat the oven to broil. Place the slices of bread on a baking sheet. In a small bowl, stir together the butter and garlic. Spread about a tablespoon of the garlic butter on each slice. Broil for 3 minutes, or until the slices are toasted and golden brown.

3. Remove the lid from the Instant Pot and top the onion mixture with 1 cup of shredded cheese. Lay the toasts on top, then top with the remaining cheese.

4. Press Sauté and cook for 5 minutes, or until the cheese is completely melted. Serve warm.

Place the onions, broth, butter, coconut aminos, thyme, and salt in a 6-quart slow cooker. Cover and cook on high for 4 hours, or until the onions are caramelized. Complete Steps 2 and 3. Turn the slow cooker to high, cover, and cook until the cheese is melted, about 20 minutes. Serve warm.

STORE in an airtight container in the fridge for up to a week or in the freezer for up to a month. To reheat, place in a preheated 350°F oven for 5 minutes, or until heated through.

NUTRITIONAL INFO (per serving)				
calories	fat	protein	carbs	fiber
278	22g	11g	11g	2g

sesame broccoli

 yield: 4 servings   *prep time:* 12 minutes   *cook time:* 5 minutes

SAUCE:

½ cup beef broth, homemade (page 320) or store-bought

¼ cup Swerve confectioners'-style sweetener or equivalent amount of liquid or powdered sweetener (see page 39)

2 tablespoons coconut aminos, or 1½ teaspoons wheat-free tamari

2 tablespoons lemon juice

1 tablespoon peeled and grated fresh ginger

1 clove Roasted Garlic (page 324)

1 teaspoon guar gum (optional, for thickening)

1 teaspoon dark (toasted) sesame oil

½ teaspoon fine sea salt

2 cups broccoli florets

2 cups cauliflower florets

2 tablespoons toasted sesame seeds, for garnish

STORE in an airtight container in the fridge for up to 5 days or in the freezer for up to a month. To reheat, place in a preheated 350°F oven for 5 minutes, or until heated through.

1. Place all of the sauce ingredients in a large bowl and stir well to combine. Add the broccoli and cauliflower and toss well to coat with the sauce.

2. Transfer the vegetable mixture to a 6-quart Instant Pot. Seal the lid, press Pressure Cook or Manual, and set the timer for 5 minutes. Once finished, turn the valve to venting for a quick release.

3. Garnish with toasted sesame seeds. Best served warm.

Complete Step 1. Place the vegetable mixture in a 6-quart slow cooker. Cover and cook on high for 30 minutes or on low for 2 hours, or until the veggies are tender. Proceed to Step 3.

NUTRITIONAL INFO (per serving)				
calories	fat	protein	carbs	fiber
78	4g	3g	9g	5g

buttery mushrooms

option option

yield: 4 servings *prep time:* 5 minutes *cook time:* 5 minutes

1 pound button mushrooms, quartered

½ cup (1 stick) unsalted butter (or coconut oil for dairy-free), melted

½ cup chicken broth, homemade (page 320) or store-bought, or vegetable broth

2 tablespoons red wine vinegar

1 tablespoon fresh thyme or marjoram leaves

1 teaspoon dried chives

Fine sea salt and ground black pepper

STORE in an airtight container in the fridge for up to a week or in the freezer for up to a month. To reheat, place in a preheated 350°F oven for 5 minutes, or until heated through.

Place the mushrooms, butter, broth, vinegar, thyme, and chives in a 3-quart or larger Instant Pot. Seal the lid, press Pressure Cook or Manual, and set the timer for 5 minutes. Once finished, turn the valve to venting for a quick release. Season with salt and pepper to taste. Serve warm.

Place the mushrooms, butter, broth, vinegar, thyme, and chives in a 3-quart or larger slow cooker. Cover and cook on high for 1 hour, or until the mushrooms are soft. Season with salt and pepper to taste. Serve warm.

NUTRITIONAL INFO (per serving)				
calories	fat	protein	carbs	fiber
256	28g	3g	3g	1g

alfredo veggies

option *yield:* 6 servings *prep time:* 12 minutes *cook time:* 5 minutes

3 broccoli crowns, cut into florets

½ head cauliflower, cut into florets

SAUCE:

½ cup shredded sharp cheddar cheese (about 2 ounces)

2 ounces cream cheese (¼ cup), softened

¼ cup grated Parmesan cheese (about ¾ ounce)

½ cup chicken broth, homemade (page 320) or store-bought, or vegetable broth

Cloves squeezed from 1 head Roasted Garlic (page 324)

1 teaspoon fine sea salt

FOR GARNISH:

Fresh oregano or basil leaves

Ground black pepper

1. Set a trivet in a 6-quart Instant Pot and pour in ½ cup of cold water.

2. Place the broccoli and cauliflower in a 1-quart casserole dish.

3. Make the sauce: Place the cheeses, broth, garlic, and salt in a food processor or blender and purée until smooth. Reserve ¼ cup of the sauce for serving. Pour the remaining sauce over the vegetables and stir well to coat. Cover the dish with the lid or a piece of aluminum foil.

4. Use a foil sling (see page 19) to lower the casserole dish onto the trivet in the Instant Pot. Tuck in the sides of the sling.

5. Seal the lid, press Pressure Cook or Manual, and set the timer for 5 minutes. Once finished, turn the valve to venting for a quick release. Lift the casserole dish out of the pot using the foil sling.

6. Top with the reserved sauce and garnish with fresh oregano or basil leaves and freshly ground pepper. Serve warm.

Complete Steps 2 and 3 using a large bowl instead of a casserole dish, then place the broccoli and cauliflower, along with any sauce remaining in the bowl, in a 6-quart slow cooker. Cover and cook on high for 30 minutes or on low for 2 hours, or until the veggies are tender. Transfer to a serving bowl and proceed to Step 6.

STORE in an airtight container in the fridge for up to 5 days or in the freezer for up to a month. To reheat, place in a preheated 350°F oven for 5 minutes, or until heated through.

NUTRITIONAL INFO (per serving)				
calories	fat	protein	carbs	fiber
128	6g	8g	10g	3g

sweet 'n' sour eggplant

 *yield:* 8 servings   *prep time:* 15 minutes   *cook time:* 12 minutes

2 pounds eggplant

2 tablespoons fine sea salt

2 tablespoons coconut oil

11 cloves garlic, minced

⅓ cup red wine vinegar

⅓ cup Swerve confectioners'-style sweetener or equivalent amount of liquid or powdered sweetener (see page 39)

2 tablespoons tomato paste

1 (28-ounce) can whole Italian tomatoes, finely chopped, with juices

5 stalks celery, cut into ½-inch pieces

1 large onion, chopped

1 large red or yellow bell pepper, cut into ½-inch pieces

½ teaspoon ground black pepper

FOR GARNISH:

2 tablespoons sliced green onions

2 tablespoons fresh cilantro leaves

2 teaspoons toasted sesame seeds

1. Cut the eggplant into ½-inch cubes and place in a colander in the sink. Sprinkle with the salt and toss to coat. Let the eggplant drain for 1 hour. It will release quite a bit of liquid.

2. Meanwhile, place the coconut oil in a 6-quart Instant Pot and press Sauté. Once melted, add the garlic and cook, stirring, until fragrant, about 1 minute. Add the vinegar, sweetener, and tomato paste and bring to a boil. Allow to boil, stirring, for 1 minute.

3. Add the tomatoes, then adjust the temperature to Less. Cook, uncovered, stirring occasionally, until thickened, about 5 minutes. (Simmering red wine vinegar makes it sweeter.) Press Cancel to stop the Sauté.

4. Add the rest of the ingredients, including the drained eggplant, to the Instant Pot. Seal the lid, press Pressure Cook or Manual, and set the timer for 5 minutes. Once finished, turn the valve to venting for a quick release.

5. Serve hot or chilled. Garnish with green onions, cilantro, and toasted sesame seeds.

Complete Step 1, then follow Steps 2 and 3 using a skillet over medium-high heat to sauté. Transfer the mixture to a 6-quart slow cooker, then add the rest of the ingredients, including the drained eggplant. Cover and cook on high for 30 minutes or on low for 2 hours, or until the eggplant is tender. Proceed to Step 5.

STORE in an airtight container in the fridge for up to 5 days or in the freezer for up to a month. To reheat, place in a skillet over medium heat for 5 minutes, or until heated through.

NUTRITIONAL INFO (per serving)				
calories	fat	protein	carbs	fiber
125	5g	4g	19g	7g

nutty "noodles"

yield: 4 servings *prep time:* 5 minutes *cook time:* 8 minutes

When my son Micah was three years old, he would gobble up a whole plate of my Nutty "Noodles." This dish is not only delicious for little ones; it is a favorite of adults, too. It also makes great leftovers.

4 cups thinly sliced cabbage

¼ cup sunflower seed butter or creamy peanut butter

¼ cup chicken broth, homemade (page 320) or store-bought, or vegetable broth

2 tablespoons coconut aminos, or 1½ teaspoons wheat-free tamari

1½ tablespoons Swerve confectioners'-style sweetener or equivalent amount of liquid or powdered sweetener (see page 39)

¼ teaspoon cayenne pepper

1½ teaspoons lemon juice

FOR GARNISH:

Sliced green onions

Lime wedges

1. Place all of the ingredients except the garnishes in a 6-quart Instant Pot. Stir well to combine. Seal the lid, press Pressure Cook or Manual, and set the timer for 8 minutes. Once finished, turn the valve to venting for a quick release. The cabbage "noodles" should be soft.

2. Serve warm or chilled. Garnish with green onions and lime wedges.

Place all of the ingredients except the garnishes in a 6-quart slow cooker. Cover and cook on low for 4 to 6 hours, until the cabbage "noodles" are very soft. You may need to stir the mixture after 1 hour so that there are no clumps of sunflower seed butter in the sauce. Proceed to Step 2.

STORE in an airtight container in the fridge for up to 5 days or in the freezer for up to a month. To reheat, place in a saucepan over medium heat, stirring occasionally, for 5 minutes, or until heated through.

NUTRITIONAL INFO (per serving)				
calories	fat	protein	carbs	fiber
128	8g	5g	9g	3g

soups
& stews

reuben soup

  yield: 4 servings *prep time:* 5 minutes *cook time:* 20 minutes

I adore a tasty Reuben sandwich, and I love a hearty soup. So I married my two favorites and created this easy Reuben soup! The leftovers taste amazing, so I suggest making a double batch.

1 (8-ounce) package cream cheese (or Kite Hill brand cream cheese style spread for dairy-free), softened

2½ cups beef broth, homemade (page 320) or store-bought

2 cups corned beef, sliced into thin strips (to resemble noodles)

1½ cups sauerkraut

1 cup finely grated Swiss cheese (omit for dairy-free)

¼ cup finely chopped onions

1 teaspoon fine sea salt

½ teaspoon ground black pepper

Fresh oregano sprigs, for garnish

1. Place the cream cheese in a 6-quart Instant Pot. Slowly add the broth while whisking. Stir in the corned beef, sauerkraut, Swiss cheese (if using), onions, salt, and pepper.

2. Seal the lid, press Soup/Broth, and set the timer for 20 minutes. Once finished, let the pressure release naturally.

3. Remove the lid and stir well. Taste and season with additional salt and pepper, if desired. Ladle the soup into bowls and garnish with oregano sprigs.

 Complete Step 1 using a 6-quart slow cooker. Cover and cook on high for 1 hour or on low for 2 hours. Proceed to Step 3.

STORE in an airtight container in the fridge for up to 5 days or in the freezer for up to a month. To reheat, place in a saucepan over medium heat, stirring occasionally, for 5 minutes, or until heated through.

NUTRITIONAL INFO (per serving)				
calories	fat	protein	carbs	fiber
427	34g	20g	4g	0.2g

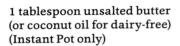

1 tablespoon unsalted butter (or coconut oil for dairy-free) (Instant Pot only)

1½ pounds fresh asparagus, woody ends trimmed, cut into 2-inch chunks, plus more for garnish

½ cup chopped onions

2 cups chopped cauliflower

4 cups chicken broth, homemade (page 320) or store-bought, or vegetable broth

½ teaspoon fine sea salt

½ teaspoon ground black pepper

4 ounces cream cheese (½ cup) (or Kite Hill brand cream cheese style spread for dairy-free)

FOR GARNISH (optional):

Asparagus tips

Purple salt

1. Place the butter in a 6-quart Instant Pot and press Sauté. Once melted, add the asparagus and onions and cook, stirring occasionally, for 4 minutes, or until the onions are soft. Press Cancel to stop the Sauté.

2. Add the cauliflower, broth, salt, and pepper. Seal the lid, press Pressure Cook or Manual, and set the timer for 10 minutes. Once finished, let the pressure release naturally.

3. Remove the lid and add the cream cheese. Transfer the soup to a food processor and process until puréed (or purée the soup right in the pot with a stick blender). Season with additional salt and pepper before serving. Garnish with asparagus tips and purple salt, if desired.

Place the asparagus, onions, cauliflower, broth, salt, and pepper in a 6-quart slow cooker. Cover and cook on high for 2 hours or on low for 6 to 7 hours, until the cauliflower is soft. Proceed to Step 3.

STORE in an airtight container in the fridge for up to 5 days or in the freezer for up to a month. To reheat, place in a saucepan over medium heat, stirring occasionally, for 5 minutes, or until heated through.

NUTRITIONAL INFO (per serving)				
calories	fat	protein	carbs	fiber
270	15g	13g	20g	5g

chicken "noodle" soup

 yield: 6 servings *prep time:* 8 minutes *cook time:* 14 minutes

¼ cup coconut oil or unsalted butter

1 cup chopped celery

¼ cup chopped onions

2 cloves garlic, minced

1 pound boneless, skinless chicken breasts, cut into 1-inch cubes

6 cups chicken broth, homemade (page 320) or store-bought

1 tablespoon dried parsley

1 teaspoon fine sea salt

½ teaspoon dried marjoram

½ teaspoon ground black pepper

1 bay leaf

2 cups zucchini noodles or daikon noodles

1. Place the coconut oil in a 6-quart Instant Pot and press Sauté. Once melted, add the celery, onions, and garlic and cook, stirring occasionally, for 4 minutes, or until the onions are soft. Press Cancel to stop the Sauté.

2. Add the cubed chicken, broth, parsley, salt, marjoram, pepper, and bay leaf. Seal the lid, press Pressure Cook or Manual, and set the timer for 10 minutes. Once finished, let the pressure release naturally.

3. Remove the lid and stir well. Place the noodles in bowls, using ⅓ cup per bowl. Ladle the soup over the noodles and serve immediately; if it sits too long, the noodles will get too soft.

Place all of the ingredients, except the noodles, in a 6-quart slow cooker. Cover and cook on high for 2 to 3 hours or on low for 6 to 8 hours, until the chicken is cooked through. Proceed to Step 3.

STORE the soup and noodles in separate airtight containers in the fridge for up to 5 days, or freeze the soup (without the noodles) for up to a month. To reheat the soup, place in a saucepan over medium heat, stirring occasionally, for 5 minutes, or until heated through. Add the noodles just before serving.

NUTRITIONAL INFO (per serving)				
calories	fat	protein	carbs	fiber
253	15g	21g	11g	1g

new england clam chowder

option

yield: 8 servings *prep time:* 5 minutes *cook time:* 13 minutes

1 pound bacon, chopped

¼ cup chopped onions

1 leek, trimmed, halved lengthwise, and sliced

2 stalks celery, diced

4 cloves garlic, minced

1 (8-ounce) package cream cheese (or Kite Hill brand cream cheese style spread for dairy-free), softened

3 (10-ounce) cans baby clams, with liquid

2 cups cauliflower florets, chopped

1½ cups chicken broth, homemade (page 320) or store-bought

2 tablespoons unsalted butter (or butter-flavored coconut oil for dairy-free)

2 teaspoons fine sea salt

1 teaspoon ground black pepper

1 teaspoon dried thyme leaves

Fresh thyme sprigs, for garnish

1. Place the bacon in a 6-quart Instant Pot and press Sauté. Cook, stirring often, for 4 minutes, or until the bacon is crisp. Remove the bacon with a slotted spoon and set aside on a paper towel–lined plate to drain, leaving the drippings in the pot.

2. Add the onions, leek, celery, and garlic to the Instant Pot and sauté in the bacon drippings for 4 minutes, or until the onions are soft. Press Cancel to stop the Sauté.

3. Add the cream cheese to the Instant Pot and whisk to loosen. (If you don't use a whisk to loosen the cream cheese, you will end up with clumps in your soup.) Add the clams (including the liquid from the cans), cauliflower, broth, butter, salt, pepper, and thyme, along with three-quarters of the bacon; reserve the rest of the bacon for garnish.

4. Seal the lid, press Pressure Cook or Manual, and set the timer for 5 minutes. Once finished, let the pressure release naturally.

5. Remove the lid and stir well. Ladle the soup into bowls and garnish with thyme sprigs and the reserved bacon.

Complete Steps 1 and 2 using a large skillet over medium-high heat. Place the onion mixture in a 6-quart slow cooker, then proceed to Step 3. Cover and cook on high for 1 hour or on low for 4 hours. Proceed to Step 5.

STORE in an airtight container in the fridge for up to 5 days or in the freezer for up to a month. To reheat, place in a saucepan over medium heat, stirring occasionally, for 5 minutes, or until heated through.

NUTRITIONAL INFO (per serving)				
calories	fat	protein	carbs	fiber
552	41g	34g	10g	1g

pumpkin chili

 yield: 4 servings   *prep time:* 5 minutes   *cook time:* 12 minutes

2 tablespoons ghee or coconut oil

1 yellow onion, diced

1 bell pepper (any color), diced

2 cloves garlic, minced

1 pound ground beef

1 (14½-ounce) can diced tomatoes

2 (4-ounce) cans diced green chilies

1 (15-ounce) can pumpkin puree

1 cup beef broth, homemade (page 320) or store-bought

1 teaspoon chili powder

1 teaspoon ground cinnamon

1 teaspoon fine sea salt

Ground black pepper

Chopped fresh Italian parsley, for garnish

1. Place the ghee in a 6-quart Instant Pot and press Sauté. Once melted, add the onion, bell pepper, and garlic and sauté for 4 minutes, or until the onion is soft. Add the ground beef and cook, breaking up the large chunks of meat, for 3 more minutes, or until the beef is starting to brown.

2. Add the tomatoes, chilies, pumpkin, broth, chili powder, cinnamon, and salt. Deglaze the pot, scraping up any bits stuck to the bottom, and stir the beef into the onion mixture well. Press Cancel to stop the Sauté.

3. Seal the lid, press Pressure Cook or Manual, and set the timer for 5 minutes. Once finished, let the pressure release naturally.

4. Remove the lid and stir well. Season with salt and pepper to taste. Ladle the soup into bowls and garnish with parsley.

Complete Step 1 using a large skillet over medium-high heat. Transfer the beef mixture to a 6-quart slow cooker. Add the tomatoes, chilies, pumpkin, broth, chili powder, cinnamon, and salt; stir well to combine. Cover and cook on high for 2 to 3 hours or on low for 5 to 6 hours, until the beef is cooked through. Proceed to Step 4.

STORE in an airtight container in the fridge for up to 5 days or in the freezer for up to a month. To reheat, place in a saucepan over medium heat, stirring occasionally, for 5 minutes, or until heated through.

NUTRITIONAL INFO (per serving)				
calories	fat	protein	carbs	fiber
431	41g	23g	15g	4g

italian chicken chili

option

yield: 12 servings   *prep time:* 7 minutes   *cook time:* 25 minutes

1 tablespoon unsalted butter (or lard or coconut oil for dairy-free)

½ cup chopped onions

Cloves squeezed from 2 heads Roasted Garlic (page 324), or 4 cloves garlic, minced

2 pounds ground chicken or turkey

2 boneless, skinless chicken breast halves (about 4 ounces each), cut into ½-inch pieces

3 cups tomato sauce

1 (28-ounce) jar stewed Italian-style tomatoes

1 cup chicken broth, homemade (page 320) or store-bought

1 tablespoon dried oregano leaves

1 tablespoon dried thyme leaves

Fine sea salt and ground black pepper

Sour cream, for garnish (omit for dairy-free)

Dried chives, for garnish

2 batches Mashed Cauliflower (page 330), for serving

1. Place the butter in a 6-quart Instant Pot and press Sauté. Once melted, add the onions and cook, stirring frequently, for 4 minutes, or until soft. Add the garlic and sauté for another minute. Press Cancel to stop the Sauté.

2. Add the chicken, tomato sauce, tomatoes, broth, oregano, and thyme. Season well with salt and pepper. Stir to combine and to break up the ground meat.

3. Seal the lid, press Pressure Cook or Manual, and set the timer for 20 minutes. Once finished, let the pressure release naturally.

4. Remove the lid and stir well. Ladle the chili into bowls and swirl in some sour cream, if desired. Garnish with chives and serve over mashed cauliflower.

Place all of the ingredients in a 6-quart slow cooker. Stir to combine and to break up the ground meat. Cover and cook on high for 3 to 4 hours or on low for 6 to 8 hours, until the chicken is cooked through. Proceed to Step 4.

STORE in an airtight container in the fridge for up to 5 days or in the freezer for up to a month. To reheat, place in a saucepan over medium heat, stirring occasionally, for 5 minutes, or until heated through.

NUTRITIONAL INFO (per serving)				
calories	fat	protein	carbs	fiber
251	12g	26g	7g	1g

tomato basil parmesan soup

 option *yield:* 12 servings *prep time:* 5 minutes *cook time:* 12 minutes

2 tablespoons unsalted butter or coconut oil (Instant Pot only)

½ cup finely diced onions

Cloves squeezed from 1 head Roasted Garlic (page 000), or 2 cloves garlic, minced

1 tablespoon dried basil leaves

1 teaspoon dried oregano leaves

1 (8-ounce) package cream cheese, softened

4 cups chicken broth, homemade (page 000) or store-bought, or vegetable broth

2 (14½-ounce) cans diced tomatoes

1 cup shredded Parmesan cheese, plus more for garnish

1 teaspoon fine sea salt

¼ teaspoon ground black pepper

Fresh basil leaves, for garnish

1. Place the butter in a 6-quart Instant Pot and press Sauté. Once melted, add the onions, garlic, basil, and oregano and cook, stirring often, for 4 minutes, or until the onions are soft. Press Cancel to stop the Sauté.

2. Add the cream cheese and whisk to loosen. (If you don't use a whisk to loosen the cream cheese, you will end up with clumps in your soup.) Slowly whisk in the broth. Add the tomatoes, Parmesan, salt, and pepper and stir to combine.

3. Seal the lid, press Pressure Cook or Manual, and set the timer for 8 minutes. Once finished, turn the valve to venting for a quick release.

4. Remove the lid and purée the soup with a stick blender, or transfer the soup to a regular blender or food processor and process until smooth. If using a regular blender, you may need to blend the soup in two batches; if you overfill the blender jar, the soup will not purée properly.

5. Season with salt and pepper to taste, if desired. Ladle the soup into bowls and garnish with more Parmesan and basil leaves.

Place the cream cheese in a 6-quart slow cooker and whisk to loosen. (If you don't use a whisk to loosen the cream cheese, you will end up with clumps in your soup.) Slowly whisk in the broth. Add the onions, garlic, basil, oregano, tomatoes, Parmesan, salt, and pepper. Cover and cook on high for 2 hours or on low for 4 hours. Proceed to Step 4.

STORE in an airtight container in the fridge for up to 5 days or in the freezer for up to a month. To reheat, place in a saucepan over medium heat, stirring occasionally, for 5 minutes, or until heated through.

NUTRITIONAL INFO (per serving)				
calories	fat	protein	carbs	fiber
146	10g	8g	4g	1g

provolone chicken soup

  yield: 4 servings *prep time:* 7 minutes *cook time:* 13 minutes

4 strips bacon, chopped

¼ cup chopped onions

2 cloves garlic, minced

2 ounces cream cheese (¼ cup), softened

1 pound boneless, skinless chicken breasts, cut into ¾-inch cubes

4 cups chicken broth, homemade (page 320) or store-bought

1 cup provolone cheese, shredded

½ teaspoon fine sea salt

½ teaspoon ground black pepper

FOR GARNISH:

Sour cream

Melted unsalted butter or ghee

Dried chives

1. Place the bacon in a 6-quart Instant Pot and press Sauté. Cook, stirring often, for 4 minutes, or until the bacon is crisp. Remove the bacon with a slotted spoon and set aside on a paper towel–lined plate to drain, leaving the drippings in the pot.

2. Add the onions and garlic to the Instant Pot and sauté in the bacon drippings for 4 minutes, or until the onions are soft. Press Cancel to stop the Sauté.

3. Add the cream cheese and whisk to loosen. (If you don't use a whisk to loosen the cream cheese, you will end up with clumps in your soup.) Add the chicken, broth, provolone, salt, and pepper and stir to combine.

4. Seal the lid, press Pressure Cook or Manual, and set the timer for 5 minutes. Once finished, let the pressure release naturally.

5. Remove the lid and stir well. Ladle the soup into bowls and garnish with sour cream, a drizzle of melted butter, the reserved bacon, and chives.

Complete Steps 1 through 3 using a large skillet over medium-high heat to sauté. Pour the mixture into a 6-quart slow cooker. Cover and cook on high for 2 hours or on low for 4 hours, or until the chicken is cooked through. Proceed to Step 5.

STORE in an airtight container in the fridge for up to 5 days or in the freezer for up to a month. To reheat, place in a saucepan over medium heat, stirring occasionally, for 5 minutes, or until heated through.

NUTRITIONAL INFO (per serving)				
calories	fat	protein	carbs	fiber
373	18g	49g	2g	0.3g

cioppino

 yield: 6 servings   *prep time:* 10 minutes   *cook time:* 38 minutes

You must use an Instant Pot for this recipe; using a slow cooker is not recommended.

4 tablespoons unsalted butter (or coconut oil for dairy-free), divided

¼ cup chopped onions

3 cloves garlic, minced

1 green bell pepper, chopped

1 (28-ounce) can crushed tomatoes, with juices

1 (8-ounce) can tomato sauce

1¼ cups chicken broth, homemade (page 320) or store-bought, or vegetable broth, divided

½ cup fresh Italian parsley, chopped

2 tablespoons red wine vinegar

2 teaspoons dried basil

1 teaspoon fine sea salt

1 teaspoon dried oregano leaves

1 teaspoon dried thyme leaves, plus more for garnish

½ teaspoon cayenne pepper

½ teaspoon smoked paprika

12 scallops

12 prawns

1 (6-ounce) fillet cod, sea bass, or other white fish, deboned and cut into bite-sized pieces

12 mussels

12 clams, or 1 (10-ounce) can baby clams with liquid

4 crab legs, cooked, or 1 (6½-ounce) can lump crab meat, rinsed and drained well

1. Place 2 tablespoons of the butter in an 8-quart Instant Pot and press Sauté. Once melted, add the onions and cook for 3 minutes, or until the onions are soft. Add the garlic and bell pepper and sauté for another 5 minutes, or until the veggies are soft. Press Cancel to stop the Sauté.

2. Add the tomatoes, tomato sauce, 1 cup of the broth, the parsley, vinegar, and seasonings and stir well. Seal the lid, press Pressure Cook or Manual, and set the timer for 30 minutes.

3. Meanwhile, place the remaining 2 tablespoons of butter in a large cast-iron skillet over medium-high heat. Season the scallops, prawns, and fish on both sides with salt. Once the butter is hot, sear the scallops for 45 seconds on each side. Remove the scallops from the skillet to a large serving bowl and set aside.

4. Add the prawns and fish to the skillet and cook over medium-high heat for 2 minutes per side or until cooked through and opaque. Remove the prawns and fish to the bowl with the scallops and set aside.

5. Pour the remaining ¼ cup of broth into the skillet and deglaze the pan, using a whisk to scrape up the bits stuck the bottom. Add the mussels and clams, cover with the lid, and cook over medium heat for 5 minutes, or until all the clams and mussels have opened; throw out any that do not open. Add crab legs to heat through. Once the Instant Pot is finished, let the pressure release naturally.

6. Remove the lid from the Instant Pot and stir in the cooked seafood. Ladle into bowls and garnish with thyme.

STORE in an airtight container in the fridge for up to 5 days or in the freezer for up to a month. To reheat, place in a saucepan over medium heat, stirring occasionally, for 5 minutes, or until heated through.

NUTRITIONAL INFO (per serving)				
calories	fat	protein	carbs	fiber
298	12g	35g	14g	2g

seafood chowder

 yield: 8 servings *prep time:* 5 minutes *cook time:* 13 minutes

2 strips bacon, chopped

2 tablespoons coconut oil, ghee, or unsalted butter (Instant Pot only)

2 cups chopped celery

½ cup diced onions

4 cloves garlic, minced

4 ounces cream cheese (½ cup), softened

3 cups chicken broth, homemade (page 320) or store-bought

1 medium head cauliflower, cut into small florets

1 pound cod or other white fish fillets, cut into 1-inch cubes

2 cups frozen raw shrimp, peeled and deveined

½ teaspoon fine sea salt

½ teaspoon ground black pepper

Extra-virgin olive oil, for drizzling (optional)

1. Place the bacon in a 6-quart Instant Pot and press Sauté. Cook, stirring often, for 4 minutes, or until the bacon is crisp. Remove the bacon with a slotted spoon and set aside on a paper towel–lined plate to drain. Wipe the pot clean.

2. Place the coconut oil in the Instant Pot. Once melted, add the celery, onions, and garlic and cook for 4 minutes, or until the onions are soft. Press Cancel to stop the Sauté.

3. Add the cream cheese and whisk to loosen. (If you don't use a whisk to loosen the cream cheese, you will end up with clumps in your soup.) Slowly whisk in the broth. Add the cauliflower, fish, shrimp, salt, and pepper and stir to combine.

4. Seal the lid, press Pressure Cook or Manual, and set the timer for 5 minutes. Once finished, let the pressure release naturally.

5. Remove the lid and stir well. Serve the soup in bowls, garnished with the bacon, freshly ground pepper, and a drizzle of olive oil, if desired.

Complete Step 1 using a small skillet to cook the bacon. Place the celery, onions, and garlic in a 6-quart slow cooker, then proceed to Step 3. Cover and cook on high for 40 minutes or on low for 2 hours, or until the cauliflower is tender and the fish is cooked through. Proceed to Step 5.

STORE in an airtight container in the fridge for up to 5 days or in the freezer for up to a month. To reheat, place in a saucepan over medium heat, stirring occasionally, for 5 minutes, or until heated through.

NUTRITIONAL INFO (per serving)				
calories	fat	protein	carbs	fiber
234	15g	17g	8g	1g

broccoli & brie soup

   yield: 6 servings   *prep time:* 5 minutes   *cook time:* 14 minutes

option   option

1 tablespoon coconut oil or unsalted butter (Instant Pot only)

1 cup finely diced onions

1 head broccoli, cut into small florets

2½ cups chicken broth, homemade (page 320) or store-bought, or vegetable broth

8 ounces Brie cheese, cut off rind and cut into chunks

1 cup unflavored unsweetened almond milk or heavy cream, plus more for drizzling

Fine sea salt and ground black pepper

Extra-virgin olive oil, for drizzling

Coarse sea salt, for garnish

1. Place the coconut oil in a 6-quart Instant Pot and press Sauté. Once hot, add the onions and sauté for 4 minutes, or until soft. Press Cancel to stop the Sauté.

2. Add the broccoli and broth. Seal the lid, press Pressure Cook or Manual, and set the timer for 10 minutes. Once finished, let the pressure release naturally.

3. Remove the lid and add the Brie and almond milk to the pot. Transfer the soup to a food processor or blender and process until smooth, or purée the soup right in the pot with a stick blender.

4. Season with salt and pepper to taste. Ladle the soup into bowls and drizzle with almond milk and olive oil. Garnish with coarse sea salt and freshly ground pepper.

Place the onions, broccoli, and broth in a 6-quart slow cooker. Cover and cook on high for 2 hours or on low for 6 hours, or until the broccoli is very soft. Proceed to Step 3.

STORE in an airtight container in the fridge for up to 5 days or in the freezer for up to a month. To reheat, place in a saucepan over medium heat, stirring occasionally, for 5 minutes, or until heated through.

NUTRITIONAL INFO (per serving)				
calories	fat	protein	carbs	fiber
210	16g	9g	7g	1g

curry beef stew

  yield: 4 servings *prep time:* 5 minutes *cook time:* 26 minutes

1 pound beef stew meat

2 teaspoons fine sea salt

1 teaspoon ground black pepper

1 tablespoon coconut oil

1 cup diced onions

2 cloves garlic, minced

1 teaspoon peeled and chopped fresh ginger

1 jalapeño pepper, diced

1 tablespoon curry powder

2 cups beef broth, homemade (page 320) or store-bought

FOR GARNISH:

Fresh cilantro leaves

Lime wedges

Sliced red jalapeño peppers

1. Cut the beef into 1-inch cubes and season on all sides with the salt and pepper.

2. Place the coconut oil in a 6-quart Instant Pot and press Sauté. Once melted, add the seasoned beef and cook for about 1 minute per side or until browned on all sides. Remove from the pot and set aside, leaving the drippings in the pot.

3. Add the onions, garlic, ginger, and jalapeño and sauté in the beef drippings for 2 minutes, until fragrant, then stir in the curry powder. Press Cancel to stop the Sauté.

4. Pour in the broth and return the browned beef to the pot. Stir to combine.

5. Seal the lid, press Pressure Cook or Manual, and set the timer for 20 minutes. Once finished, let the pressure release naturally.

6. Remove the lid and stir well. Serve the stew in bowls, garnish with cilantro, lime wedges, red jalapeño slices, and freshly ground black pepper.

Complete Step 1. Then follow Steps 2 and 3 using a skillet over medium heat. Transfer the onion mixture to a 6-quart slow cooker and add the broth and browned beef. Cover and cook on high for 3 to 4 hours or on low for 6 to 8 hours, until the beef is very tender. Proceed to Step 6.

STORE in an airtight container in the fridge for up to a week or in the freezer for up to a month. To reheat, place in a saucepan over medium heat, stirring occasionally, for 5 minutes, or until heated through.

NUTRITIONAL INFO (per serving)				
calories	fat	protein	carbs	fiber
394	26g	33g	5g	1g

spicy chicken stew

 yield: 10 servings *prep time:* 10 minutes *cook time:* 25 minutes

1 tablespoon coconut oil

2 pounds bulk Italian sausage

2 boneless, skinless chicken thighs, cut into ½-inch pieces

½ cup chopped onions

1 (28-ounce) can whole peeled tomatoes, drained

1 cup tomato sauce

1 (4½-ounce) can green chilies

3 tablespoons minced garlic

2 tablespoons smoked paprika

1 tablespoon ground cumin

1 tablespoon dried oregano leaves

2 teaspoons fine sea salt

1 teaspoon cayenne pepper

1 cup chicken broth, homemade (page 320) or store-bought

1 ounce unsweetened baking chocolate, chopped

¼ cup lime juice

Chopped fresh cilantro leaves, for garnish

Red pepper flakes, for garnish

1. Place the coconut oil in a 6-quart Instant Pot and press Sauté. Once melted, add the sausage, chicken, and onions and cook, stirring to break up the sausage, until the sausage is starting to cook through and the onions are soft, about 5 minutes.

2. Meanwhile, make the tomato puree: Place the tomatoes, tomato sauce, and chilies in a food processor and process until smooth.

3. Add the garlic, paprika, cumin, oregano, salt, and cayenne pepper to the Instant Pot and stir to combine. Then add the tomato puree, broth, and chocolate and stir well. Press Cancel to stop the Sauté.

4. Seal the lid, press Pressure Cook or Manual, and set the timer for 20 minutes. Once finished, let the pressure release naturally.

5. Just before serving, stir in the lime juice. Ladle the stew into bowls and garnish with cilantro and red pepper flakes.

 Place the oil, sausage, chicken, and onions in a 6-quart slow cooker. Stir well to break up the sausage. Add the remaining ingredients and stir well. Cover and cook on high for 1 hour or on low for 2 hours. Proceed to Step 5.

STORE in an airtight container in the fridge for up to 5 days or in the freezer for up to a month. To reheat, place in a saucepan over medium heat, stirring occasionally, for 5 minutes, or until heated through.

NUTRITIONAL INFO (per serving)				
calories	fat	protein	carbs	fiber
341	23g	21g	10g	2g

african "nut" stew

option option *yield:* 12 servings *prep time:* 15 minutes *cook time:* 8 minutes

1 tablespoon coconut oil, preferably butter-flavored (Instant Pot only)

2 red bell peppers, chopped

¼ cup diced onions

4 cloves garlic, minced

3½ cups Keto "Rice" (page 328)

1 cup natural sunflower seed butter or peanut butter

8 cups chicken broth, homemade (page 320) or store-bought, or vegetable broth

1 (28-ounce) can crushed tomatoes, with juices

¼ teaspoon chili powder

¼ teaspoon ground black pepper

Fine sea salt (optional)

Sliced green onions, for garnish

1. Place the coconut oil in a 6-quart Instant Pot and press Sauté. Once melted, add the bell peppers and onions and cook for 4 minutes, or until the onions are soft. Add the garlic and "rice" and sauté for another 3 minutes. Press Cancel to stop the Sauté.

2. Add the sunflower seed butter and stir until softened. Slowly whisk in the broth. Add the tomatoes, chili powder, and black pepper.

3. Seal the lid, press Pressure Cook or Manual, and set the timer for 1 minute. Once finished, turn the valve to venting for a quick release.

4. Remove the lid and stir well. Taste and season with salt, if needed. Ladle the stew into bowls and garnish with sliced green onions.

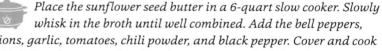 *Place the sunflower seed butter in a 6-quart slow cooker. Slowly whisk in the broth until well combined. Add the bell peppers, onions, garlic, tomatoes, chili powder, and black pepper. Cover and cook on high for 1 hour or on low for 3 hours. Remove the lid and stir in the "rice." Cover and cook on high for another 20 minutes, or until the "rice" is tender. Proceed to Step 4.*

STORE in an airtight container in the fridge for up to 5 days or in the freezer for up to a month. To reheat, place in a saucepan over medium heat, stirring occasionally, for 5 minutes, or until heated through.

NUTRITIONAL INFO (per serving)				
calories	fat	protein	carbs	fiber
290	19g	14g	14g	2g

venison stew

option

yield: 8 servings   *prep time:* 12 minutes   *cook time:* 42 minutes

I am often asked to write wild game recipes. If you do not have venison or prefer not to use it, you can use beef roast in this stew instead.

1 tablespoon unsalted butter (or lard for dairy-free) (Instant Pot only)

1 cup diced onions

2 cups button mushrooms, sliced in half

2 large stalks celery, cut into ¼-inch pieces

Cloves squeezed from 2 heads Roasted Garlic (page 324) or 4 cloves garlic, minced

2 pounds boneless venison or beef roast, cut into 4 large pieces

5 cups beef broth, homemade (page 320) or store-bought

1 (14½-ounce) can diced tomatoes

1 teaspoon fine sea salt

1 teaspoon ground black pepper

½ teaspoon dried rosemary, or 1 teaspoon fresh rosemary, finely chopped

½ teaspoon dried thyme leaves, or 1 teaspoon fresh thyme leaves, finely chopped

½ head cauliflower, cut into large florets

Fresh thyme leaves, for garnish

1. Place the butter in a 6-quart Instant Pot and press Sauté. Once melted, add the onions and sauté for 4 minutes, or until soft.

2. Add the mushrooms, celery, and garlic and sauté for another 3 minutes, or until the mushrooms are golden brown. Press Cancel to stop the Sauté. Add the roast, broth, tomatoes, salt, pepper, rosemary, and thyme.

3. Seal the lid, press Pressure Cook or Manual, and set the timer for 30 minutes. Once finished, turn the valve to venting for a quick release.

4. Add the cauliflower. Seal the lid, press Pressure Cook or Manual, and set the timer for 5 minutes. Once finished, let the pressure release naturally.

5. Remove the lid and shred the meat with two forks. Taste the liquid and add more salt, if needed. Ladle the stew into bowls. Garnish with thyme leaves.

Place the onions, mushrooms, celery, garlic, roast, broth, tomatoes, salt, pepper, rosemary, and thyme in a 6-quart slow cooker. Cover and cook on high for 4 to 5 hours or on low for 8 hours, until the meat is fork-tender. Add the cauliflower, then cover and cook on high for another 20 minutes, or until the cauliflower is soft. Proceed to Step 5.

NUTRITIONAL INFO (per serving)				
calories	fat	protein	carbs	fiber
359	21g	32g	9g	3g

french onion soup

yield: 12 servings *prep time:* 10 minutes *cook time:* 22 minutes

6 tablespoons (¾ stick) unsalted butter

4 large onions, sliced and separated into rings

1 tablespoon Swerve granular-style sweetener or equivalent amount of liquid or powdered sweetener (see page 39)

Cloves squeezed from 1 head Roasted Garlic (page 324) or 2 cloves garlic, minced

7 cups beef broth, homemade (page 320) or store-bought, divided

1 teaspoon fine sea salt

¼ teaspoon dried thyme leaves

1 bay leaf

12 slices Low-Carb Loaf Bread (page 326)

½ cup shredded Gruyère cheese

¼ cup grated Parmesan cheese (about ¾ ounce)

2 tablespoons shredded mozzarella cheese

Fresh thyme sprigs, for garnish

Freshly ground black pepper, for garnish

1. Place the butter in a 6-quart Instant Pot and press Sauté. Once melted, add the onions and sprinkle with the sweetener. Cook, stirring frequently, until the onions are golden brown and soft, about 10 minutes.

2. Stir in the garlic and cook until fragrant, about 1 minute. Add ½ cup of the broth and use a whisk to scrape up the bits stuck to the bottom of the pot. Press Cancel to stop the Sauté. Pour in the rest of the broth. Add the salt, thyme, and bay leaf and stir to combine.

3. Seal the lid, press Pressure Cook or Manual, and set the timer for 10 minutes. Once finished, let the pressure release naturally.

4. Meanwhile, preheat the oven to broil. Arrange the bread slices on a baking sheet. Broil until toasted, 1 to 2 minutes per side. Place the cheeses in a small bowl and combine well with a fork.

5. Just before serving, remove the lid and discard the bay leaf. Fill oven-safe soup crocks three-quarters full with the soup and top each crock with a slice of toasted bread. Sprinkle about 2 tablespoons of the cheese mixture on each slice of bread. Place the filled crocks on a rimmed baking sheet and broil until the cheese topping is lightly browned and bubbling, about 2 minutes. Garnish with thyme and freshly ground pepper.

Melt the butter in a large, heavy pot over medium-high heat. Add the onions and cook, stirring frequently, until they are golden brown and soft, about 10 minutes. Sprinkle the onions with the sweetener and reduce the heat to medium. Add the garlic and cook until fragrant, about 1 minute. Stir in ½ cup of the broth and use a whisk to scrape up the bits stuck to the bottom of the pot. Transfer the onion mixture to a 6-quart slow cooker and pour in the remaining broth. Add the salt, thyme, and bay leaf and stir to combine. Cover and cook on low for 8 to 10 hours, until the onions are very soft. Proceed to Step 4.

STORE the soup and toppings in separate airtight containers in the fridge for up to 5 days, or freeze the soup for up to a month. To reheat the soup, place in a saucepan over medium heat, stirring occasionally, for 5 minutes, or until heated through. Just before serving, top the soup with the toasted bread and cheeses and place under the oven broiler until the cheese topping is lightly browned and bubbling.

NUTRITIONAL INFO (per serving)				
calories	fat	protein	carbs	fiber
329	11g	15g	11g	4g

creamy chicken & tomato soup

option

yield: 4 servings   *prep time:* 10 minutes   *cook time:* 19 minutes

1 tablespoon unsalted butter (or coconut oil for dairy-free)

¼ cup finely chopped onions

2 cloves garlic, minced

2 large boneless, skinless chicken breasts (see Note)

1 cup chicken broth, homemade (page 320) or store-bought

1 cup heavy cream (or full-fat coconut milk for dairy-free)

1 (14½-ounce) can diced tomatoes, drained

2 tablespoons tomato paste

3 tablespoons Italian seasoning

1 teaspoon fine sea salt

½ teaspoon ground black pepper

Chopped fresh basil leaves, for garnish

Extra-virgin olive oil, for drizzling

1. Place the butter in a 6-quart Instant Pot and press Sauté. Once melted, add the onions and garlic and sauté for 4 minutes, or until the onions are soft. Press Cancel to stop the Sauté.

2. Add the chicken, broth, cream, tomatoes, tomato paste, Italian seasoning, salt, and pepper to the Instant Pot and stir to combine. Seal the lid, press Pressure Cook or Manual, and set the timer for 15 minutes. Once finished, turn the valve to venting for a quick release.

3. Remove the lid and shred the chicken with two forks. Taste and adjust the seasoning to your liking. Ladle the soup into bowls and garnish with basil and a drizzle of olive oil.

Place all of the ingredients except the basil and olive oil in a 6-quart slow cooker. Cover and cook on low for 8 hours, or until the chicken is fork-tender. Proceed to Step 3.

STORE in an airtight container in the fridge for up to 5 days or in the freezer for up to a month. To reheat, place in a saucepan over medium heat, stirring occasionally, for 5 minutes, or until heated through.

NOTE: You can use frozen chicken breasts instead of fresh—just set the cook time to 20 minutes instead of 15.

NUTRITIONAL INFO (per serving)				
calories	fat	protein	carbs	fiber
382	29g	24g	11g	2g

belgian booyah

 yield: 8 servings   *prep time:* 10 minutes   *cook time:* 16 minutes

1 tablespoon unsalted butter (or coconut oil for dairy-free)

2 cups sliced button mushrooms

1 medium onion, diced

Cloves squeezed from 1 head Roasted Garlic (page 324), or 2 cloves garlic, minced

1 pound ground beef

4 boneless, skinless chicken thighs, cut into ¾-inch pieces

1 head cauliflower, cut into 1-inch pieces

2 cups beef broth, homemade (page 320) or store-bought

2 cups tomato sauce

1 (14½-ounce) can diced tomatoes

2 teaspoons dried basil leaves

2 teaspoons dried oregano leaves

1 teaspoon celery salt

1 teaspoon ground black pepper

1. Place the butter in a 6-quart Instant Pot and press Sauté. Once melted, add the mushrooms, onion, and garlic and cook for 4 minutes, or until the onions are soft.

2. Add the ground beef and continue to cook, crumbling the meat to break up the large chunks, for 2 minutes, or until the beef is starting to cook through. Press Cancel to stop the Sauté.

3. Add the chicken, cauliflower, broth, tomato sauce, tomatoes, basil, oregano, celery salt, and pepper. Stir well to combine.

4. Seal the lid, press Pressure Cook or Manual, and set the timer for 10 minutes. Once finished, turn the valve to venting for a quick release.

5. Remove the lid and stir well. Ladle the soup into bowls and serve.

Complete Steps 1 and 2 using a large skillet over medium-high heat. Transfer the mixture to a 6-quart slow cooker and proceed to Step 3. Cover and cook on high for 3 hours or on low for 7 hours, until the meats are fully cooked through. Proceed to Step 5.

STORE in an airtight container in the fridge for up to 5 days or in the freezer for up to a month. To reheat, place in a saucepan over medium heat, stirring occasionally, for 5 minutes, or until heated through.

NUTRITIONAL INFO (per serving)				
calories	fat	protein	carbs	fiber
273	15g	22g	13g	4g

supreme pizza soup

yield: 6 servings   *prep time:* 10 minutes   *cook time:* 13 minutes

1 tablespoon unsalted butter (or coconut oil for dairy-free)

¼ cup diced onions

1 cup button or cremini mushrooms (fresh or canned), thinly sliced

¼ cup diced red bell peppers

1½ pounds bulk Italian sausage

5 cups marinara sauce, homemade (page 332) or store-bought

1 cup beef broth, homemade (page 320) or store-bought

½ cup sliced pepperoni

1 teaspoon dried oregano leaves

Fine sea salt and ground black pepper

½ cup sliced black olives, plus more for garnish

¼ cup shredded mozzarella, for garnish (optional; omit for dairy-free)

Fresh oregano leaves, for garnish (optional)

1. Place the butter in a 6-quart Instant Pot and press Sauté. Once melted, add the onions and cook for 3 minutes, or until soft. Add the mushrooms and bell peppers and cook for another 3 minutes, or until the peppers are soft.

2. Add the sausage and cook, crumbling the meat to break up the large chunks, for 5 minutes, or until almost completely cooked through. Add the marinara, broth, pepperoni, and dried oregano and stir to combine. Press Cancel to stop the Sauté.

3. Seal the lid, press Pressure Cook or Manual, and set the timer for 2 minutes. Once finished, turn the valve to venting for a quick release.

4. Remove the lid and stir well. Season with salt and pepper to taste and stir in the olives. Ladle the soup into bowls and top each bowl with a couple of olive slices and some shredded cheese, if using. Garnish with oregano leaves, if desired.

Place the butter, onions, mushrooms, bell peppers, and sausage in a 6-quart slow cooker. Cover and cook on high for 20 minutes, or until the sausage is almost cooked through. Stir well to break up the meat. Add the marinara, broth, pepperoni, and dried oregano and stir to combine. Cover and cook on high for 3 to 4 hours or on low for 6 to 8 hours, until the veggies are soft. Proceed to Step 4.

STORE in an airtight container in the fridge for up to 5 days or in the freezer for up to a month. To reheat, place in a saucepan over medium heat, stirring occasionally, for 5 minutes, or until heated through.

NUTRITIONAL INFO (per serving)				
calories	fat	protein	carbs	fiber
260	21g	6g	9g	2g

green borscht

    yield: 4 servings *prep time:* 10 minutes *cook time:* 15 minutes

I love anything topped with an egg, so when I heard a chef talk about a traditional Russian soup called green borscht that often has hard-boiled eggs in it, I knew I had to try it! I always store hard-boiled eggs in the fridge for easy additions to recipes like this one.

2 tablespoons unsalted butter (or coconut oil for dairy-free) (Instant Pot only)

½ cup diced onions

3 cups chopped sorrel or spinach

4 boneless, skinless chicken breasts, cut into ¾-inch chunks

1 head cauliflower, cut into ¾-inch pieces

6 cups chicken broth, homemade (page 320) or store-bought

1 tablespoon chopped fresh dill, plus more for garnish

1 tablespoon lemon juice

Fine sea salt and ground black pepper

6 hard-boiled eggs (page 331), halved (omit for egg-free)

Sour cream, for garnish (omit for dairy-free)

1. Place the butter in a 6-quart Instant Pot and press Sauté. Once melted, add the onions and cook for 2 minutes. Add the sorrel and cook for another 3 minutes, or until the onions are soft.

2. Add the chicken, cauliflower, broth, and dill and stir to combine. Press Cancel to stop the Sauté.

3. Seal the lid, press Pressure Cook or Manual, and set the timer for 10 minutes. Once finished, let the pressure release naturally.

4. Remove the lid and stir in the lemon juice. Season with salt and pepper to taste. Ladle the soup into bowls, then place the halved hard-boiled eggs in the bowls. Garnish with a dollop of sour cream (if using) and more dill.

Place the onions, sorrel, chicken, cauliflower, broth, dill, and lemon juice in a 6-quart slow cooker. Cover and cook on high for 3 hours or on low for 6 hours, or until the chicken is cooked through. Proceed to Step 4.

STORE the soup and hard-boiled eggs in separate airtight containers in the fridge for up to 5 days; the soup can be frozen (without the eggs) for up to a month. To reheat the soup, place in a saucepan over medium heat, stirring occasionally, for 5 minutes, or until heated through. Then add the hard-boiled eggs.

NUTRITIONAL INFO (per serving)				
calories	fat	protein	carbs	fiber
519	24g	52g	23g	4g

egg roll soup

  yield: 4 servings   *prep time:* 10 minutes   *cook time:* 20 minutes

1 pound ground pork

2 cups thinly sliced cabbage, for "noodles"

4 cups beef broth, homemade (page 320) or store-bought

½ cup coconut aminos, or 2 tablespoons wheat-free tamari

½ teaspoon toasted sesame oil

¼ cup Swerve confectioners'-style sweetener or equivalent amount of liquid or powdered sweetener (see page 39)

4 green onions, thinly sliced, plus more for garnish

Cloves squeezed from 1 head Roasted Garlic (page 324), or 2 teaspoons garlic paste

1 (2-inch) piece fresh ginger, peeled and finely grated

4 poached eggs, for serving (see Tip)

1. Place the ground pork and cabbage "noodles" in a 6-quart Instant Pot. Add the broth, coconut aminos, sesame oil, sweetener, green onions, garlic, and ginger. Stir well to break up the meat.

2. Seal the lid, press Pressure Cook or Manual, and set the timer for 20 minutes. Once finished, let the pressure release naturally.

3. Remove the lid and stir well. Ladle the soup into bowls and add a poached egg to each bowl. Garnish with more sliced green onions.

 Complete Step 1 in a 6-quart slow cooker. Cover and cook on high for 4 to 5 hours or on low for 6 to 8 hours, until the pork is cooked through and no longer pink. Proceed to Step 3.

STORE the soup and poached eggs in separate airtight containers in the fridge for up to 5 days; the soup can be frozen (without the eggs) for up to a month. To reheat the soup, place in a saucepan over medium heat, stirring occasionally, for 5 minutes, or until heated through.

TIP: If you are in a hurry and need a poached egg quickly, all you have to do is put ½ cup of water in a microwave-safe mug, crack an egg into the water, and cover the mug with a saucer. Microwave on high for 1 minute to make a perfect poached egg!

NUTRITIONAL INFO (per serving)				
calories	fat	protein	carbs	fiber
425	30g	26g	11g	8g

chicken cordon bleu soup

 yield: 12 servings *prep time:* 10 minutes *cook time:* 14 minutes

3 tablespoons unsalted butter or coconut oil (Instant Pot only)

2 cups button or cremini mushrooms, sliced

¼ cup chopped onions

Cloves squeezed from 1 head Roasted Garlic (page 324) or 3 cloves garlic, minced

4 ounces cream cheese (¼ cup), softened

6 cups chicken broth, homemade (page 320) or store-bought

1 pound boneless, skinless chicken breasts, cut into 1-inch cubes

2 cups ham "noodles" (ham cut into long strips)

4 ounces Swiss cheese, shredded (about 1 cup)

½ cup grated Parmesan cheese (about 1½ ounces)

2 teaspoons dried tarragon

1 teaspoon fine sea salt

1 teaspoon ground black pepper

Extra-virgin olive oil, for drizzling

Fresh tarragon, for garnish

1. Place the butter in a 6-quart Instant Pot and press Sauté. Once melted, add the mushrooms, onions, and garlic and cook, stirring frequently, for 4 minutes, or until the onions are soft. Press Cancel to stop the Sauté.

2. Add the cream cheese and whisk to loosen. (If you don't use a whisk to loosen the cream cheese, you will end up with clumps in your soup.) Slowly whisk in the broth. Add the chicken, ham, cheeses, tarragon, salt, and pepper and stir to combine.

3. Seal the lid, press Pressure Cook or Manual, and set the timer for 10 minutes. Once finished, turn the valve to venting for a quick release.

4. Remove the lid and stir well. Ladle the soup into bowls and garnish with a drizzle of olive oil and some fresh tarragon.

Place the cream cheese in a 6-quart slow cooker. Slowly whisk in the broth. Add the mushrooms, onions, garlic, chicken, ham, cheeses, tarragon, salt, and pepper. Cover and cook on high for 3 hours or on low for 6 hours, or until the chicken is tender. Proceed to Step 4.

STORE in an airtight container in the fridge for up to 5 days or in the freezer for up to a month. To reheat, place in a saucepan over medium heat, stirring occasionally, for 5 minutes, or until heated through.

NUTRITIONAL INFO (per serving)				
calories	fat	protein	carbs	fiber
274	18g	22g	6g	0.3g

immune-boosting soup

  yield: 4 servings   *prep time:* 7 minutes   *cook time:* 10 minutes

I'm often asked, "What should I eat when I'm sick and don't have much of an appetite?" This soup is my answer. It is a great healthy meal that gives you the immune-boosting benefits of ginger and garlic as well as enough protein to help with muscle building.

4 large boneless, skinless chicken breasts, cut into 1-inch cubes

1 (1-inch) piece fresh ginger, unpeeled, cut into 4 thick slices

Cloves squeezed from 1 head Roasted Garlic (page 324), or 2 cloves garlic, crushed to a paste

8 cups chicken broth, homemade (page 320) or store-bought

Fine sea salt and ground black pepper

Fresh thyme or parsley leaves, for garnish

1. Place the chicken, ginger, garlic, and broth in a 6-quart Instant Pot. Stir to combine.

2. Seal the lid, press Pressure Cook or Manual, and set the timer for 10 minutes. Once finished, let the pressure release naturally.

3. Remove the lid and discard the ginger. Shred the chicken with two forks. Season with salt and pepper to taste.

4. Ladle the soup into bowls and garnish with fresh thyme.

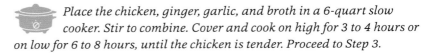 *Place the chicken, ginger, garlic, and broth in a 6-quart slow cooker. Stir to combine. Cover and cook on high for 3 to 4 hours or on low for 6 to 8 hours, until the chicken is tender. Proceed to Step 3.*

STORE in an airtight container in the fridge for up to 4 days or in the freezer for up to a month. To reheat, place in a saucepan over medium heat, stirring occasionally, for 5 minutes, or until heated through.

NUTRITIONAL INFO (per serving)				
calories	fat	protein	carbs	fiber
230	7g	23g	18g	0.1g

mexican beef soup

 yield: 8 servings *prep time:* 12 minutes *cook time:* 42 minutes

This simple twist on beef stew is packed with flavor! If you prefer a spicy soup, add one or two seeded and chopped jalapeños. If you like lots of heat, include some of the seeds as well. One of my recipe testers messaged me right after making this recipe and said, "I want to rename this 'Mexican Beef Soup of Deliciousness' since I can't seem to put down my, uhhh, 'tasting spoon' and get to bed!"

10 strips bacon, chopped

1 medium white onion, chopped

Cloves squeezed from 3 heads Roasted Garlic (page 324), or 6 cloves garlic, minced

1 to 2 jalapeño peppers, seeded and chopped (optional; see above)

2 pounds boneless beef chuck roast, cut into 4 equal-sized pieces

5 cups beef broth, homemade (page 320) or store-bought

1 cup chopped fresh cilantro, plus more for garnish

2 teaspoons fine sea salt

1 teaspoon ground black pepper

FOR GARNISH:

1 avocado, peeled, pitted, and diced

2 radishes, very thinly sliced

2 tablespoons chopped fresh chives

1. Place the bacon in a 6-quart Instant Pot and press Sauté. Cook, stirring occasionally, for 4 minutes, or until the bacon is crisp. Remove the bacon with a slotted spoon, leaving the drippings in the pot. Set the bacon on a paper towel–lined plate to drain.

2. Add the onion, garlic, and jalapeños, if using, to the Instant Pot and sauté for 3 minutes, or until the onion is soft. Press Cancel to stop the Sauté.

3. Add the beef, broth, cilantro, salt, and pepper. Stir to combine.

4. Seal the lid, press Pressure Cook or Manual, and set the timer for 35 minutes. Once finished, let the pressure release naturally.

5. Remove the lid and shred the beef with two forks. Taste the liquid and add more salt, if needed.

6. Ladle the soup into bowls. Garnish with the reserved bacon, avocado, radishes, chives, and more cilantro.

Place the onion, garlic, jalapeños (if using), beef, broth, cilantro, salt, and pepper in a 6-quart slow cooker. Cover and cook on high for 4 to 5 hours or on low for 8 hours, until the beef is fork-tender. Meanwhile, place the bacon in a large skillet and fry over medium heat for 4 minutes, or until crisp. Proceed to Step 5.

STORE in an airtight container in the fridge for up to 5 days or in the freezer for up to a month. To reheat, place in a saucepan over medium heat, stirring occasionally, for 3 minutes, or until heated through.

NUTRITIONAL INFO (per serving)				
calories	fat	protein	carbs	fiber
456	36g	25g	6g	2g

broccoli cheddar soup

option *yield:* 6 servings *prep time:* 10 minutes *cook time:* 12 minutes

1 tablespoon unsalted butter
(Instant Pot only)

½ cup diced onions

2 cloves garlic, chopped

2 ounces cream cheese (¼ cup),
softened

3 cups chicken broth, homemade
(page 320) or store-bought, or
vegetable broth

6 ounces aged white cheddar,
shredded (1½ cups)

1 small head broccoli, cut into
florets

Fine sea salt and ground black
pepper (optional)

1. Place the butter in a 6-quart Instant Pot and press Sauté. Once melted, add the onions and garlic and cook for 4 minutes, stirring often, or until the onions are soft. Press Cancel to stop the Sauté.

2. Add the cream cheese and whisk to loosen. (If you don't use a whisk to loosen the cream cheese, you will end up with clumps in your soup.) Slowly whisk in the broth.

3. Add the cheese and use a stick blender to purée the soup until smooth. Alternatively, you can pour the soup into a regular blender or food processor and purée until smooth, then return it to the Instant Pot. If using a regular blender, you may need to blend the soup in two batches; if you overfill the blender jar, the soup will not purée properly.

4. Add the broccoli to the puréed soup in the Instant Pot and stir to combine. Seal the lid, press Pressure Cook or Manual, and set the timer for 8 minutes. Once finished, turn the valve to venting for a quick release.

5. Remove the lid and stir well. Taste and add salt and pepper, if desired. Ladle into bowls for serving.

Place all of the ingredients, except the broccoli, in a 6-quart slow cooker. Cover and cook on high for 30 minutes. Remove the lid and use a stick blender to purée the soup until smooth (or transfer the soup to a regular blender or food processor and purée). Add the broccoli, cover, and cook on high for 1 hour or on low for 3 hours, or until the broccoli is tender. Proceed to Step 5.

STORE in an airtight container in the fridge for up to 5 days or in the freezer for up to a month. To reheat, place in a saucepan over medium heat, stirring occasionally, for 5 minutes, or until heated through.

NUTRITIONAL INFO (per serving)				
calories	fat	protein	carbs	fiber
227	16g	12g	9g	1g

cheesy bacon noodle soup

  yield: 6 servings *prep time:* 12 minutes *cook time:* 12 minutes

Broccoli cheese soup is my favorite broccoli dish. I also adore noodles in soup, so I combined the two ideas to create this recipe. The noodles are made from the broccoli stem, which has a mild flavor and is just as nutrient-rich as the florets. Even if you don't like broccoli, you will love this soup!

2 large heads broccoli

2 strips bacon, chopped

2 tablespoons unsalted butter

¼ cup diced onions

Cloves squeezed from 1 head Roasted Garlic (page 324), or 2 cloves garlic, minced

3 cups chicken broth or beef broth, homemade (page 320) or store-bought

6 ounces extra-sharp cheddar cheese, shredded (about 1½ cups)

2 ounces cream cheese (¼ cup), softened

½ teaspoon fine sea salt

¼ teaspoon ground black pepper

Pinch of ground nutmeg

SPECIAL EQUIPMENT:

Spiral slicer

STORE in an airtight container in the fridge for up to 5 days or in the freezer for up to a month. To reheat, place in a saucepan over medium heat, stirring occasionally, for 5 minutes, or until heated through.

1. Cut the broccoli florets off the stems, leaving as much of the stems intact as possible. Reserve the florets for another recipe. Trim the bottom end of each stem so that it is flat. Using a spiral slicer, cut the stems into "noodles."

2. Place the bacon in a 6-quart Instant Pot and press Sauté. Cook, stirring occasionally, for 4 minutes, or until crisp. Remove the bacon with a slotted spoon and set aside on a paper towel–lined plate to drain, leaving the drippings in the pot.

3. Add the butter and onions to the Instant Pot and cook for 4 minutes, or until the onions are soft. Add the garlic (and, if using raw garlic, sauté for another minute). Add the broth, cheddar cheese, cream cheese, salt, pepper, and nutmeg and sauté until the cheeses are melted, about 3 minutes. Press Cancel to stop the Sauté.

4. Use a stick blender to purée the soup until smooth. Alternatively, you can pour the soup into a regular blender or food processor and purée until smooth, then return it to the Instant Pot. If using a regular blender, you may need to blend the soup in two batches; if you overfill the blender jar, the soup will not purée properly.

5. Add the broccoli noodles to the puréed soup in the Instant Pot. Seal the lid, press Pressure Cook or Manual, and set the timer for 1 minute. Once finished, let the pressure release naturally.

6. Remove the lid and stir well. Ladle the soup into bowls and sprinkle some of the bacon on top of each serving.

Complete Step 1, then follow Step 2 using a small skillet over medium heat to cook the bacon. Place the butter, onions, garlic, broth, cheddar cheese, cream cheese, salt, pepper, and nutmeg in a 6-quart slow cooker. Cover and cook on low for 3 to 5 hours, until the onions are soft and the soup is fragrant. Proceed to Step 4. Add the broccoli noodles to the puréed soup in the slow cooker, cover, and cook on low for another 30 minutes, or until the noodles are soft. Proceed to Step 6.

NUTRITIONAL INFO (per serving)				
calories	fat	protein	carbs	fiber
258	19g	13g	9g	1g

chicken & asparagus red curry soup

  yield: 8 servings *prep time:* 7 minutes *cook time:* 11 minutes

1 tablespoon unsalted butter (or coconut oil for dairy-free)

¼ cup finely chopped onions

2 cloves garlic, minced

1 (14-ounce) can full-fat coconut milk

1 (14-ounce) can tomato sauce

1 cup chicken broth, homemade (page 320) or store-bought

1 tablespoon red curry paste

1 teaspoon fish sauce or fine sea salt

½ teaspoon ground black pepper

2 pounds boneless, skinless chicken breasts, cut into ½-inch chunks

2 cups asparagus, trimmed and cut into 2-inch pieces

Fresh cilantro leaves, for garnish

Lime wedges, for garnish

1. Place the butter in a 6-quart Instant Pot and press Sauté. Once melted, add the onions and garlic and sauté for 4 minutes, or until the onions are soft. Press Cancel to stop the Sauté.

2. Add the coconut milk, tomato sauce, broth, curry paste, fish sauce, and pepper and whisk to combine well. Stir in the chicken and asparagus.

3. Seal the lid, press Pressure Cook or Manual, and set the timer for 7 minutes. Once finished, turn the valve to venting for a quick release.

4. Remove the lid and stir well. Taste and adjust the seasoning to your liking. Ladle the soup into bowls and garnish with cilantro. Serve with lime wedges or a squirt of lime juice.

Place all of the ingredients, except the asparagus and garnishes, in a 6-quart slow cooker. Cover and cook on high for 2 hours or on low for 4 hours, or until the chicken is fork-tender. Add the asparagus and cook on low for another 20 minutes, or until the asparagus is tender. Proceed to Step 4.

STORE in an airtight container in the fridge for up to 5 days or in the freezer for up to a month. To reheat, place in a saucepan over medium heat, stirring occasionally, for 5 minutes, or until heated through.

NUTRITIONAL INFO (per serving)				
calories	fat	protein	carbs	fiber
235	13g	24g	8g	2g

lasagna soup

yield: 6 servings *prep time:* 5 minutes *cook time:* 7 minutes

1½ pounds bulk Italian sausage

5 cups marinara sauce, homemade (page 332) or store-bought

1 cup beef broth, homemade (page 320) or store-bought

1 cup finely sliced cabbage or thinly sliced deli turkey breast, for "noodles"

1 teaspoon dried oregano leaves

Fine sea salt and ground black pepper (optional)

1 cup ricotta cheese (8 ounces), homemade (see page 322) or store-bought

½ cup grated Parmesan cheese (about 1½ ounces)

2 cups shredded mozzarella cheese

Fresh basil and/or oregano leaves, for garnish

1. Place the sausage in a 6-quart Instant Pot and press Sauté. Cook, while crumbling, for 5 minutes, or until almost completely cooked through. Add the marinara, broth, "noodles," and dried oregano. Press Cancel to stop the Sauté.

2. Seal the lid, press Pressure Cook or Manual, and set the timer for 2 minutes. Once finished, turn the valve to venting for a quick release.

3. Remove the lid and stir well. Taste and add salt and pepper, if desired. Ladle the soup into bowls, place a dollop of ricotta in the center of each bowl, and top with the cheeses. Garnish with fresh basil and/or oregano.

Place the sausage in a 6-quart slow cooker. Cover and cook on high for 20 minutes, or until the meat is starting to crumble. Stir well to break up the meat. Add the marinara, broth, "noodles," and dried oregano. Cover and cook on high for 3 to 4 hours or on low for 6 to 8 hours, until the cabbage is very tender. Proceed to Step 3.

STORE in an airtight container in the fridge for up to 5 days or in the freezer for up to a month. To reheat, place in a saucepan over medium heat, stirring occasionally, for 5 minutes, or until heated through.

NUTRITIONAL INFO (per serving)				
calories	fat	protein	carbs	fiber
622	48g	35g	9g	2g

beef
& lamb

santa fe meatloaf

  yield: 6 servings   *prep time:* 10 minutes   *cook time:* 30 minutes

---

1½ pounds ground beef

⅔ cup salsa, plus more for serving

½ cup finely chopped button or cremini mushrooms

½ cup chopped green onions

1 teaspoon fine sea salt

1 teaspoon chili powder

1 teaspoon smoked paprika

½ teaspoon ground cumin

½ teaspoon garlic powder

½ teaspoon onion powder

1 (4-ounce) can chopped mild green chilies, drained well

1 large egg, lightly beaten

1 jalapeño pepper, thinly sliced (optional)

Fresh cilantro leaves, for garnish

Guacamole, for serving (optional)

1. Place a 15 by 9-inch sheet of parchment paper on a 15 by 9-inch piece of aluminum foil and set aside.

2. Place all of the ingredients, except the jalapeño slices and garnishes, in a large bowl and mix well with your hands. Shape the mixture into a 9 by 5-inch loaf, then place the loaf on the parchment-lined foil. Top the meatloaf with the jalapeño slices, if using.

3. To make the loaf pan, use the foil on the outside of the loaf to hold its shape, then tuck in the sides of the foil around the loaf.

4. Set a trivet in an 8-quart Instant Pot and pour in 1 cup of cold water. Grasp the sides of the foil loaf pan and place the meatloaf on the trivet.

5. Seal the lid, press Pressure Cook or Manual, and set the timer for 30 minutes. Once finished, let the pressure release naturally.

6. Remove the lid and lift the meatloaf out of the pot. Place on a serving dish and top with additional salsa or guacamole, if using. Garnish with cilantro, slice, and serve.

 Complete Steps 1 through 3. Then grasp the sides of the foil loaf pan and place the meatloaf in a 6-quart slow cooker. Cover and cook on low for 5½ hours, or until cooked through. Proceed to Step 6.

STORE in an airtight container in the fridge for up to 5 days or in the freezer for up to a month. To reheat, place meatloaf slices on a rimmed baking sheet in a preheated 350°F oven for 5 minutes, or until heated through.

VARIATION: Santa Fe Meatloaf Cupcakes. Whether or not you have kids, little meat cupcakes are the cutest entrees to serve. To make, place all of the ingredients for the meatloaf in a large bowl and mix well with your hands. Grease six 4-ounce ramekins and press equal portions of the meatloaf mixture into the ramekins. Set a trivet in an 8-quart Instant Pot and pour in 1 cup of cold water. Place the ramekins on the trivet. Seal the lid, press Pressure Cook or Manual, and set the timer for 20 minutes. Once finished, let the pressure release naturally. Alternatively, place the ramekins in an 8-quart slow cooker and carefully pour water around the ramekins until it comes halfway up the sides of the ramekins. Cover and cook on high for 2 hours or on low for 4 hours, or until cooked through. Top each cupcake with guacamole and a cherry tomato.

NUTRITIONAL INFO (per serving)				
calories	fat	protein	carbs	fiber
318	24g	21g	4g	1g

mocha pot roast

   option   *yield:* 4 servings   *prep time:* 6 minutes   *cook time:* 30 minutes

My son Kai is a true Ethiopian: he loves coffee! This recipe combines his two favorites—coffee and beef.

2 tablespoons finely ground decaf coffee

2 tablespoons unsweetened cocoa powder

1 tablespoon smoked paprika

2 teaspoons fine sea salt

2 pounds boneless beef chuck roast, cut into 1½- to 2-inch cubes

2 cups beef broth, homemade (page 320) or store-bought

1 cup chopped onions

3 tablespoons coconut vinegar or apple cider vinegar

Keto "Rice" (page 328), for serving (optional; omit for egg-free)

1. Place the coffee, cocoa powder, paprika, and salt in a small bowl and stir to combine well. Add the beef cubes in batches and rub the seasoning mixture onto the meat with your hands.

2. Place the seasoned beef in a 6-quart Instant Pot. Add the broth, onions, and vinegar. Seal the lid, press Pressure Cook or Manual, and set the timer for 30 minutes. Once finished, turn the valve to venting for a quick release.

3. Remove the lid and shred the meat with two forks. Serve over keto "rice," if desired.

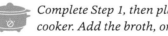 *Complete Step 1, then place the seasoned beef in a 6-quart slow cooker. Add the broth, onions, and vinegar. Cover and cook on low for 6 to 8 hours, until the meat is fork-tender. Proceed to Step 3.*

STORE in an airtight container in the fridge for up to 5 days or in the freezer for up to a month. To reheat, place in a casserole dish in a preheated 350°F oven for 5 minutes, or until heated through.

NUTRITIONAL INFO (per serving)				
calories	fat	protein	carbs	fiber
698	56g	41g	6g	2g

lamb vindaloo

option   option

yield: 4 servings   *prep time:* 10 minutes   *cook time:* 34 minutes

If you cannot find lamb or prefer to use beef, this vindaloo tastes great when made with beef, too.

1 tablespoon unsalted butter (or coconut oil for dairy-free) (Instant Pot only)

¼ cup diced onions

6 cloves garlic, minced

3 tablespoons grainy mustard

2 teaspoons ground cumin

2 teaspoons turmeric powder

½ teaspoon cayenne pepper

2 pounds boneless lamb shoulder, cut into 1½-inch cubes

1 (14-ounce) can full-fat coconut milk

1 tablespoon lime juice

Keto "Rice" (page 328), for serving (optional; omit for egg-free)

Fresh cilantro leaves, for garnish

1. Place the butter in a 6-quart Instant Pot and press Sauté. Once melted, add the onions and garlic and cook, stirring often, for 4 minutes, or until the onions are soft. Press Cancel to stop the Sauté.

2. Place the mustard, cumin, turmeric, and cayenne in a small bowl and stir well. Place the lamb in the Instant Pot and cover with the mustard mixture. Pour in the coconut milk.

3. Seal the lid, press Pressure Cook or Manual, and set the timer for 30 minutes. Once finished, let the pressure release naturally.

4. Remove the lid and stir in the lime juice. Serve over keto "rice," if desired. Garnish with cilantro.

Place the mustard, cumin, turmeric, cayenne, and vinegar in a small bowl and stir well, then transfer this mixture to a 4-quart or larger slow cooker. Add the lamb, coconut milk, onions, and garlic and stir to combine. Cover and cook on high for 3 hours or on low for 6 hours, or until the meat is very tender. Proceed to Step 4.

STORE in an airtight container in the fridge for up to 5 days or in the freezer for up to a month. To reheat, place in a cast-iron skillet over medium heat, stirring occasionally, for 5 minutes, or until heated through.

NUTRITIONAL INFO (per serving)				
calories	fat	protein	carbs	fiber
535	35g	46g	5g	1g

mushroom & swiss mini meatloaves

 yield: 8 servings   *prep time:* 5 minutes   *cook time:* 20 minutes

1½ pounds ground beef

1½ cups sliced mushrooms, plus more for topping

½ cup diced onions

½ cup powdered Parmesan cheese (see Note)

¼ cup tomato sauce

2 tablespoons prepared yellow mustard

1 large egg

1 clove garlic, crushed to a paste

2 teaspoons paprika

½ teaspoon fine sea salt

6 ounces Swiss cheese, cut into ¼-inch chunks (1½ cups)

SPECIAL EQUIPMENT:

3 mini loaf pans (6 by 3½ inches) or 6 (4-ounce) ramekins

1. Place all of the ingredients, except the Swiss cheese, in a large bowl and mix well with your hands. Press into 3 mini loaf pans or six 4-ounce ramekins.

2. Set a trivet in an 8-quart Instant Pot and pour in 1 cup of cold water. Place the mini loaves on the trivet. Seal the lid, press Pressure Cook or Manual, and set the timer for 20 minutes (or 15 minutes if using ramekins). Once finished, let the pressure release naturally.

3. Preheat the oven to broil.

4. Remove the lid and lift the mini meatloaves out of the pot. Sprinkle the Swiss cheese over the tops of the loaves and top with extra mushroom slices. Place the loaves under the broiler for a few minutes to melt the cheese.

5. Cut into slices and serve.

Complete Step 1 using ramekins. Place the ramekins in an 8-quart slow cooker. Carefully pour water around the ramekins until it comes halfway up the sides of the ramekins. Cover and cook on high for 2 hours or on low for 4 hours, or until the meatloaves are cooked through. Proceed to Step 3.

STORE in an airtight container in the fridge for up to 5 days or in the freezer for up to a month. To reheat, place meatloaf slices on a rimmed baking sheet in a preheated 350°F oven for 5 minutes, or until heated through.

NOTE: Powdered Parmesan is simply Parmesan cheese that has been grated to the point of being light, fluffy, and powdery. Fresh pregrated Parmesan cheese available at supermarket cheese counters usually has a powdery texture and can be a convenient option in recipes such as this one that call for powdered Parmesan. To make powdered Parmesan at home, place grated Parmesan cheese in a food processor or clean spice grinder and pulse until fluffy and powdery.

NUTRITIONAL INFO (per serving)				
calories	fat	protein	carbs	fiber
282	21g	20g	3g	0.3g

mama maria's italian meatballs

 yield: 4 servings *prep time:* 10 minutes *cook time:* 10 minutes

I know what you're thinking: I called these meatballs Mama Maria's because that's my name, but there are two other reasons for this recipe title. One, I am a mama who loves meatballs. And two, Craig and I used to eat at a wonderful Italian restaurant called Mama Maria's.

1½ pounds ground beef

3½ cups marinara sauce, homemade (page 000) or store-bought, divided

¼ cup chopped fresh Italian parsley

¼ cup chopped onions

2 cloves garlic, minced

1 large egg, beaten

1 tablespoon coconut flour, or 3 tablespoons powdered Parmesan cheese (see Note, page 152)

1¼ teaspoons Italian seasoning

1 teaspoon fine sea salt

FOR GARNISH:

Shredded mozzarella cheese (omit for dairy-free)

Fresh basil and/or oregano leaves

1. Put the ground beef, ¼ cup of the marinara, the parsley, onions, garlic, egg, coconut flour, Italian seasoning, and salt in a large bowl and thoroughly combine using your hands. (To check the seasoning, see the tip below.) Shape the meat mixture into 16 balls about 1¼ inches in diameter.

2. Place the meatballs in a 6-quart Instant Pot, leaving a little space between them. Pour the remaining marinara around the meatballs.

3. Seal the lid, press Pressure Cook or Manual, and set the timer for 10 minutes. Once finished, let the pressure release naturally.

4. Serve the sauce and meatballs topped with shredded mozzarella, if using, and fresh herbs.

Complete Step 1. Place the meatballs in a 4-quart or larger slow cooker. Cover and cook on low for 6 to 8 hours, until the meatballs are cooked through. Drain any fat from the slow cooker. Add the remaining marinara and cook for 30 more minutes. Proceed to Step 4.

STORE in an airtight container in the fridge for up to a week or in the freezer for up to a month. To reheat, place in a preheated 350°F oven for 5 minutes, or until heated through.

TIP: To check the seasoning of the meatball mixture, cook a smidgen of the mixture in a small skillet and taste it. It should taste amazing! If it doesn't, it likely needs more salt. Adjust the seasoning, then proceed with the recipe.

NUTRITIONAL INFO (per serving)				
calories	fat	protein	carbs	fiber
583	45g	33g	10g	3g

swedish meatballs

 yield: 12 servings *prep time:* 5 minutes *cook time:* 10 minutes

MEATBALLS:

1½ pounds ground beef

¼ pound bulk pork sausage

1 large egg

¼ cup tomato sauce

¼ cup minced onions

1 tablespoon mustard powder

1 clove garlic, minced

2 teaspoons fine sea salt

1 teaspoon ground black pepper

SAUCE:

1 cup beef broth, homemade
(page 320) or store-bought

1 (8-ounce) package cream cheese
(1 cup), softened

⅛ teaspoon ground nutmeg

Cabbage pasta (see Note) or
zucchini noodles, for serving

1. Make the meatballs: Place all of the meatball ingredients in a large bowl and mix well with your hands. Shape the meat mixture into 1½-inch balls.

2. Put the meatballs in an 8-quart Instant Pot, leaving a little space around each meatball.

3. Make the sauce: Place the broth, cream cheese, and nutmeg in a medium-sized bowl and whisk to combine. Pour the sauce around the meatballs in the pot.

4. Seal the lid, press Pressure Cook or Manual, and set the timer for 10 minutes. Once finished, let the pressure release naturally.

5. Serve the meatballs with the sauce over cabbage pasta.

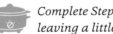 *Complete Step 1, then put the meatballs in an 8-quart slow cooker, leaving a little space around each meatball. Complete Step 3. Cover and cook on high for 2 hours or on low for 4 hours, or until the meatballs are cooked through. Proceed to Step 5.*

STORE in an airtight container in the fridge for up to 5 days or in the freezer for up to a month. To reheat, place in a baking dish in a preheated 350°F oven for 5 minutes, or until heated through.

NOTE: To make cabbage pasta, melt some coconut oil in a large sauté pan over medium heat. Add very thinly sliced green cabbage (1 cup per person) and sauté until very tender, about 15 minutes, stirring often to keep it from burning.

NUTRITIONAL INFO (per serving)				
calories	fat	protein	carbs	fiber
249	20g	13g	1g	0.2g

ranch mini meatloaves

 yield: 8 servings   *prep time:* 6 minutes   *cook time:* 20 minutes (for 2 mini loaves)

The mushrooms in this recipe reduce the calories while adding moisture and umami taste. Don't worry if you don't like mushrooms; you won't even taste them! This recipe makes four mini meatloaves. Because two mini loaves are enough to serve my family of four, I like to store the remaining two in an airtight container in the fridge or freezer for an easy meal later.

RANCH DRESSING:

4 ounces cream cheese (½ cup) (or ½ cup mayonnaise for dairy-free)

⅓ cup beef or chicken broth, homemade (page 320) or store-bought

¼ teaspoon dried chives

¼ teaspoon dried parsley

¼ teaspoon dried dill weed

⅛ teaspoon garlic powder

⅛ teaspoon onion powder

⅛ teaspoon fine sea salt

⅛ teaspoon ground black pepper

MEATLOAF:

1½ pounds ground beef

1 large egg, beaten

1 cup finely chopped button or cremini mushrooms

1 teaspoon fine sea salt

¾ teaspoon dried chives

¾ teaspoon dried parsley

½ teaspoon dried dill weed

½ teaspoon garlic powder

½ teaspoon onion powder

½ teaspoon ground black pepper

4 slices bacon, chopped and cooked crisp, for garnish

SPECIAL EQUIPMENT:

4 mini loaf pans (6 by 3½ inches)

1. Make the ranch dressing: Place all of the ingredients in a blender or food processor and purée until well combined. Cover and refrigerate for 2 hours before serving; the dressing will thicken in the fridge. It will keep for up to 5 days.

2. Make the meatloaf: Place all of the meatloaf ingredients in a large bowl and mix well with your hands. Divide the mixture into 4 equal portions and shape each portion into a loaf.

3. Place each loaf in a mini loaf pan. If desired, wrap up 2 of the uncooked loaves and store in the fridge or freezer to cook later.

4. Set a trivet in an 8-quart Instant Pot and pour in 1 cup of cold water. Place 2 of the filled mini loaf pans on the trivet. Seal the lid, press Pressure Cook or Manual, and set the timer for 20 minutes. Once finished, let the pressure release naturally. If cooking all 4 mini loaves, repeat with the remaining 2 loaves.

5. Remove the lid and lift the mini meatloaves out of the pot. Top with the ranch dressing and garnish with the bacon. Cut into slices and serve.

Place four 10 by 6-inch sheets of parchment paper on four 10 by 6-inch pieces of aluminum foil and set aside. Complete Steps 1 and 2. Place each mini loaf on a piece of parchment-lined foil. For 2 of the mini loaves, make a foil loaf pan: Use the foil on the outside to hold the loaf shape, tucking in the sides of the foil around each loaf. Wrap the 2 remaining loaves completely in the parchment-lined foil and store in the fridge or freezer to cook later. Grasp the sides of each foil loaf pan and place the loaves side by side in a 6-quart or larger slow cooker. Cover and cook on low for 3 hours, or until cooked through. Proceed to Step 5.

NUTRITIONAL INFO (per serving)				
calories	fat	protein	carbs	fiber
314	25g	19g	1g	0.2g

STORE in an airtight container in the fridge for up to 5 days or in the freezer for up to a month. To reheat, place meatloaf slices on a rimmed baking sheet in a preheated 350°F oven for 5 minutes, or until heated through.

bbq short ribs

 yield: 8 servings   *prep time:* 10 minutes   *cook time:* 35 minutes

1 cup tomato sauce

⅓ cup Swerve confectioners'-style sweetener or equivalent amount of liquid or powdered sweetener (see page 39)

¼ cup beef broth, homemade (page 320) or store-bought

¼ cup apple cider vinegar

2 teaspoons liquid smoke

8 beef short ribs (about 4 pounds)

1. Place the tomato sauce, sweetener, broth, vinegar, and liquid smoke in a 6-quart Instant Pot and stir until smooth. Add the short ribs.

2. Seal the lid, press Pressure Cook or Manual, and set the timer for 35 minutes. Once finished, let the pressure release naturally.

3. Remove the ribs from the pot. If you prefer a thicker sauce, press Sauté and cook the sauce for 5 to 15 minutes, until thickened to your liking. Press Cancel to stop the Sauté.

4. To serve, place the short ribs on plates and spoon the sauce over the ribs.

Complete Step 1 using a 6-quart slow cooker. Cover and cook on low for 7 to 8 hours, until the meat is tender and easily pulls away from the bones. If you prefer a thicker sauce, transfer the sauce from the slow cooker to a saucepan and cook over medium-high heat, stirring often, for 5 to 15 minutes, until thickened to your liking. Proceed to Step 4.

STORE in an airtight container in the fridge for up to 5 days or in the freezer for up to a month. To reheat, place in a baking dish in a preheated 350°F oven for 5 minutes, or until heated through.

NUTRITIONAL INFO (per serving)				
calories	fat	protein	carbs	fiber
569	50g	26g	2g	0.3g

beef stroganoff

  yield: 4 servings *prep time:* 5 minutes *cook time:* 34 minutes

1 tablespoon coconut oil

2 cups sliced mushrooms

½ cup diced onions

Cloves squeezed from 1 head Roasted Garlic (page 324), or 2 cloves garlic, minced

1 pound boneless beef roast, cut into 2-inch cubes

1½ teaspoons fine sea salt

½ teaspoon ground black pepper

4 ounces cream cheese (½ cup), softened

1 cup beef broth, homemade (page 320) or store-bought

1 teaspoon tomato paste

4 cups thinly sliced cabbage, for "noodles"

Fresh thyme leaves, for garnish

1. Place the coconut oil in a 6-quart Instant Pot and press Sauté. Once melted, add the mushrooms, onions, and garlic and cook for 4 minutes, or until the onions are soft. Remove the mushroom mixture to a small bowl and set aside.

2. Pat the beef cubes dry and season well on all sides with the salt and pepper. Place the beef in the Instant Pot, still on Sauté mode, and brown on all sides, about 4 minutes. Press Cancel to stop the Sauté.

3. Place the cream cheese in a medium-sized bowl and whisk to loosen. (If you don't use a whisk to loosen the cream cheese, you will end up with clumps in your sauce.) Slowly whisk in the broth and tomato paste until smooth. Pour the mixture into the Instant Pot. Add the mushroom mixture and stir to combine.

4. Seal the lid, press Pressure Cook or Manual, and set the timer for 20 minutes. Once finished, let the pressure release naturally.

5. Remove the lid and shred the beef with two forks. Lay the cabbage on top of the shredded beef.

6. Seal the lid, press Pressure Cook or Manual, and set the timer for 6 minutes. Once finished, turn the valve to venting for a quick release.

7. Transfer the stroganoff to a large serving dish, garnish with thyme, and enjoy!

Pat the beef cubes dry and season on all sides with the salt and pepper. Heat the coconut oil in a skillet over medium heat. Add the beef and brown on all sides. Transfer the meat to a 6-quart slow cooker, leaving the drippings in the pan. Add the mushrooms, onions, and garlic to the skillet and sauté for 3 minutes, or until the onions are tender. Add the onion mixture to the slow cooker. Proceed to Step 3, pouring the cream cheese mixture into the slow cooker. Cover and cook on low for 6 hours or until the beef is fork-tender. Proceed to Step 5, then stir to coat the cabbage "noodles." Cover and cook on high for 30 minutes to 1 hour, until the cabbage is very tender. Proceed to Step 7.

STORE in an airtight container in the fridge for up to 5 days or in the freezer for up to a month. To reheat, place in a saucepan over medium heat, stirring occasionally, for 5 minutes, or until heated through.

NUTRITIONAL INFO (per serving)				
calories	fat	protein	carbs	fiber
469	32g	34g	9g	3g

corned b

3

beef & cabbage

pounds brisket

2 cups beef broth, homemade (page 320) or store-bought

1 teaspoon mustard seeds

3 bay leaves

10 allspice berries

Cloves squeezed from 2 heads Roasted Garlic (page 324), or 4 cloves garlic, minced

1 teaspoon fine sea salt

1 teaspoon ground black pepper

1 head red cabbage, cut into large wedges

1. Place all of the ingredients, except the cabbage wedges, in a 6-quart Instant Pot. Seal the lid, press Pressure Cook or Manual, and set the timer for 90 minutes. Once finished, let the pressure release naturally.

2. Remove the lid and lay the cabbage wedges on top of the corned beef. Seal the lid, press Pressure Cook or Manual, and set the timer for 4 minutes. Once finished, turn the valve to venting for a quick release.

3. Put the cabbage in a serving dish or on the outer edges of a serving platter. Place the corned beef on a cutting board and cut across the grain into ¼-inch-thick slices. Move the slices to the center of the serving dish with the cabbage.

Place all of the ingredients, except the cabbage wedges, in a 6-quart slow cooker. Cover and cook on low for 8 hours, or until the corned beef is very tender. Lay the cabbage wedges on top of the corned beef. Cover and cook for 20 more minutes, or until the cabbage is tender. Proceed to Step 3.

STORE in an airtight container in the fridge for up to 5 days. To reheat, place in a lightly greased skillet over medium heat for 5 minutes, or until heated through.

NUTRITIONAL INFO (per serving)				
calories	fat	protein	carbs	fiber
548	40g	39g	7g	3g

smoky bbq brisket

4 pounds brisket

2 teaspoons celery salt

1½ teaspoons garlic powder

½ teaspoon ground black pepper

½ cup tomato sauce

½ cup liquid smoke

1. Place all of the ingredients in a 6-quart Instant Pot. Seal the lid, press Pressure Cook or Manual, and set the timer for 70 minutes. Once finished, let the pressure release naturally.

2. Place the brisket on a cutting board. Cut the meat across the grain into ¼-inch-thick slices.

 Place all of the ingredients in a 6-quart slow cooker. Cover and cook on low for 8 hours, or until the brisket is very tender. Proceed to Step 2.

STORE in an airtight container in the fridge for up to 5 days or in the freezer for up to a month. To reheat, place in a lightly greased skillet over medium heat for 5 minutes, or until heated through.

NUTRITIONAL INFO (per serving)				
calories	fat	protein	carbs	fiber
522	40g	38g	1g	0.1g

blue cheese steak roll-ups

  yield: 6 servings *prep time:* 5 minutes *cook time:* 15 minutes

1 (1½-pound) beef round tip roast, sliced into 6 steaks of equal thickness

6 ounces blue cheese, crumbled

½ cup beef broth, homemade (page 320) or store-bought

¼ cup coconut aminos, or 1 tablespoon wheat-free tamari

4 cloves garlic, minced

Chopped fresh Italian parsley, for garnish

Cracked black pepper, for garnish

1. Place each steak in a resealable plastic bag and pound with a rolling pin or meat mallet until it is ½ inch thick. Lay the pounded steaks flat on a cutting board or other work surface.

2. Divide the blue cheese evenly among the steaks, placing the cheese on one side. Roll up each steak, starting at a shorter end, and secure with toothpicks.

3. Combine the broth, coconut aminos, and garlic in a 6-quart Instant Pot. Add the steak roll-ups to the broth mixture.

4. Seal the lid, press Pressure Cook or Manual, and set the timer for 15 minutes. Once finished, turn the valve to venting for a quick release.

5. Remove the toothpicks from the steak roll-ups before serving. Garnish the roll-ups with chopped parsley and cracked black pepper.

 Complete Steps 1 through 3 using a 6-quart slow cooker. Cover and cook on low for 3 hours, or until the beef is cooked to your liking. Proceed to Step 5.

STORE in an airtight container in the fridge for up to 5 days. To reheat, place in a lightly greased skillet over medium heat for 5 minutes, or until heated through.

NUTRITIONAL INFO (per serving)				
calories	fat	protein	carbs	fiber
417	28g	37g	3g	2g

asian orange short ribs

  yield: 4 servings *prep time:* 5 minutes *cook time:* 38 minutes

½ cup coconut aminos, or
2 tablespoons wheat-free tamari

⅓ cup Swerve confectioners'-style
sweetener or equivalent amount
of liquid or powdered sweetener
(see page 39)

¼ cup beef broth, homemade
(page 320) or store-bought

¼ cup lime juice

Cloves squeezed from 1 head
Roasted Garlic (page 324), or
2 cloves garlic, peeled and
smashed with the side of a knife

1 tablespoon peeled and grated
fresh ginger

¼ teaspoon food-grade orange oil,
or 1 teaspoon orange extract

8 beef short ribs (about 4 pounds)

½ head green cabbage, quartered

½ teaspoon guar gum

Lime wedges, for serving

1. Place the coconut aminos, sweetener, broth, lime juice, garlic, ginger, and orange oil in a 6-quart Instant Pot. Add the short ribs, arranging them in a single layer. Lay the cabbage quarters on top.

2. Seal the lid, press Pressure Cook or Manual, and set the timer for 35 minutes. Once finished, let the pressure release naturally.

3. Remove the lid and transfer the cabbage and short ribs to plates. With a large spoon or ladle, skim the fat from the cooking liquid, keeping the cooking liquid in the pot.

4. Press Sauté. In a small bowl, whisk together the guar gum and 1 tablespoon of cold water until smooth. Whisk the guar gum mixture into the cooking liquid and cook until the sauce has thickened, 2 to 3 minutes.

5. Spoon the sauce over the short ribs and cabbage. Serve with lime wedges.

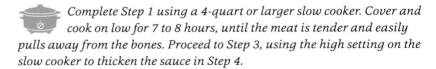 *Complete Step 1 using a 4-quart or larger slow cooker. Cover and cook on low for 7 to 8 hours, until the meat is tender and easily pulls away from the bones. Proceed to Step 3, using the high setting on the slow cooker to thicken the sauce in Step 4.*

STORE in an airtight container in the fridge for up to 5 days or in the freezer for up to a month. To reheat, place on a rimmed baking sheet in a preheated 350°F oven for 5 minutes, or until heated through.

NUTRITIONAL INFO (per serving)				
calories	fat	protein	carbs	fiber
460	38g	21g	9g	2g

protein noodle lasagnas

 yield: 8 servings   *prep time:* 10 minutes   *cook time:* 15 minutes

I grew up getting to choose any dinner I wanted for my birthday, but I usually made it myself. I remember my brothers and sister gathered around my parents' huge table, gobbling up my lasagna. Back then, my lasagna wasn't keto. And for years, I craved lasagna on my birthday, which led me to test different ideas for replacing the high-carb noodles. A simple swap of deli chicken slices really hits the spot. This recipe is my family's favorite—my boys would eat it every night!

The ingredients listed below make two lasagnas. My suggestion is to fill two 7-cup round casserole dishes and cook one. Cover the second dish tightly and store it, uncooked, in the freezer for up to a month. You can take the lasagna out of the freezer and pressure-cook it frozen; just add 15 minutes to the cooking time.

1 pound ground beef

1 pound bulk Italian sausage

3 tablespoons chopped onions

Cloves squeezed from 1 head Roasted Garlic (page 324), or 2 cloves garlic, minced

2 cups marinara sauce, homemade (page 332) or store-bought

2 cups whole-milk ricotta cheese (1 pound), homemade (page 322) or store-bought

1 large egg

½ teaspoon fine sea salt

16 thin slices deli chicken breast (about 8 ounces), divided

12 ounces mozzarella cheese, sliced, divided

¾ cup grated Parmesan cheese (about 2¼ ounces), divided

1. Put the ground beef, sausage, onions, and garlic in a Dutch oven over medium heat. Cook until the meats are well browned, about 5 minutes, stirring often to crumble them. Stir in the marinara and remove from the heat.

2. Put the ricotta, egg, and salt in a medium-sized bowl and stir to combine.

3. Set a trivet in a 6-quart Instant Pot and pour in 1 cup of cold water.

4. To assemble the lasagnas, spread one-quarter of the meat sauce in a 7-cup round casserole dish. Arrange one-quarter of the chicken slices over the meat sauce. Spread one-quarter of the ricotta mixture over the chicken. Top with 2 ounces of the mozzarella. Spoon ¾ cup of the meat sauce over the mozzarella and sprinkle with 2 tablespoons of the Parmesan cheese. Repeat the layers, then make a second lasagna in another 7-cup round casserole dish. Freeze one of the lasagnas to cook later.

5. Make a foil sling (see page 19) and use it to lower the dish onto the trivet in the Instant Pot. Tuck in the sides of the sling.

6. Seal the lid, press Pressure Cook or Manual, and set the timer for 10 minutes. Once finished, let the pressure release naturally. Remove the lid and lift the casserole dish out of the pot using the foil sling.

7. Let cool for 15 minutes before serving.

NUTRITIONAL INFO (per serving)				
calories	fat	protein	carbs	fiber
613	44g	45g	6g	1g

Place a large sheet of parchment paper in a 6-quart slow cooker so that the edges come up out of the slow cooker (for easy lifting of the lasagna out of the slow cooker). Complete Steps 1, 2, and 4, layering the lasagna ingredients directly in the slow cooker. Cover and cook on low for 4 to 5 hours, until the cheese is fully melted. Let cool for 15 minutes before serving.

STORE in an airtight container in the fridge for up to 4 days or in the freezer for up to a month. To reheat, place the casserole dish in a preheated 375°F oven for 8 minutes, or until heated through.

TIP: If you use part-skim mozzarella, there will be excess moisture in the dish after cooking; you may have to drain some of that moisture.

korean rib wraps

   yield: 4 servings *prep time:* 7 minutes *cook time:* 25 minutes

¼ cup coconut aminos, or
1 tablespoon wheat-free tamari

2 tablespoons coconut vinegar

2 tablespoons sesame oil

3 green onions, thinly sliced, plus
more for garnish

2 teaspoons peeled and grated
fresh ginger

2 teaspoons minced garlic

½ teaspoon fine sea salt

½ teaspoon red pepper flakes,
plus more for garnish

1 pound boneless beef short ribs,
sliced ½ inch thick

FOR SERVING:

1 head radicchio, thinly sliced

Butter lettuce leaves

1. Place the coconut aminos, vinegar, sesame oil, green onions, ginger, garlic, salt, and red pepper flakes in a 6-quart Instant Pot and stir to combine. Add the short ribs and toss to coat well.

2. Seal the lid, press Pressure Cook or Manual, and set the timer for 20 minutes. Once finished, let the pressure release naturally.

3. Remove the ribs from the Instant Pot and set aside on a warm plate, leaving the sauce in the pot.

4. Press Sauté and cook the sauce, whisking often, until thickened to your liking, about 5 minutes.

5. Put the sliced radicchio on a serving platter, then lay the short ribs on top. Pour the thickened sauce over the ribs. Garnish with more sliced green onions and red pepper flakes. Serve wrapped in lettuce leaves.

Complete Step 1 using a 6-quart slow cooker. Cover and cook on high for 4 hours or on low for 8 hours, or until the short ribs are very tender. Remove the ribs from the slow cooker, set aside on a warm plate, and pour the reserved sauce from the slow cooker into a small saucepan. Cook over medium-high heat, whisking often, until the sauce is thickened to your liking, about 5 minutes. Proceed to Step 5.

STORE in an airtight container in the fridge for up to 4 days. To reheat, place in a lightly greased skillet over medium heat, stirring occasionally, for 5 minutes, or until heated through.

NUTRITIONAL INFO (per serving)				
calories	fat	protein	carbs	fiber
547	48g	18g	9g	5g

spaghetti bolognese

BOLOGNESE SAUCE:

4 slices bacon, chopped

½ cup chopped onions

Cloves squeezed from 1 head Roasted Garlic (page 324), or 1 clove garlic, minced

¼ cup fresh flat-leaf parsley

3 tablespoons fresh oregano leaves

3 tablespoons fresh thyme leaves

2 bay leaves

1 teaspoon fine sea salt

½ teaspoon ground black pepper

1 pound ground beef

½ pound ground Italian sausage

2 cups marinara sauce, homemade (page 332) or store-bought

4 cups crushed tomatoes, with juices

1 cup beef broth, homemade (page 320) or store-bought

½ teaspoon stevia glycerite (optional)

¼ cup heavy cream (omit for dairy-free)

2 tablespoons unsalted butter (omit for dairy-free)

FOR SERVING:

2 medium zucchini, cut into thin noodles, warmed

1 cup grated Parmesan cheese (about 4 ounces) (omit for dairy-free)

1. Place the bacon in a 6-quart Instant Pot and press Sauté. Cook, stirring occasionally, for 4 minutes, or until the bacon is starting to crisp and the fat is rendered. Add the onions and cook, stirring frequently, for 4 more minutes, or until soft. Add the garlic, herbs, salt, and pepper. Cook, stirring, for 30 seconds.

2. Add the ground beef and Italian sausage and stir well to combine. Add the marinara, tomatoes, broth, and stevia, if using. Press Cancel to stop the Sauté.

3. Seal the lid, press Pressure Cook or Manual, and set the timer for 10 minutes. Once finished, let the pressure release naturally.

4. Remove the lid, add the cream and butter, if using, and stir to combine. Cover to keep warm until ready to serve. Before serving, adjust the seasoning to taste and discard the bay leaves. Serve the Bolognese sauce over the zucchini noodles and top with the Parmesan cheese, if desired.

Complete Step 1 using a large skillet over medium-high heat. Transfer the bacon mixture to a 6-quart slow cooker, add the ground beef and Italian sausage, and stir well to combine and to break up the meats. Add the marinara, tomatoes, broth, and stevia, if using. Cover and cook on high for 4 hours or on low for 8 hours, or until the meats are cooked through. Proceed to Step 4.

STORE the noodles and Bolognese sauce in separate airtight containers in the fridge for up to 4 days or in the freezer for up to a month. To reheat, place in a skillet over medium heat for 5 minutes, or until heated through.

NUTRITIONAL INFO (per serving)				
calories	fat	protein	carbs	fiber
460	34g	24g	13g	3g

barbacoa

yield: 8 servings *prep time:* 10 minutes *cook time:* 42 minutes

This dish is a great one to make ahead on a lazy Sunday for weekday meals. After shredding the meat, place it back in the Instant Pot, cover the inner pot with the lid, and refrigerate. Then use the reheating instructions below when ready to eat!

1 tablespoon coconut oil (Instant Pot only)

1 large onion, diced

Cloves squeezed from 1 head Roasted Garlic (page 324), or 2 cloves garlic, minced

1 (3-pound) boneless beef chuck roast, cut into 4 equal pieces

4 canned chipotle chilies

2 cups beef broth, homemade (page 320) or store-bought

½ cup lime juice

1 teaspoon liquid smoke (optional)

1½ tablespoons chili powder

2 teaspoons dried oregano leaves

1½ teaspoons ground cumin

1 teaspoon fine sea salt

¼ teaspoon ground black pepper

16 large Boston lettuce leaves

TOPPING SUGGESTIONS:

Lime wedges

Diced tomatoes

Sliced olives

Shredded red cabbage

Guacamole

Sour cream (omit for dairy-free)

Shredded cheddar cheese (omit for dairy-free)

1. Place the coconut oil in a 6-quart Instant Pot and press Sauté. Once melted, add the onion and cook for 4 minutes, or until soft. If using raw garlic instead of roasted, add the garlic and cook for another minute. If using roasted garlic, add it with the other ingredients in Step 2.

2. Add the roast, chilies, broth, lime juice, liquid smoke (if using), chili powder, oregano, cumin, salt, and pepper and stir to combine.

3. Seal the lid, press Pressure Cook or Manual, and set the timer for 38 minutes. Once finished, let the pressure release naturally.

4. Transfer the roast to a cutting board and shred the meat with two forks.

5. Serve the barbacoa wrapped in lettuce leaves with your desired toppings.

Spread the onion in a 4-quart or larger slow cooker. Place the roast and chilies on top of the onion. Pour the broth, lime juice, and liquid smoke, if using, over the beef, then add the garlic, chili powder, oregano, cumin, salt, and pepper. Cover and cook on high for 5 to 6 hours or on low for 6 to 8 hours, until the beef is fork-tender. Proceed to Step 4.

STORE in an airtight container in the fridge for up to 5 days or in the freezer for up to a month. To reheat, place in a saucepan over medium heat, stirring occasionally, for 5 minutes, or until heated through. If reheating in the Instant Pot, press Slow Cook and set the timer for 15 to 30 minutes.

NOTE: The nutritional information at left does not account for any toppings. Higher-fat toppings such as guacamole, olives, sour cream, and cheese will help increase the fat ratio.

NUTRITIONAL INFO (per serving)				
calories	fat	protein	carbs	fiber
539	43g	32g	4g	2g

chili cheese dog casserole

 yield: 6 servings *prep time:* 5 minutes *cook time:* 11 minutes

1 tablespoon unsalted butter or coconut oil

½ cup diced onions

Cloves squeezed from 1 head Roasted Garlic (page 324), or 2 cloves garlic, minced

1 pound ground beef

1 cup diced tomatoes (fresh preferred)

1 cup tomato sauce

1 cup beef broth, homemade (page 320) or store-bought

2 teaspoons Swerve confectioners'-style sweetener or equivalent amount of liquid or powdered sweetener (see page 39) (optional)

2 teaspoons chili powder

1 teaspoon fine sea salt

½ teaspoon ground cumin

¼ teaspoon ground black pepper

8 uncured hot dogs (see Note), sliced lengthwise and then cut in half

1 cup shredded Monterey Jack or cheddar cheese (about 4 ounces)

1. Place the butter in a 6-quart Instant Pot and press Sauté. Once melted, add the onions and garlic and cook, stirring often, for 4 minutes, or until the onions are soft.

2. Add the ground beef, tomatoes, tomato sauce, broth, sweetener (if using), chili powder, salt, cumin, and pepper and stir well.

3. Seal the lid, press Pressure Cook or Manual, and set the timer for 5 minutes. Once finished, turn the valve to venting for a quick release.

4. Remove the lid and stir well to combine. Lay the hot dog slices on top of the casserole mixture. Cover everything with the shredded cheese. Cover loosely with the lid, press Sauté, and cook for 2 minutes, or until the cheese is melted.

5. Scoop the casserole into bowls to serve.

Complete Step 1 using a large skillet over medium-high heat. Place the onion mixture in a 6-quart slow cooker and follow Step 2. Cover and cook on high for 2 hours or on low for 5 hours, or until the hot dogs are cooked through. Complete Step 4, covering and cooking on high for 15 minutes, or until the cheese is melted. Proceed to Step 5.

STORE in an airtight container in the fridge for up to 5 days or in the freezer for up to a month. To reheat, place in a skillet over medium heat for 5 minutes, or until heated through.

NOTE: I prefer Applegate Farms brand organic hot dogs.

NUTRITIONAL INFO (per serving)				
calories	fat	protein	carbs	fiber
541	41g	33g	7g	2g

unagi ribs

   yield: 6 servings *prep time:* 5 minutes *cook time:* 25 minutes

This recipe was inspired by my son Kai. He loves to go for sushi with his dad and fill up on unagi, which is eel—crazy, I know! Unagi is traditionally served with a yummy glaze, but we ask for it without the glaze because the glaze contains lots of sugar. Kai also adores ribs! Because eel isn't something I can easily find here in Wisconsin, I thought I would marry the two and make ribs with an unagi-like sauce. You can also make this recipe with boneless country-style pork ribs.

1 cup coconut aminos, or ¼ cup wheat-free tamari

¼ cup beef broth, homemade (page 320) or store-bought

3 tablespoons Swerve confectioners'-style sweetener or equivalent amount of liquid or powdered sweetener (see page 39)

1 tablespoon tomato sauce

1 teaspoon stevia glycerite (optional)

⅛ teaspoon guar gum or xanthan gum (optional, for thickening)

2 pounds boneless beef ribs

Sliced green onions, for garnish

1. Place the coconut aminos, broth, Swerve sweetener, tomato sauce, and stevia, if using, in a 6-quart Instant Pot. Slowly whisk in the guar gum, if using. Add the ribs and stir to coat.

2. Seal the lid, press Meat/Stew, and set the timer for 25 minutes. Once finished, let the pressure release naturally for 10 minutes, then turn the valve to venting for a quick release.

3. Remove the lid and remove the ribs from the pot. Serve with the sauce from the pot. Garnish with green onions.

Complete Step 1 using a 4-quart or larger slow cooker. Cover and cook on high for 3 to 4 hours or on low for 6 to 8 hours, until the meat is fork-tender. Proceed to Step 3.

STORE in an airtight container in the fridge for up to 5 days. To reheat, place on a rimmed baking sheet in a preheated 350°F oven for 5 minutes, or until heated through.

NUTRITIONAL INFO (per serving)				
calories	fat	protein	carbs	fiber
594	55g	23g	1g	0.1g

pork

pork lettuce cups

yield: 4 servings *prep time:* 5 minutes *cook time:* 10 minutes

1 tablespoon coconut oil

1 pound ground pork

1 cup chopped button or cremini mushrooms

½ cup chopped white onions

2 cloves garlic, minced

1 tablespoon coconut aminos, or ¾ teaspoon wheat-free tamari

1 tablespoon coconut vinegar or unseasoned rice vinegar

2 teaspoons toasted (dark) sesame oil

2 teaspoons peeled and finely grated fresh ginger

1 bunch green onions, chopped

DIPPING SAUCE:

½ cup lime juice

2 tablespoons fish sauce

1 teaspoon Asian chili sauce (such as sambal oelek)

1 teaspoon peeled and finely grated fresh ginger

1 clove garlic, minced

3 tablespoons Swerve confectioners'-style sweetener or equivalent amount of liquid or powdered sweetener (see page 39)

Fine sea salt, to taste

FOR SERVING:

Red leaf or Boston lettuce leaves

Mint, basil, and/or cilantro leaves

1 orange bell pepper, seeded and chopped, for garnish

Sliced green onions, for garnish

1. Place the coconut oil in a 6-quart Instant Pot and press Sauté. Once melted, add the pork, mushrooms, white onions, and garlic and cook, while crumbling the pork, for 5 minutes, or until the meat is almost cooked through. Press Cancel to stop the Sauté.

2. Stir in the coconut aminos, vinegar, sesame oil, ginger, and green onions. Seal the lid, press Pressure Cook or Manual, and set the timer for 5 minutes. Once finished, let the pressure release naturally.

3. Meanwhile, prepare the dipping sauce: Place all of the sauce ingredients in a serving dish and stir to combine.

4. Arrange the lettuce leaves around the outer edges of a large serving platter and pile the meat mixture in the center. Spoon a portion of the pork filling in a lettuce leaf and add the desired herbs. Garnish with bell peppers and green onions. Then wrap the lettuce around the filling like a burrito and serve with the dipping sauce.

Grease a 4-quart or larger slow cooker with the coconut oil. Place the pork, white onions, garlic, coconut aminos, vinegar, sesame oil, ginger, and green onions in the greased slow cooker. Cover and cook on low for 4 hours, or until the pork is fully cooked. After 30 minutes, stir and crumble the pork. Proceed to Step 3.

STORE the pork and dipping sauce in separate airtight containers in the fridge for up to a week, or freeze the pork for up to a month. To reheat the pork, place in a saucepan over medium heat, stirring occasionally, for 5 minutes, or until heated through.

NUTRITIONAL INFO (per serving)				
calories	fat	protein	carbs	fiber
385	30g	22g	9g	2g

smoky baby back ribs

 yield: 4 servings *prep time:* 3 minutes *cook time:* 23 minutes

How do you like your ribs—chewy, or slightly falling apart, or so tender that the meat falls off the bone when you blow on them? I prefer the latter, but no matter your preference, this recipe is perfect! If you want chewier ribs, cook them for 17 minutes. The longer you cook them, the more tender the ribs will be.

2 pounds baby back pork ribs

2 teaspoons fine sea salt

2 teaspoons smoked paprika

GLAZE:

½ cup tomato sauce

¼ cup Swerve confectioners'-style sweetener or equivalent amount of liquid or powdered sweetener (see page 39)

2 teaspoons liquid smoke

1. Season the ribs on all sides with the salt and paprika.

2. Place a trivet in an 8-quart Instant Pot and pour in 1 cup of cold water. Place the seasoned ribs on the trivet.

3. Seal the lid, press Pressure Cook or Manual, and set the timer for 20 minutes. Once finished, turn the valve to venting for a quick release.

4. Meanwhile, preheat the oven to broil. Place the glaze ingredients in a small bowl and stir well to combine.

5. Place the cooked ribs on a rimmed baking sheet. Brush the glaze over the ribs, reserving some to pour over the ribs after broiling, if desired. Broil the ribs for 3 minutes, or until crispy on the edges.

6. Serve with the reserved glaze poured over the top of the ribs, if desired.

Complete Step 1, then place the seasoned ribs in a 6-quart or larger slow cooker and pour in ½ cup of ham or chicken broth. Cover and cook on high for 4 to 5 hours or on low for 8 hours, until the ribs are cooked to your liking.

STORE in an airtight container in the fridge for up to 5 days. To reheat, place on a rimmed baking sheet in a preheated 350°F oven for 5 minutes, or until heated through.

NUTRITIONAL INFO (per serving)				
calories	fat	protein	carbs	fiber
518	41g	37g	2g	1g

perfect bbq pulled pork

  yield: 8 servings *prep time:* 5 minutes *cook time:* 60 minutes

1 (5-pound) boneless pork shoulder roast

5 cloves garlic, sliced

1 medium onion, diced

2 cups chicken broth, homemade (page 320) or store-bought

1 cup tomato sauce

2 teaspoons liquid smoke

2 tablespoons paprika

1 teaspoon fine sea salt

1 teaspoon ground black pepper

½ teaspoon chili powder

1. Use a sharp paring knife to cut deep slits in the pork roast. Push the garlic slices into the slits.

2. Place the roast in a 6-quart Instant Pot. Add the onion, broth, tomato sauce, liquid smoke, paprika, salt, pepper, and chili powder.

3. Seal the lid, press Pressure Cook or Manual, and set the timer for 60 minutes. Once finished, let the pressure release naturally.

4. Remove the lid and shred the meat with two forks. Stir before serving.

 Complete Step 1. Place the pork roast in a 4-quart or larger slow cooker. Add the rest of the ingredients. Cover and cook on low for 8 hours, or until the meat reaches an internal temperature of 160°F. Proceed to Step 4.

STORE in an airtight container in the fridge for up to 5 days. To reheat, place in a saucepan over medium heat, stirring occasionally, for 5 minutes, or until heated through.

NUTRITIONAL INFO (per serving)				
calories	fat	protein	carbs	fiber
584	34g	60g	7g	1g

melt-

in-your-mouth pork belly

yield: 8 servings   *prep time:* 6 minutes   *cook time:* 44 minutes

1 (2-pound) pork belly

1 cup beef or chicken broth, homemade (page 320) or store-bought

2 green onions, thinly sliced

2 tablespoons peeled and grated fresh ginger

1 tablespoon coconut oil

2 teaspoons fine sea salt

½ teaspoon ground black pepper

Kimchi (see Note) or Keto "Rice" (page 328), for serving (optional) (use kimchi for egg-free)

1. Place the pork belly, broth, green onions, and ginger in a 6-quart Instant Pot.

2. Seal the lid, press Pressure Cook or Manual, and set the timer for 35 minutes. Once finished, turn the valve to venting for a quick release.

3. Remove the pork belly from the pot and discard the cooking liquid. Place the coconut oil in the pot and press Sauté. Season the cooked pork belly on all sides with the salt and pepper. When the oil is hot, add the pork belly to the pot and sauté on all sides until crispy, about 2 minutes per side. Press Cancel to stop the Sauté.

4. Place the crispy pork belly on a cutting board and allow to rest for 5 minutes. Cut into ½-inch slices. Serve over kimchi or keto "rice," if desired.

Complete Step 1 using a 6-quart slow cooker. Cover and cook on high for 4 to 5 hours or on low for 7 to 8 hours, until the meat is fork-tender. Remove the pork belly from the slow cooker and discard the cooking liquid. Place the coconut oil in a cast-iron skillet over medium-high heat. Season the cooked pork belly on all sides with the salt and pepper. When the oil is hot, add the pork belly to the skillet and sauté on all sides until crispy, about 2 minutes per side. Proceed to Step 4.

STORE in an airtight container in the fridge for up to 5 days or in the freezer for up to a month. To reheat, place in a lightly greased skillet over medium heat for 5 minutes, or until heated through.

NOTE: When buying premade kimchi, check the label to make sure that there are no added sugars or MSG. You can find my homemade kimchi recipe in my book Quick & Easy Ketogenic Cooking.

NUTRITIONAL INFO (per serving)				
calories	fat	protein	carbs	fiber
349	30g	18g	2g	0.2g

sweet 'n' sour pork

   yield: 4 servings *prep time:* 6 minutes *cook time:* 15 minutes

6 ounces tomato paste

1½ cups beef or chicken broth, homemade (page 320) or store-bought

⅓ cup Swerve confectioners'-style sweetener or equivalent amount of liquid or powdered sweetener (see page 39)

¼ cup coconut vinegar

¾ tablespoon lime or lemon juice

¾ teaspoon fish sauce

½ teaspoon fine sea salt

½ teaspoon garlic powder

⅛ teaspoon peeled and grated fresh ginger

1 pound boneless pork shoulder roast

½ cup (½-inch chunks) green bell peppers

Butter lettuce leaves, for serving

Sliced green onions, for garnish

1. Place the tomato paste, broth, sweetener, vinegar, lime juice, fish sauce, salt, garlic powder, and ginger in a 6-quart Instant Pot. Stir well. Add the pork roast and bell peppers and stir to coat in the sauce.

2. Seal the lid, press Pressure Cook or Manual, and set the timer for 15 minutes. Once finished, turn the valve to venting for a quick release.

3. Remove the lid and shred the meat with two forks. Serve the shredded pork wrapped in lettuce leaves. Garnish with sliced green onions.

Complete Step 1 using a 4-quart or larger slow cooker. Cover and cook on high for 4 hours or on low for 6 to 8 hours, until the pork is fork-tender. Proceed to Step 3.

STORE in an airtight container in the fridge for up to 5 days. To reheat, place in a lightly greased skillet over medium heat for 5 minutes, or until heated through.

NOTE: You can make this recipe with brisket if you prefer beef or choose not to consume pork.

NUTRITIONAL INFO (per serving)				
calories	fat	protein	carbs	fiber
294	14g	27g	11g	3g

five-ingredient pork roast

  yield: 4 servings   *prep time:* 5 minutes   *cook time:* 35 minutes

1 (2½-pound) boneless pork loin roast

2 teaspoons fine sea salt

1 large onion, cut into thick slices

2 cloves garlic, minced

2 cups chicken broth, homemade (page 320) or store-brought

Fresh herbs, such as rosemary, for garnish

Lemon wedges, for garnish

1. Season the pork roast on all sides with the salt, then place the roast in a 6-quart Instant Pot. Add the onion slices and garlic, then pour in the broth.

2. Seal the lid, press Pressure Cook or Manual, and set the timer for 35 minutes. Once finished, turn the valve to venting for a quick release.

3. Remove the roast to a serving platter and shred the meat with two forks. Serve with the onion slices and juices from the pot. Garnish with fresh herbs and lemon wedges.

Complete Step 1 using a 6-quart slow cooker. Cover and cook on high for 3 to 4 hours or on low for 6 to 8 hours, until the pork shreds easily. Proceed to Step 3.

STORE in an airtight container in the fridge for up to 5 days or in the freezer for up to a month. To reheat, place in a baking dish in a preheated 350°F oven for 5 minutes, or until heated through.

NUTRITIONAL INFO (per serving)				
calories	fat	protein	carbs	fiber
560	33g	58g	5g	1g

pork tenderloin

yield: 8 servings *prep time:* 5 minutes *cook time:* 17 minutes

1 (2-pound) pork tenderloin

½ cup crumbled Gorgonzola cheese (3 ounces)

½ cup crumbled feta cheese (3 ounces)

2 cloves garlic, minced

2 tablespoons finely crushed raw almonds

1 tablespoon finely chopped onions

½ teaspoon fine sea salt

½ teaspoon ground black pepper

1. Use a sharp knife to cut a large pocket in the tenderloin; starting at a short end, slice the meat lengthwise to leave a ½-inch edge on one long side and both short ends.

2. Place the cheeses, garlic, almonds, and onions in a medium-sized bowl and stir to combine. Stuff the cheese mixture into the pocket in the pork.

3. Secure the cut side of the tenderloin with toothpicks to seal in the stuffing. Season on all sides with the salt and pepper. Wrap the stuffed tenderloin in parchment paper.

4. Set a trivet in a 6-quart Instant Pot and pour in 1 cup of cold water. Place the wrapped tenderloin on the trivet.

5. Seal the lid, press Pressure Cook or Manual, and set the timer for 17 minutes. Once finished, let the pressure release naturally.

6. Remove the tenderloin to a cutting board and allow to rest for 10 minutes, then cut into 1-inch-thick slices and serve.

Complete Steps 1 through 3. Place the wrapped tenderloin in a 6-quart or larger slow cooker. Pour in ½ cup beef broth. Cover and cook on low for 4 hours, or until the tenderloin is cooked through but still slightly pink inside. Proceed to Step 6.

STORE in an airtight container in the fridge for up to 5 days. To reheat, place slices on a rimmed baking sheet in preheated 350°F oven for 5 minutes, or until heated through.

NUTRITIONAL INFO (per serving)				
calories	fat	protein	carbs	fiber
253	14g	29g	1g	0.3g

pot roast pork

 yield: 14 servings *prep time:* 6 minutes *cook time:* 60 minutes

Sometimes people look at my recipes and get nervous because they see ingredients they've never heard of before. Fish sauce? What is that?! I was like that once, too! If you've never tried a recipe with fish sauce in it, you're missing out. It's an ingredient that makes food taste extra-special, and it's a staple that every cook should have in the fridge. Fish sauce, along with mushrooms and aged cheeses, has something called umami. *Umami is a pleasant savory taste produced by glutamate and ribonucleotides, which are chemicals that occur naturally in many foods. Umami is subtle and not generally identifiable to people when they encounter it, but it blends well with other tastes to intensify and enhance flavors.*

I prefer Red Boat fish sauce, which is traditionally fermented without wheat, unlike most other brands. A bottle will last you a long time. You use only a little bit in a dish; it's strong stuff!

1 (4-pound) boneless pork loin roast

12 cloves garlic

½ cup sliced onions

1 cup ham or chicken broth, homemade (page 320) or store-bought

3 tablespoons lime or lemon juice

3 teaspoons fish sauce

3 bay leaves

2 teaspoons fine sea salt

½ teaspoon ground black pepper

Lime slices, for garnish

Fresh flat-leaf parsley, for garnish

1. Use a sharp paring knife to cut deep slits in the pork roast. Push the garlic cloves into the slits.

2. Place the roast in a 6-quart Instant Pot and lay the onions on top. Add the broth, lime juice, fish sauce, bay leaves, salt, and pepper.

3. Seal the lid, press Pressure Cook or Manual, and set the timer for 60 minutes. Once finished, let the pressure release naturally.

4. Remove the roast to a cutting board and allow to rest for 10 minutes, then cut into ½-inch slices. Season with additional salt and a squirt of lime juice, then garnish with lime slices and parsley.

Complete Steps 1 and 2 using a 6-quart slow cooker. Cover and cook on high for 3 hours or on low for 6 hours, or until the pork is tender and no longer pink inside. Proceed to Step 4.

STORE in an airtight container in the fridge for up to 5 days or in the freezer for up to a month. To reheat, place slices on a rimmed baking sheet in a preheated 350°F oven for 5 minutes, or until heated through.

NUTRITIONAL INFO (per serving)				
calories	fat	protein	carbs	fiber
261	15g	27g	2g	0.2g

sausa

...ge fajita bowls

yield: 6 servings   *prep time:* 5 minutes   *cook time:* 8 minutes

1 tablespoon unsalted butter (or coconut oil for dairy-free)

½ cup sliced onions

½ cup sliced orange bell peppers

½ cup sliced yellow bell peppers

2 cloves garlic, minced

6 (5-inch-long) smoked sausages, cut into ¼-inch slices

½ cup salsa, plus more for serving

1 teaspoon fine sea salt

½ teaspoon ground cumin

½ teaspoon smoked paprika

½ cup shredded sharp cheddar cheese, for garnish (optional; omit for dairy-free)

Finely chopped fresh cilantro leaves, for garnish

Sour cream, for serving (optional; omit for dairy-free)

1. Place the butter in a 3-quart or larger Instant Pot and press Sauté. Once melted, add the onions, bell peppers, and garlic. Cook for 5 minutes, or until the onions and peppers are soft. Press Cancel to stop the Sauté. Add the sausage, salsa, salt, cumin, and paprika and stir to combine.

2. Seal the lid, press Pressure Cook or Manual, and set the timer for 3 minutes. Once finished, turn the valve to venting for a quick release.

3. Remove the lid and stir well. Place the sausage mixture in bowls, top with the shredded cheese (if using) and additional salsa, and garnish with cilantro. Serve with sour cream on the side, if desired.

 Complete Step 1 using a 3-quart or larger slow cooker. Cover and cook on high for 1 hour or on low for 2 hours, or until the onions and peppers are soft.

STORE in an airtight container in the fridge for up to 5 days or in the freezer for up to a month. To reheat, place in a skillet over medium heat, stirring occasionally, for 5 minutes, or until heated through.

NUTRITIONAL INFO (per serving)				
calories	fat	protein	carbs	fiber
204	16g	9g	4g	1g

sweet 'n' sour ribs

 yield: 6 servings *prep time:* 5 minutes *cook time:* 27 minutes

4 pounds bone-in pork ribs

¾ cup coconut aminos, or
3 tablespoons wheat-free tamari

½ cup Swerve confectioners'-style
sweetener or equivalent amount
of liquid or powdered sweetener
(see page 39)

2 tablespoons unseasoned rice
vinegar

6 cloves garlic, minced

2 teaspoons peeled and finely
grated fresh ginger

1 teaspoon fish sauce (optional)

½ teaspoon red pepper flakes
(optional)

4 drops food-grade orange oil, or
2 teaspoons orange extract

¼ teaspoon guar gum (optional,
for thickening the sauce)

Sliced green onions, for garnish

Toasted sesame seeds, for garnish

1. Place the ribs in a 6-quart Instant Pot. In a medium-sized bowl, whisk together the coconut aminos, sweetener, vinegar, garlic, ginger, fish sauce (if using), red pepper flakes (if using), and orange oil. Pour the sauce over the ribs.

2. Seal the lid, press Pressure Cook or Manual, and set the timer for 20 minutes. Once finished, let the pressure release naturally.

3. Before serving, preheat the oven to broil. Transfer the ribs to a rimmed baking sheet, leaving the sauce in the pot.

4. If you desire a thicker sauce, slowly whisk in the guar gum. Press Sauté and cook the sauce for about 4 minutes, or until thickened a little. Press Cancel to stop the Sauté.

5. Baste the ribs with a few tablespoons of the sauce. Broil the ribs for about 3 minutes, until the sauce is bubbling and slightly caramelized.

6. Serve the ribs with extra sauce and garnish with green onions and toasted sesame seeds.

Complete Steps 1 and 2 using a 6-quart slow cooker, then cover and cook on high for 4 to 5 hours or on low for 7 to 8 hours, until the meat is tender. Before serving, preheat the oven to broil and transfer the ribs to a rimmed baking sheet. If using guar gum to thicken the sauce, transfer the sauce in the slow cooker to a small saucepan and slowly whisk in the guar gum. Boil the sauce over high heat for about 4 minutes, or until thickened a little. Proceed to Step 5.

STORE in an airtight container in the fridge for up to 4 days or in the freezer for up to a month. To reheat, place on a rimmed baking sheet in a preheated 350°F oven for 5 minutes, or until heated through.

NUTRITIONAL INFO (per serving)				
calories	fat	protein	carbs	fiber
695	35g	88g	3g	1g

...ticker bowls

This dish is amazing! It makes the most delicious leftovers to take with you for lunch the next day. You can make it with ground chicken instead of pork if you prefer.

4 cups finely shredded cabbage

1 pound ground pork

½ cup finely chopped red bell peppers

½ cup sliced green onions (about 1 bunch), plus more for garnish

2 cloves garlic, minced

½ teaspoon peeled and grated fresh ginger

½ cup coconut aminos, or 2 tablespoons wheat-free tamari

¼ cup chicken broth, homemade (page 320) or store-bought

2 tablespoons lime juice

2 teaspoons coconut vinegar or unseasoned rice vinegar

⅛ teaspoon red pepper flakes

2 large eggs, lightly beaten

Fine sea salt

Black sesame seeds, for garnish

1. Place all of the ingredients, except the eggs, salt, and sesame seeds, in a 6-quart Instant Pot. Stir well.

2. Seal the lid, press Pressure Cook or Manual, and set the timer for 7 minutes. Once finished, let the pressure release naturally.

3. Remove the lid and make a well in the center of the pork mixture. Pour the eggs into the well and press Sauté. Scramble the eggs for 2 minutes, or until set. Stir the eggs into the pork mixture until well combined. Press Cancel to stop the Sauté.

4. Taste and season with salt, if needed. Serve in bowls, garnished with more sliced green onions and black sesame seeds.

Complete Step 1 using a 6-quart slow cooker. Cover and cook on high for 2 hours or on low for 4 hours, or until the pork is cooked through and the cabbage is soft. Complete Step 3 with the slow cooker set to high. Proceed to Step 4.

STORE in an airtight container in the fridge for up to 4 days. To reheat, place in a lightly greased skillet over medium heat, stirring occasionally, for 5 minutes, or until heated through.

NUTRITIONAL INFO (per serving)				
calories	fat	protein	carbs	fiber
267	19g	17g	8g	4g

toscana

paglia e fieno

I often ordered this fantastic Italian dish at restaurants when Craig and I first started dating. It is a pasta dish with ham and asparagus in a delicious cream sauce. Here is my keto version.

½ cup diced ham

4 cups thinly sliced cabbage, for "noodles"

¼ cup diced asparagus (about 4 spears)

Cloves squeezed from 1 head Roasted Garlic (page 324), or 2 teaspoons crushed garlic

1 cup heavy cream

2 tablespoons unsalted butter

½ cup grated Parmesan cheese (about 1½ ounces)

2 large egg yolks, lightly beaten

Sliced green onions, for garnish

Fresh herbs of choice, for garnish

1. Place the ham, cabbage, asparagus, garlic, heavy cream, and butter in a 6-quart Instant Pot. Stir well to combine.

2. Seal the lid, press Pressure Cook or Manual, and set the timer for 10 minutes. Once finished, let the pressure release naturally.

3. Remove the lid and stir in the Parmesan cheese and beaten egg yolks. Press Sauté and cook for 1 minute, or until the sauce has thickened a bit.

4. Serve garnished with green onions and fresh herbs.

Complete Step 1 using a 6-quart slow cooker. Cover and cook on high for 3 to 4 hours or on low for 6 to 8 hours, until the cabbage is very soft. Complete Step 3 with the slow cooker set to high. Proceed to Step 4.

STORE *in an airtight container in the fridge for up to 4 days. To reheat, place in a lightly greased skillet over medium heat for about 3 minutes, until heated through.*

NUTRITIONAL INFO (per serving)				
calories	fat	protein	carbs	fiber
378	34g	13g	9g	3g

with onion gravy

  yield: 4 servings *prep time:* 5 minutes *cook time:* 24 minutes

2 tablespoons unsalted butter (or coconut oil for dairy-free)

1 cup sliced onions

2 cups beef broth, homemade (page 320) or store-bought

1 teaspoon chopped fresh thyme or other herb of choice

Fine sea salt and ground black pepper

4 (4-ounce) bratwursts

2 cups Mashed Cauliflower (page 330), for serving

Fresh flat-leaf parsley, for garnish (optional)

1. Place the butter in a 6-quart Instant Pot and press Sauté. Once melted, add the onions and cook until translucent and just starting to brown, about 6 minutes. Add the broth and thyme and cook for another 10 minutes. Season with salt and pepper. Press Cancel to stop the Sauté.

2. Add the brats to the pot. Seal the lid, press Pressure Cook or Manual, and set the timer for 8 minutes. Once finished, let the pressure release naturally.

3. To serve, place ½ cup of mashed cauliflower on each plate. Top with a brat and cover with the onion gravy from the pot. Garnish with parsley, if desired.

Complete Step 1 using a large skillet over medium-high heat. Transfer the onion mixture to a 6-quart slow cooker and add the brats. Cover and cook on high for 2 hours or on low for 4 hours, or until the brats are cooked through. Proceed to Step 3.

STORE in an airtight container in the fridge for up to 3 days. To reheat the brats, place on a rimmed baking sheet in a preheated 350°F oven for 5 minutes, or until heated through. Reheat the gravy in a small saucepan over medium heat until warmed. Or reheat in the Instant Pot by placing the brats with the onion gravy in one steamer basket and the mashed cauliflower in another steamer basket. Seal the lid, press Pressure Cook or Manual, and set the timer for 3 minutes. Once finished, turn the valve to venting for a quick release.

NUTRITIONAL INFO (per serving)				
calories	fat	protein	carbs	fiber
424	45g	17g	11g	3g

amazing asian-inspired pulled pork

   yield: 8 servings *prep time:* 10 minutes *cook time:* 40 minutes

¾ cup coconut aminos, or 3 tablespoons wheat-free tamari

½ cup beef broth, homemade (page 320) or store-bought

⅓ cup Swerve confectioners'-style sweetener or equivalent amount of liquid or powdered sweetener (see page 39)

2 tablespoons unseasoned rice vinegar

Cloves squeezed from 2 heads Roasted Garlic (page 324), or 4 cloves garlic, minced

1 tablespoon fish sauce (optional)

2 teaspoons peeled and grated fresh ginger

4 drops food-grade orange oil, or 2 teaspoons orange extract

1 (4-pound) boneless pork shoulder roast, cut into 4 equal pieces

Bibb lettuce leaves, for serving

Sliced green onions, for garnish

Finely chopped red cabbage, for garnish

1. Place the coconut aminos, broth, sweetener, vinegar, garlic, fish sauce (if using), ginger, and orange oil in a 6-quart Instant Pot. Stir well, then add the pork roast.

2. Seal the lid, press Pressure Cook or Manual, and set the timer for 40 minutes. Once finished, turn the valve to venting for a quick release.

3. Remove the lid and use two forks to shred the meat. Stir well to incorporate the flavorful sauce.

4. Serve in lettuce leaves and garnish with green onions and red cabbage.

 Place the pork roast in a 4-quart or larger slow cooker. Add the coconut aminos, broth, sweetener, vinegar, garlic, fish sauce, ginger, and orange oil. Cover and cook on low for 7 to 8 hours, until the meat is fork-tender and falls apart easily. Proceed to Step 3.

STORE in an airtight container in the fridge for up to 4 days or in the freezer for up to a month. To reheat, place in a saucepan over medium heat for 5 minutes, or until heated through.

NUTRITIONAL INFO (per serving)				
calories	fat	protein	carbs	fiber
559	41g	40g	5g	3g

poultry

chicken adobo

  yield: 6 servings *prep time:* 6 minutes *cook time:* 21 minutes

6 cloves garlic, minced

2 shallots, minced

3 tablespoons Swerve confectioners'-style sweetener or equivalent amount of liquid or powdered sweetener (see page 39)

½ teaspoon ground black pepper

¼ teaspoon cayenne pepper

2 bay leaves

½ cup chicken broth, homemade (page 320) or store-bought

⅓ cup coconut aminos, or 4 teaspoons wheat-free tamari

¼ cup coconut vinegar or apple cider vinegar

2 pounds bone-in, skin-on chicken thighs

FOR GARNISH:

Chopped fresh cilantro leaves

Whole peppercorns (any color)

Lime wedges

1. Place the garlic, shallots, sweetener, black pepper, cayenne, and bay leaves in a 6-quart Instant Pot. Add the broth, coconut aminos, vinegar, and chicken and stir to combine.

2. Seal the lid, press Pressure Cook or Manual, and set the timer for 10 minutes. Once finished, turn the valve to venting for a quick release.

3. Preheat the oven to broil. Remove the chicken from the pot and place in a cast-iron skillet or on a rimmed baking sheet.

4. Strain the remaining sauce from the pot into a saucepan and cook over medium-high heat, stirring frequently, until reduced by half, about 8 minutes.

5. Brush both sides of the chicken thighs with the reduced sauce. Place in the oven and broil for 2 to 3 minutes, until slightly charred and crispy. Serve the chicken with the sauce and garnish with cilantro, peppercorns, and lime wedges.

 Complete Step 1 using a 6-quart slow cooker. Cover and cook on low for 6 hours. Proceed to Step 3.

STORE in an airtight container in the fridge for up to 5 days or in the freezer for up to a month. To reheat, place in a baking dish in a preheated 350°F oven for 5 minutes, or until heated through.

NUTRITIONAL INFO (per serving)				
calories	fat	protein	carbs	fiber
318	21g	25g	5g	3g

maria's italian chicken cupcakes

yield: 5 servings (2 cupcakes per serving)   *prep time:* 6 minutes   *cook time:* 22 minutes

This recipe makes ten cupcakes, and eight will fit into an 8-quart Instant Pot. I store the remaining two uncooked in the fridge for up to 3 days or in the freezer for up to a month. They make a quick and easy dinner for one when you are looking for something comforting and delicious!

1½ pounds ground chicken

¾ cup finely chopped button or cremini mushrooms

½ cup grated Parmesan cheese (about 1½ ounces)

½ cup chopped fresh basil leaves

¼ cup marinara sauce, homemade (page 332) or store-bought, plus more for serving

1 teaspoon Italian seasoning

1 teaspoon dried oregano leaves

2 cloves garlic, minced

1½ cups (¼-inch chunks) fontina or mozzarella cheese

10 slices fresh mozzarella cheese, for topping (optional)

Fresh oregano leaves, for garnish

1. Place the chicken, mushrooms, Parmesan cheese, basil, and marinara in a large bowl. Add the Italian seasoning, oregano, garlic, and chunks of cheese and stir well.

2. Divide the meat mixture into 10 equal portions and press each portion into a greased 4-ounce ramekin or mason jar.

3. Set a trivet in an 8-quart Instant Pot and pour in 1 cup of cold water. Place eight of the ramekins on the trivet; cover and refrigerate or freeze the other two to cook later. Seal the lid, press Pressure Cook or Manual, and set the timer for 20 minutes. Once finished, let the pressure release naturally.

4. Remove the ramekins with tongs and preheat the oven to broil.

5. Remove the cupcakes from the ramekins. If desired, top each with a mozzarella slice, place on a rimmed baking sheet, and broil for 2 minutes, or until the cheese is melted. To serve, spoon some warmed marinara onto a serving platter. Place the cupcakes on top of the sauce. Garnish with oregano.

Complete Steps 1 and 2. Pour 3 cups of hot water into an 8-quart slow cooker. Set four of the ramekins in the slow cooker, making sure the water comes about halfway up the sides of the ramekins. Cover and cook on high for 2 to 3 hours or on low for 5 to 6 hours, until the "cupcakes" are cooked through. Repeat the process with the remaining four ramekins, or cover and refrigerate or freeze them to cook later. Proceed to Step 4.

STORE in an airtight container in the fridge for up to 5 days or in the freezer for up to a month. To reheat, place in a baking dish in a preheated 350°F oven for 6 minutes, or until the cheese topping (if used) is melted and the cupcakes are heated through.

NUTRITIONAL INFO (per serving)				
calories	fat	protein	carbs	fiber
637	41g	74g	1g	0.2g

greek chicken

  yield: 4 servings *prep time:* 10 minutes *cook time:* 14 minutes

2 tablespoons unsalted butter (or butter-flavored coconut oil for dairy-free) (Instant Pot only)

4 bone-in, skin-on chicken thighs

1 teaspoon fine sea salt

¾ teaspoon ground black pepper

Cloves squeezed from 1 head Roasted Garlic (page 324), or 2 cloves garlic, minced

¼ cup red wine vinegar or apple cider vinegar

2 tablespoons lemon or lime juice

2 teaspoons Dijon mustard

½ teaspoon dried basil leaves

½ teaspoon dried oregano leaves

GREEK SALAD:

2 cups Greek olives, pitted

1 medium cucumber, diced

1 medium tomato, diced

¼ cup diced red onions

4 sprigs fresh oregano

Extra-virgin olive oil or Greek Vinaigrette (page 260), for drizzling

1 cup crumbled feta cheese, for garnish (omit for dairy-free)

1. Place the butter in a 6-quart Instant Pot and press Sauté. Season the chicken thighs on all sides with the salt and pepper. When the butter is hot, place the chicken in the pot, skin side down. Add the garlic and cook for 4 minutes, or until golden brown. Flip the chicken over and add the vinegar, lemon juice, mustard, basil, and oregano. Stir to combine the ingredients. Press Cancel to stop the Sauté.

2. Seal the lid, press Pressure Cook or Manual, and set the timer for 10 minutes. Once finished, turn the valve to venting for a quick release.

3. Meanwhile, make the salad: Place the olives, cucumber, tomato, onions, and oregano in a large serving dish or on a large serving platter. Drizzle with olive oil. When the chicken is finished, take ¼ cup of the liquid from the pot and stir it into the salad.

4. Serve the chicken on top of the salad. Garnish with crumbled feta cheese, if desired.

Season the chicken thighs on all sides with the salt and pepper and place in a 6-quart slow cooker. Add the garlic, vinegar, lemon juice, mustard, basil, and oregano and stir to combine. Cover and cook on high for 3 to 4 hours or on low for 4 to 5 hours, until the chicken is no longer pink inside. Preheat the oven to broil. Transfer the chicken thighs to a rimmed baking sheet. Broil for 4 minutes, or until the skin is crispy. Proceed to Step 3.

TIP: If you forgot to plan ahead and have only frozen chicken thighs, this recipe will still work. Just increase the cook time to 15 minutes in an Instant Pot or 6 to 7 hours on low in a slow cooker.

STORE the chicken and salad in separate airtight containers in the fridge for up to 5 days; the chicken can be frozen for up to a month. To reheat the chicken, place on a rimmed baking sheet in a preheated 375°F oven for 8 minutes, or until heated through.

NUTRITIONAL INFO (per serving)				
calories	fat	protein	carbs	fiber
764	63g	40g	13g	7g

roast chicken

  yield: 6 servings *prep time:* 5 minutes *cook time:* 28 minutes

1 (4-pound) whole chicken

1 lemon, halved

1 medium onion, quartered

1 tablespoon paprika

2 teaspoons fine sea salt

1 teaspoon ground black pepper

1 cup chicken broth, homemade (page 320) or store-bought

Fresh thyme leaves, for garnish

1. Pat the chicken dry with a paper towel. Stuff the lemon halves and onion quarters inside the cavity. Rub the paprika all over the chicken. Sprinkle the chicken with the salt and pepper. Tie the legs together with kitchen twine.

2. Place the prepared chicken, breast side down (see Note), in a 6-quart Instant Pot. Pour the broth around the chicken.

3. Seal the lid, press Pressure Cook or Manual, and set the timer for 20 minutes. Once finished, let the pressure release naturally.

4. Preheat the oven to 425°F. Remove the chicken from the pot and place on a rimmed baking sheet. Roast for 8 minutes, or until the skin is crispy and golden brown. Place on a cutting board to rest for 10 minutes, then garnish with thyme before slicing and serving.

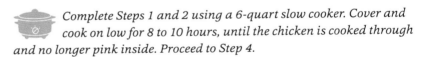 *Complete Steps 1 and 2 using a 6-quart slow cooker. Cover and cook on low for 8 to 10 hours, until the chicken is cooked through and no longer pink inside. Proceed to Step 4.*

NOTE: When cooking a whole bird, I always cook it with the breast side down. I used to think that the driest part of the meat should sit in the most liquid, but then I learned that it doesn't have anything to do with the breast being in liquid. When the breast is at the bottom, the juices in the bird drain down into the breast.

STORE in an airtight container in the fridge for up to 5 days or in the freezer for up to a month. To reheat, place slices on a baking sheet in a preheated 350°F oven for 5 minutes, or until heated through.

NUTRITIONAL INFO (per serving)				
calories	fat	protein	carbs	fiber
593	23g	88g	4g	1g

buffalo chicken lettuce wraps

  yield: 4 servings *prep time:* 5 minutes *cook time:* 24 minutes

1 tablespoon coconut oil or ghee (Instant Pot only)

2 stalks celery, thinly sliced

¼ cup diced onions

1 clove garlic, minced

1 pound boneless, skinless chicken breasts

2 cups chicken broth, homemade (page 320) or store-bought

1 teaspoon fine sea salt

½ cup hot sauce

FOR SERVING:

Boston or romaine lettuce leaves

Ranch Dressing (page 158)

Crumbled blue cheese (optional; omit for dairy-free)

Sliced celery

1. Place the coconut oil in a 6-quart Instant Pot and press Sauté. When hot, add the celery, onions, and garlic and sauté for 4 minutes, or until the onions are soft. Press Cancel to stop the Sauté.

2. Add the chicken, broth, and salt to the Instant Pot and stir to combine the ingredients. Seal the lid, press Pressure Cook or Manual, and set the timer for 20 minutes. Once finished, turn the valve to venting for a quick release.

3. Remove the lid and shred the chicken with two forks. Place the shredded chicken in a serving bowl and add ½ of cup the liquid from the pot. Add the hot sauce and stir well.

4. To serve, place ½ cup of the Buffalo chicken in a lettuce leaf. Top with ranch dressing and blue cheese crumbles, if using, and serve with sliced celery.

Place the celery, onions, garlic, chicken, broth, and salt in a 6-quart slow cooker. Cover and cook on low for 6 to 8 hours, until the chicken is tender and shreds easily. Proceed to Step 3.

STORE the chicken in an airtight container in the fridge for up to a week or in the freezer for up to a month. To reheat, place in a baking dish in a preheated 350°F oven for 5 minutes, or until heated through.

NUTRITIONAL INFO (per serving)				
calories	fat	protein	carbs	fiber
190	7g	24g	8g	2g

sesame c

2 tab
coo

...hicken

...lespoons avocado oil or
...onut oil (Instant Pot only)

... pound boneless, skinless
chicken thighs, cut into bite-sized
pieces

Fine sea salt

½ cup chicken broth, homemade
(page 320) or store-bought

⅓ cup Swerve confectioners'-style
sweetener or equivalent amount
of liquid or powdered sweetener
(see page 39)

½ cup coconut aminos, or
2 tablespoons wheat-free tamari

2 tablespoons toasted (dark)
sesame oil

2 tablespoons tomato sauce

1 tablespoon lime juice

¼ teaspoon peeled and grated
fresh ginger

Cloves squeezed from 1 head
Roasted Garlic (page 324), or
1 clove garlic, smashed to a paste

FOR GARNISH:

Sesame seeds

Sliced green onions

Lime wedges

1. Place the oil in a 6-quart Instant Pot and press Sauté. Pat the chicken pieces dry with a paper towel and season well on all sides with salt. When the oil is hot, add the chicken and cook, stirring often, until light golden brown on all sides, about 4 minutes.

2. Remove the chicken and set aside. Add the remaining ingredients to the pot and cook, stirring occasionally, until the sauce is reduced and thickened, about 10 minutes.

3. Return the chicken to the pot and cook, stirring occasionally, for 10 minutes, or until cooked through and no longer pink inside. Press Cancel to stop the Sauté.

4. Serve garnished with sesame seeds, sliced green onions, and lime wedges.

Season the chicken on all sides with salt. Place in a 6-quart slow cooker and add the remaining ingredients. Cover and cook on high for 2 hours or on low for 4 hours, or until the chicken is cooked through and no longer pink inside. If you desire a thicker sauce, use a slotted spoon to transfer the chicken to a serving platter. Transfer the sauce to a saucepan over high heat and cook, stirring often, for 5 minutes, or until thickened to your liking. Proceed to Step 4.

STORE in an airtight container in the fridge for up to 3 days or in the freezer for up to a month. To reheat, place in a greased skillet over medium heat for 5 minutes, or until warmed to your liking.

NUTRITIONAL INFO (per serving)				
calories	fat	protein	carbs	fiber
355	29g	20g	3g	0.1g

bbq chic

ken & "cornbread" casserole

6 servings   *prep time:* 5 minutes   *cook time:* 28 minutes

Q CHICKEN:

½ pounds boneless, skinless chicken breasts

2 cups tomato sauce

½ cup diced onions

¼ cup Swerve confectioners'-style sweetener or equivalent amount of liquid or powdered sweetener (see page 39)

1 teaspoon liquid smoke

1 teaspoon fine sea salt

"CORNBREAD" TOPPING:

1¼ cups whole-milk ricotta cheese (10 ounces), homemade (page 322) or store-bought

5 large eggs

½ cup coconut flour

1 teaspoon baking powder

1 teaspoon fine sea salt

1 teaspoon Mexican seasoning

Cherry tomatoes, for serving (optional)

1. Make the BBQ chicken: Grease a 6-quart Instant Pot. Place the chicken, tomato sauce, onions, sweetener, liquid smoke, and salt in the pot.

2. Seal the lid, press Pressure Cook or Manual, and set the timer for 20 minutes. Once finished, turn the valve to venting for a quick release.

3. Meanwhile, make the "cornbread" topping: Place the ricotta, eggs, coconut flour, baking powder, salt, and Mexican seasoning in a food processor or large bowl and mix until very smooth.

4. Remove the lid from the Instant Pot and shred the chicken with two forks. Top the shredded chicken with the topping mixture.

5. Seal the lid, press Pressure Cook or Manual, and set the timer for 8 minutes. Once finished, let the pressure release naturally.

6. Serve the casserole with cherry tomatoes, if desired.

Grease a 6-quart slow cooker. Place the ingredients for the BBQ chicken in the slow cooker. Cover and cook on low for 4 to 5 hours, until the chicken is tender. While the chicken is cooking, complete Step 3, then proceed to Step 4. Cook on low for 4 more hours, or until the topping is cooked through. Serve the casserole with cherry tomatoes, if desired.

STORE in an airtight container in the fridge for up to 5 days or in the freezer for up to a month. To reheat, place in a baking dish in a preheated 350°F oven for 5 minutes, or until heated through.

NUTRITIONAL INFO (per serving)				
calories	fat	protein	carbs	fiber
240	14g	15g	13g	4g

hot chicken caesar sandwiches

yield: 8 servings *prep time:* 10 minutes *cook time:* 22 minutes

---

2 pounds boneless, skinless chicken thighs

2 cups chicken broth, homemade (page 320) or store-bought

1 teaspoon fine sea salt

1 teaspoon ground black pepper

CAESAR DRESSING:

1 tablespoon Dijon mustard

1 tablespoon coconut vinegar or apple cider vinegar

Cloves squeezed from ½ head Roasted Garlic (page 324), or 1 clove garlic, minced

¼ teaspoon fine sea salt

¼ teaspoon ground black pepper

½ cup MCT oil or extra-virgin olive oil

2 tablespoons mayonnaise

1 teaspoon lemon juice

1 (2-ounce) can anchovies, finely chopped

½ cup shredded Parmesan cheese (about 2 ounces), plus more for garnish

¼ cup chopped fresh parsley

½ teaspoon ground black pepper, plus more for garnish

FOR SERVING:

8 romaine lettuce leaves, or 8 slices Low-Carb Loaf Bread (page 326) (use lettuce for nut-free)

1 tomato, thinly sliced

1. Place the chicken, broth, salt, and pepper in a 3-quart Instant Pot. Seal the lid, press Pressure Cook or Manual, and set the timer for 20 minutes. Once finished, turn the valve to venting for a quick release.

2. While the chicken is cooking, make the dressing: Place the mustard, vinegar, garlic, salt, and pepper in a blender and blend until smooth and thick. With the blender running on low speed, slowly add the oil, then the mayonnaise. Scrape down the sides of the jar as needed. Add the lemon juice and blend well. Add the anchovies and purée until smooth. Taste and add up to ¾ teaspoon more salt, adding it in ¼-teaspoon increments and blending and tasting after each addition. Season with additional pepper, if needed.

3. Remove the lid from the Instant Pot and drain the broth, leaving the chicken in the pot. Shred the chicken with two forks. Add ½ cup of the Caesar dressing, the Parmesan cheese, parsley, and pepper. (Refrigerate the remaining dressing for later use.) Stir until thoroughly combined.

4. Press Sauté and cook for 2 minutes, or until the Caesar chicken mixture is heated through and the cheese is melted.

5. To serve, spoon ¼ cup of the Caesar chicken onto a lettuce leaf (or slice of bread). Top with extra shredded Parmesan, a slice of tomato, and freshly ground pepper. Repeat with the remaining ingredients to make 8 sandwiches.

Place the chicken, broth, salt, and pepper a 3-quart slow cooker. Cover and cook on high for 2 hours or on low for 4 hours, or until the chicken shreds easily. Follow Steps 2 and 3, using the slow cooker in Step 3. Cover and cook on high for 20 minutes, or until the cheese is melted. Proceed to Step 5.

STORE the chicken mixture in an airtight container in the fridge for up to 5 days or in the freezer for up to a month. The leftover dressing will keep in the fridge for up to 4 days. To reheat the chicken, place in a saucepan over medium heat, stirring occasionally, for 5 minutes, or until heated through.

NUTRITIONAL INFO (per serving)				
calories	fat	protein	carbs	fiber
577	49g	32g	10g	4g

easy reuben chicken

option

yield: 6 servings *prep time:* 5 minutes *cook time:* 15 minutes

DRESSING:

⅔ cup mayonnaise

⅓ cup tomato sauce

¼ cup finely diced dill pickles or dill pickle relish

½ teaspoon fine sea salt

½ teaspoon ground black pepper

¼ teaspoon onion powder

32 ounces sauerkraut, with juices

6 boneless, skinless chicken breast halves (about 4 ounces each)

Fine sea salt and ground black pepper

3 ounces Swiss cheese, shredded (¾ cup) (omit for dairy-free)

Prepared yellow mustard, for drizzling

1. Make the dressing: Put the mayonnaise, tomato sauce, dill pickles, salt, pepper, and onion powder in a medium-sized bowl and stir until well combined. Set aside in the fridge; the dressing can be made up to 3 days ahead.

2. Grease a 6-quart Instant Pot. Place the sauerkraut with juices in the pot. Season the chicken on all sides with salt and pepper. Place the chicken on top of the sauerkraut.

3. Seal the lid, press Pressure Cook or Manual, and set the timer for 15 minutes. (If you use larger chicken breasts, they may need closer to 20 minutes.) Once finished, turn the valve to venting for a quick release.

4. Divide the sauerkraut among 6 plates. Place a chicken breast on top of each serving, then add the shredded Swiss cheese and a scoop of the dressing. Garnish with a drizzle of mustard and some freshly ground pepper.

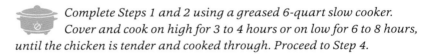

Complete Steps 1 and 2 using a greased 6-quart slow cooker. Cover and cook on high for 3 to 4 hours or on low for 6 to 8 hours, until the chicken is tender and cooked through. Proceed to Step 4.

STORE in an airtight container in the fridge for up to 5 days. To reheat, place in a baking dish in a preheated 350°F oven for 5 minutes, or until heated through.

NUTRITIONAL INFO (per serving)				
calories	fat	protein	carbs	fiber
303	22g	22g	4g	0.2g

chicken asparagus rolls

 yield: 4 servings *prep time:* 12 minutes *cook time:* 24 minutes

I like to serve these Chicken Asparagus Rolls over Mashed Cauliflower (page 330); it makes a comforting and hearty meal!

½ cup mayonnaise

3 tablespoons Dijon mustard

Zest and juice of 1 lemon

2 teaspoons dried tarragon

1 teaspoon ground black pepper

½ teaspoon fine sea salt

1 tablespoon unsalted butter or coconut oil

16 spears fresh asparagus, trimmed

4 boneless, skinless chicken breast halves (about 4 ounces each)

2 ounces provolone cheese, shredded (½ cup)

Fresh thyme leaves, for garnish

1. Place the mayonnaise, mustard, lemon zest, lemon juice, tarragon, pepper, and salt in a medium-sized bowl and stir until well combined. Set aside.

2. Place the butter in a 6-quart Instant Pot and press Sauté. Once melted, add the asparagus and sauté for 4 minutes, or until tender. Press Cancel to stop the Sauté. Remove the asparagus from the pot and set aside.

3. Place a chicken breast between two sheets of parchment paper. Using a cast-iron skillet, a rolling pin, or the smooth side of a meat mallet, pound the chicken until it is about ¼ inch thick. Remove the parchment and repeat with the remaining chicken breasts.

4. Place a quarter of the shredded cheese on top of each chicken breast, then top with 4 asparagus spears. Roll the chicken around the asparagus and cheese. Secure with a few toothpicks.

5. Pour half of the mayonnaise mixture into the Instant Pot and add the chicken rolls. Seal the lid, press Pressure Cook or Manual, and set the timer for 20 minutes. Once finished, turn the valve to venting for a quick release.

6. Serve the chicken rolls with the sauce from the pot. Garnish with thyme leaves and the rest of the mayonnaise mixture.

Complete Step 1. Melt the butter in a large skillet over medium heat. Add the asparagus and sauté for 4 minutes, or until tender. Remove from the skillet and set aside. Follow Steps 3 and 4. Pour half of the mayonnaise mixture into a 6-quart slow cooker and add the chicken rolls. Cover and cook on high for 3 to 4 hours or on low for 6 to 8 hours, until the chicken is tender and cooked through. Proceed to Step 6.

STORE in an airtight container in the fridge for up to 5 days. To reheat, place in a baking dish in a preheated 350°F oven for 5 minutes, or until heated through.

TIP: I ask my butcher to pound chicken breasts to a ¼-inch thickness to save me time when making this recipe!

NUTRITIONAL INFO (per serving)				
calories	fat	protein	carbs	fiber
392	29g	26g	5g	2g

cornish game hens

yield: 4 servings   *prep time:* 12 minutes   *cook time:* 33 minutes

4 cloves garlic, minced

1 teaspoon lemon pepper

½ teaspoon fine sea salt

½ teaspoon dried basil

Leaves from 1 sprig fresh rosemary

2 (1-pound) Cornish game hens, skin removed, patted dry

1 small onion, cut into thick slices

½ cup chicken broth, homemade (page 320) or store-bought

1. Put the garlic, lemon pepper, salt, basil, and rosemary in a small bowl and stir to combine. Rub the mixture all over the hens.

2. Place the onion slices and broth in a 6-quart Instant Pot. Lay the hens on top of the onions, breast side down (see Note, page 222).

3. Seal the lid, press Pressure Cook or Manual, and set the timer for 25 minutes. Once finished, let the pressure release naturally.

4. Preheat the oven to 425°F.

5. Transfer the hens to a rimmed baking sheet, breast side up, and place in the oven. Roast for 8 minutes, or until the skin is crispy and golden brown. Place on a cutting board to rest for 10 minutes before slicing and serving.

Complete Steps 1 and 2 using a 6-quart slow cooker. Cover and cook on high for 3 to 4 hours or on low for 6 to 8 hours, until the hens are cooked through and no longer pink inside. Proceed to Step 4.

STORE in an airtight container in the fridge for up to 5 days or in the freezer for up to a month. To reheat, place in a baking dish in a preheated 350°F oven for 5 minutes, or until heated through.

NUTRITIONAL INFO (per serving)				
calories	fat	protein	carbs	fiber
611	42g	51g	4g	0.4g

broccoli casserole

1 (8-ounce) package cream cheese, softened

1 cup chicken broth, homemade (page 320) or store-bought

1 cup mayonnaise

1 pound boneless, skinless chicken breasts, cut into 1-inch cubes

4 cups frozen broccoli florets

1 teaspoon fine sea salt

½ teaspoon ground black pepper

4 ounces cheddar cheese, shredded (1 cup)

4 ounces provolone cheese, shredded (1 cup)

Dried chives, for garnish

1. Place the cream cheese in a 6-quart Instant Pot and whisk to loosen. (If you don't use a whisk to loosen the cream cheese, you will end up with clumps in your casserole.) Slowly whisk in the broth, then the mayonnaise. Add the chicken, broccoli, salt, and pepper and stir to combine.

2. Seal the lid, press Pressure Cook or Manual, and set the timer for 9 minutes. Once finished, let the pressure release naturally.

3. Remove the lid and stir in the cheddar and provolone cheeses until melted.

4. Spoon the casserole onto plates or into bowls and garnish with chives.

Complete Step 1 using a 6-quart slow cooker. Cover and cook on high for 2 hours or on low for 4 hours, or until the chicken is cooked through and no longer pink. Proceed to Step 3.

STORE in an airtight container in the fridge for up to 5 days or in the freezer for up to a month. To reheat, place in a baking dish in a preheated 350°F oven for 5 minutes, or until heated through.

NUTRITIONAL INFO (per serving)				
calories	fat	protein	carbs	fiber
583	49g	26g	6g	2g

...th mushroom cream sauce

...d: 4 servings *prep time:* 8 minutes *cook time:* 14 minutes

...lespoons unsalted butter or
...conut oil (Instant Pot only)

2 cups sliced button or cremini
mushrooms

¼ cup diced onions

2 cloves garlic, minced

4 boneless, skinless chicken
breast halves (about 4 ounces
each)

½ cup chicken broth, homemade
(page 320) or store-bought

¼ cup heavy cream

1 teaspoon dried tarragon leaves

1 teaspoon fine sea salt

½ teaspoon ground black pepper

½ teaspoon dried thyme leaves

2 bay leaves

½ cup grated Parmesan cheese
(about 1½ ounces)

Fresh thyme leaves, for garnish

1. Place the butter in a 6-quart Instant Pot and press Sauté. Once melted, add the mushrooms, onions, and garlic and cook, stirring often, for 4 minutes, or until the onions are soft. Press Cancel to stop the Sauté.

2. Add the chicken, broth, heavy cream, tarragon, salt, pepper, thyme, and bay leaves and stir to combine.

3. Seal the lid, press Pressure Cook or Manual, and set the timer for 10 minutes. Once finished, let the pressure release naturally.

4. Remove the lid and discard the bay leaves. Transfer the chicken to a serving platter. Add the Parmesan cheese to the pot with the sauce and stir well until the cheese is melted.

5. Top the chicken with the mushroom sauce from the pot. Garnish with fresh thyme.

 Place all the ingredients except the Parmesan cheese in a 6-quart slow cooker. Cover and cook on high for 2 to 4 hours or on low for 6 to 7 hours, until the chicken is cooked through and no longer pink. Proceed to Step 4.

STORE in an airtight container in the fridge for up to 5 days or in the freezer for up to a month. To reheat, place in a lightly greased skillet over medium-high heat for 5 minutes, or until heated through.

NUTRITIONAL INFO (per serving)				
calories	fat	protein	carbs	fiber
275	17g	27g	5g	1g

...n piccata

yield: 2 servings   *prep time:* 8 minutes   *cook time:* 3 minutes

This easy recipe makes a quick dinner for two, or you can make a double batch (or more) for a family meal.

2 boneless, skinless chicken thighs

1 teaspoon Italian seasoning

½ teaspoon fine sea salt

2 tablespoons unsalted butter (or coconut oil for dairy-free)

½ cup chicken broth, homemade (page 320) or store-bought

2 tablespoons lemon juice

2 tablespoons capers, rinsed and drained

1 lemon, thinly sliced, for garnish

2 tablespoons chopped fresh Italian parsley leaves, for garnish

1. Place the chicken thighs between two sheets of parchment paper. Using a cast-iron skillet, a rolling pin, or the smooth side of a meat mallet, pound the thighs until they are about ¼ inch thick. Remove the parchment. Season the chicken on both sides with the Italian seasoning and salt.

2. Place the butter in a 6-quart Instant Pot and press Sauté. Once melted, add the chicken and cook for 2 minutes per side or until golden brown but not cooked through. Add the broth, lemon juice, and capers to the pot. Whisk the sauce well to scrape up the bits stuck to the bottom of the pot. Press Cancel to stop the Sauté.

3. Seal the lid, press Pressure Cook or Manual, and set the timer for 1 minute. Once finished, turn the valve to venting for a quick release.

4. Remove the chicken to a serving platter and pour the sauce over the thighs. Garnish with the lemon slices and parsley.

 Complete Step 1. Place the seasoned chicken, butter, broth, lemon juice, and capers in a 6-quart slow cooker. Cover and cook on high for 2 hours or on low for 4 hours, or until the chicken is cooked through and no longer pink. Proceed to Step 4.

STORE in an airtight container in the fridge for up to 4 days. To reheat, place in a lightly greased skillet over medium heat for about 3 minutes, until heated through.

NUTRITIONAL INFO (per serving)				
calories	fat	protein	carbs	fiber
442	23g	54g	6g	1g

& bacon lasagna roll-ups

yield: 8 servings *prep time:* 10 minutes *cook time:* 26 minutes

SAUCE:

1 (8-ounce) package cream cheese, softened

½ cup chicken broth, homemade (page 320) or store-bought

½ cup shredded cheddar cheese (about 2 ounces)

2 teaspoons garlic powder

2 teaspoons onion powder

1 pound bacon, chopped

FILLING:

2 boneless, skinless chicken thighs

½ cup diced yellow onions

6 cloves garlic, crushed

½ cup shredded cheddar cheese (about 2 ounces)

8 long slices shaved deli chicken breast

Ground black pepper

1. Make the sauce: Place the cream cheese in a medium-sized bowl and whisk to loosen. (If you don't use a whisk to loosen the cream cheese, you will end up with clumps in your sauce.) Slowly whisk in the broth. Add the cheddar cheese, garlic powder, and onion powder and stir well to combine. Set the sauce aside in the fridge.

2. Cook the bacon: Place the bacon in a 6-quart Instant Pot and press Sauté. Cook, stirring occasionally, until crisp, about 4 minutes. Remove the bacon using a slotted spoon, leaving the drippings in the pot. Reserve 3 tablespoons of the bacon for the topping and set the rest aside.

3. Make the filling: Add the chicken thighs, onions, and garlic to the Instant Pot. Seal the lid, press Pressure Cook or Manual, and set the timer for 20 minutes. Once finished, turn the valve to venting for a quick release.

4. Remove the lid. Shred the chicken with two forks and transfer to a medium-sized bowl or container. (The filling can be made up to 2 days ahead.)

5. Pour the sauce into the Instant Pot.

6. Lay a slice of shaved chicken on a clean work surface. Place a few tablespoons of the shredded chicken filling, 1½ teaspoons of the cheddar cheese, and a teaspoon of the cooked bacon in the center. Wrap the shaved chicken around the filling and set in the sauce. Repeat with the remaining filling and chicken "tortillas." Top the roll-ups with the remaining cheddar cheese.

7. Seal the lid, press Pressure Cook or Manual, and set the timer for 2 minutes. Once finished, let the pressure release naturally.

8. Remove the roll-ups to a serving plate or dish using a large serving spoon. Top with the reserved bacon and freshly ground pepper.

NUTRITIONAL INFO (per serving)				
calories	fat	protein	carbs	fiber
644	46g	51g	4g	0.3g

Complete Step 1. Place the bacon in a cast-iron skillet over medium-high heat and sauté for 4 minutes, or until crisp. Place the chicken thighs, onions, and garlic in a 6-quart slow cooker. Cover and cook on high for 4 hours or on low for 6 to 8 hours, until the chicken is tender. Follow Steps 4 through 6 using the slow cooker. Cover and cook on high for 30 minutes, or until the roll-ups are heated through and the cheese is melted. Proceed to Step 8.

STORE in an airtight container in the fridge for up to 5 days or in the freezer for up to a month. To reheat, place in a casserole dish in a preheated 350°F oven for 6 minutes, or until the cheese is melted and the roll-ups are heated through.

chicken cacciatore

yield: 8 servings   *prep time:* 10 minutes   *cook time:* 29 minutes

1 tablespoon unsalted butter (or coconut oil for dairy-free)

2½ pounds bone-in, skin-on chicken thighs

1 cup chopped onions

1 medium-sized green bell pepper, chopped

8 ounces cremini or button mushrooms, sliced

4 cloves garlic, minced

1 (14½-ounce) can diced tomatoes

1 tablespoon Italian seasoning

1 teaspoon fine sea salt

1 teaspoon ground black pepper

1 drop stevia glycerite (optional)

⅓ cup tomato sauce

⅓ cup grated Parmesan cheese (about 1 ounce) (omit for dairy-free)

Capers, rinsed and drained, for garnish (optional)

Fresh thyme leaves, for garnish (optional)

1. Place the butter in a 6-quart Instant Pot and press Sauté. Season the chicken on all sides with salt and pepper. Once the butter is melted, place the chicken skin side down in the pot and cook for 4 minutes, or until the skin is golden brown. Remove from the pot and set aside, leaving the drippings in the pot.

2. Place the onions, bell pepper, mushrooms, and garlic in the pot and cook, stirring often, for 5 minutes, or until the onions are soft. Add the tomatoes, Italian seasoning, salt, and pepper and cook for another 10 minutes. Taste and adjust the seasonings; if the sauce tastes too acidic, add the stevia glycerite. Press Cancel to stop the Sauté.

3. Add the tomato sauce and Parmesan cheese and stir to combine. Return the chicken to the pot with the sauce.

4. Seal the lid, press Pressure Cook or Manual, and set the timer for 10 minutes. Once finished, turn the valve to venting for a quick release.

5. Transfer the chicken to a serving dish and top with the sauce from the pot. Garnish with capers and thyme leaves, if desired.

Complete Steps 1 and 2 using a large skillet over medium-high heat. Transfer the vegetable mixture to a 6-quart slow cooker, add the chicken, tomato sauce, and Parmesan cheese, and stir to combine. Cover and cook on high for 3 hours or on low for 6 to 8 hours, until the chicken is cooked through and no longer pink inside. Proceed to Step 5.

STORE in an airtight container in the fridge for up to 5 days or in the freezer for up to a month. To reheat, place in a casserole dish in a preheated 350°F oven for 6 minutes, or until heated through.

NUTRITIONAL INFO (per serving)				
calories	fat	protein	carbs	fiber
333	22g	25g	7g	1g

chicken cordon bleu

  yield: 6 servings   *prep time:* 12 minutes   *cook time:* 18 minutes

This recipe was such a hit in my book Keto Comfort Foods *that I decided to modify it for the Instant Pot and slow cooker and include it here, too! Serve the chicken rolls on a bed of lettuce if you like.*

4 boneless, skinless chicken breast halves (about 4 ounces each)

4 (1-ounce) slices Swiss cheese

8 (1-ounce) slices ham

SAUCE:

¼ cup chicken broth, homemade (page 320) or store-bought

1½ ounces cream cheese (3 tablespoons)

1 tablespoon unsalted butter

¼ teaspoon fine sea salt

¼ teaspoon ground black pepper

Chopped fresh flat-leaf parsley, for garnish

1. Place a chicken breast between two sheets of parchment paper. Using a cast-iron skillet, a rolling pin, or the smooth side of a meat mallet, pound the chicken until it is about ¼ inch thick. Repeat with the remaining chicken.

2. Place a slice of Swiss cheese on each pounded chicken breast, then top with 2 slices of ham. Roll the chicken around the ham and cheese. Secure with toothpicks and set aside.

3. Make the sauce: Whisk together all of the sauce ingredients in a small saucepan over medium heat, stirring until the cream cheese is melted and the sauce is smooth.

4. Set the chicken rolls, seam side down, in a 1-quart casserole dish. Pour half of the sauce over the chicken. Set the remaining sauce aside.

5. Set a trivet in a 6-quart Instant Pot and pour in 1 cup of cold water. Use a foil sling (see page 19) to lower the casserole dish onto the trivet. Tuck in the sides of the sling.

6. Seal the lid, press Pressure Cook or Manual, and set the timer for 15 minutes. Once finished, let the pressure release naturally. Lift the casserole dish out of the Instant Pot using the foil sling.

7. Transfer the chicken rolls to a serving plate and top with the reserved sauce. Garnish with parsley.

Complete Steps 1 through 3. Set the chicken rolls seam side down in a 6-quart slow cooker. Pour half of the sauce over the chicken. Cover and cook on high for 2 to 3 hours or on low for 6 to 8 hours, until the chicken is cooked through. Proceed to Step 7, rewarming the reserved sauce in a small saucepan before serving.

STORE in an airtight container in the fridge for up to 5 days or in the freezer for up to a month. To reheat, place in a preheated 350°F oven for 6 minutes, or until the cheese is melted and the rolls are heated through.

NUTRITIONAL INFO (per serving)				
calories	fat	protein	carbs	fiber
239	15g	25g	1g	0g

chicken fajita bowls

   yield: 2 servings *prep time:* 5 minutes *cook time:* 10 minutes

2 cups chicken broth, homemade (page 320) or store-bought

1 cup salsa

1 teaspoon fine sea salt

1 teaspoon chili powder

1 teaspoon paprika

½ teaspoon ground black pepper

½ teaspoon ground cumin

1 pound boneless, skinless chicken breasts, cut into 1-inch pieces

1 lime, halved

FOR GARNISH:

Sour cream (omit for dairy-free)

Crumbled Cotija cheese (omit for dairy-free)

Chopped fresh cilantro leaves

Sliced avocado

Lime slices

Extra-virgin olive oil or avocado oil

1. Place the broth, salsa, salt, and spices in a 6-quart Instant Pot. Set the chicken on top.

2. Seal the lid, press Pressure Cook or Manual, and set the timer for 10 minutes. Once finished, turn the valve to venting for a quick release.

3. Remove the lid and shred the chicken with two forks. Squeeze the lime juice into the chicken mixture. Taste and add more salt, if desired. Stir well.

4. Ladle the chicken mixture into bowls. Garnish with sour cream (if using), Cotija cheese crumbles, cilantro, avocado slices, lime slices, and freshly ground black pepper. Drizzle with olive oil.

 Complete Step 1 using a 6-quart slow cooker. Cover and cook on high for 3 hours or on low for 6 hours, or until the chicken is tender. Proceed to Step 3.

STORE in an airtight container in the fridge for up to 5 days or in the freezer for up to a month. To reheat, place in a saucepan over medium heat for 7 minutes, or until heated through.

NUTRITIONAL INFO (per serving)				
calories	fat	protein	carbs	fiber
278	6g	51g	6g	1g

chicken parmigiana

 yield: 4 servings   *prep time:* 10 minutes   *cook time:* 5 minutes

4 boneless, skinless chicken thighs

Fine sea salt and ground black pepper

2 large eggs

1 cup powdered Parmesan cheese (see Note, page 152)

2 teaspoons Italian seasoning

3 tablespoons avocado oil or coconut oil, for frying

1 cup marinara sauce, homemade (page 332) or store-bought

4 ounces fresh mozzarella cheese, cut into 4 thin slices

Finely chopped fresh basil, for garnish

1. Place a chicken thigh between two sheets of parchment paper. Using a cast-iron skillet, a rolling pin, or the smooth side of a meat mallet, pound the chicken until it is about ¼ inch thick. Repeat with the remaining chicken. Season the pounded thighs well on both sides with salt and pepper.

2. Crack the eggs into a shallow dish. Beat in 1 tablespoon of water and season with a pinch each of salt and pepper. Place the powdered Parmesan cheese and Italian seasoning in another shallow dish and mix until well combined.

3. Dip each chicken thigh in the eggs and let any excess drip off, then dredge both sides of the chicken in the Parmesan mixture.

4. Pour the oil into a 6-quart Instant Pot and press Sauté. Once hot, place a chicken thigh in the hot oil and sear until golden brown, about 2 minutes per side. Repeat with the remaining thighs. After all of the chicken is fried, wipe the pot clean.

5. Meanwhile, spoon the marinara into a 1-quart casserole dish. Set the chicken on top of the marinara. Top each thigh with a mozzarella slice.

6. Set a trivet in the Instant Pot and pour in 1 cup of cold water. Use a foil sling (see page 19) to lower the casserole dish onto the trivet. Tuck in the sides of the sling.

7. Seal the lid, press Pressure Cook or Manual, and set the timer for 1 minute. Once finished, turn the valve to venting for a quick release. Lift the casserole dish out of the Instant Pot using the foil sling.

8. Garnish with basil and serve.

NUTRITIONAL INFO (per serving)				
calories	fat	protein	carbs	fiber
604	46g	41g	6g	2g

Complete Steps 1 through 3. Pour the oil into a large skillet over medium-high heat. Place a chicken thigh in the hot oil and sear until golden brown, about 2 minutes per side. Repeat with the remaining chicken. Meanwhile, pour the marinara into a 6-quart slow cooker. Set the fried chicken thighs on top of the marinara. Top each thigh with a mozzarella slice. Cover and cook on high for 45 minutes or on low for 2 hours, or until the chicken is cooked through. Proceed to Step 8.

STORE in an airtight container in the fridge for up to 4 days or in the freezer for up to a month. To reheat, place in a lightly greased skillet over medium heat for about 3 minutes, until heated through.

fish
& seafood

crab-stuffed avocados

  yield: 3 servings (2 halves per serving) *prep time:* 5 minutes *cook time:* 10 minutes

1 (6½-ounce) can lump crab meat, rinsed and drained well

4 ounces cream cheese (½ cup), softened

¼ cup fresh or canned diced tomatoes

1 tablespoon chopped green onions (green part only), plus more for garnish

¼ teaspoon fine sea salt

¼ teaspoon ground black pepper

⅛ teaspoon cayenne pepper

3 large ripe avocados, halved and pitted

½ cup shredded Parmesan or sharp cheddar cheese (about 2 ounces)

1. Place the crab meat, cream cheese, tomatoes, green onions, salt, pepper, and cayenne in a large bowl and mix until well combined.

2. Fill the 6 avocado halves with equal portions of the crab mixture and top with equal amounts of the shredded cheese. Place the stuffed avocados in two 1-quart round casserole dishes.

3. Set a trivet in a 6-quart Instant Pot and pour in ½ cup of cold water. Use a foil sling (see page 19) to lower the casserole dishes onto the trivet, stacking one on top of the other. Tuck in the sides of the sling.

4. Seal the lid, press Pressure Cook or Manual, and set the timer for 10 minutes. Once finished, turn the valve to venting for a quick release. Lift the casserole dishes out of the pot using the foil sling.

5. Serve warm, garnished with extra green onions.

Complete Steps 1 and 2 and place the stuffed avocados in an oval-shaped 6-quart slow cooker. (It might be difficult to fit the 6 halves in a round cooker.) Cover and cook on low for 2 to 3 hours, until the avocados are soft and the cheese is melted. Proceed to Step 5.

STORE in an airtight container in the fridge for up to a week or in the freezer for up to a month. To reheat, place in a baking dish in a preheated 350°F oven for 5 minutes, or until heated through.

NUTRITIONAL INFO (per serving)				
calories	fat	protein	carbs	fiber
549	46g	19g	19g	14g

italian salmon

yield: 4 servings   *prep time:* 7 minutes   *cook time:* 21 minutes

1 tablespoon unsalted butter (or coconut oil for dairy-free) (Instant Pot only)

Cloves squeezed from 1 head Roasted Garlic (page 324), or 3 cloves garlic, minced

1¼ cups fresh or canned diced tomatoes

¼ cup lemon juice

2 tablespoons capers, rinsed and drained

1 tablespoon chopped fresh flat-leaf parsley, plus more for garnish

¼ teaspoon ground black pepper

4 (6-ounce) skinless salmon fillets

1 teaspoon fine sea salt

Lemon wedges, for garnish

1. Place the butter in a 6-quart Instant Pot and press Sauté. Once melted, if using raw garlic, add the garlic and sauté for 1 minute. Otherwise, move on to Step 2.

2. Add the roasted garlic, tomatoes, lemon juice, capers, parsley, and pepper. Simmer for 5 minutes, until the liquid has reduced a bit.

3. While the sauce is simmering, rinse the salmon and pat dry with a paper towel. Season on all sides with the salt.

4. Use a spatula to push the reduced sauce to one side of the pot and place the salmon on the other side. Spoon the sauce over the salmon. Leave uncovered and cook, still in Sauté mode, for 15 minutes, or until the salmon flakes easily with a fork. The timing will depend on the thickness of the fillets.

5. Transfer the salmon to a platter. Serve with the sauce and garnish with parsley and lemon wedges.

Place the garlic, tomatoes, lemon juice, capers, parsley, and pepper in a 6-quart slow cooker and stir well. Turn the cooker to high. Rinse the salmon and pat dry with a paper towel. Season on all sides with the salt. Use a spatula to push the sauce to one side of the slow cooker and place the salmon on the other side. Spoon the sauce over the salmon. Cook, uncovered, for 40 minutes, or until the salmon flakes easily with a fork. The timing will depend on the thickness of the fillets. Proceed to Step 5.

STORE in an airtight container in the fridge for up to 4 days. To reheat, place in a lightly greased skillet over medium heat for about 3 minutes, until heated through.

NUTRITIONAL INFO (per serving)				
calories	fat	protein	carbs	fiber
243	9g	34g	5g	1g

easy greek fish

  yield: 4 servings *prep time:* 5 minutes *cook time:* 6 minutes

4 (5-ounce) sablefish or tilapia fillets

½ teaspoon fine sea salt

¼ teaspoon ground black pepper

1 lemon, cut into 12 thin slices

GREEK VINAIGRETTE:

½ cup avocado oil or extra-virgin olive oil

¼ cup plus 1 tablespoon red wine vinegar or apple cider vinegar

2 tablespoons lemon or lime juice

2 cloves garlic, minced

2 teaspoons Dijon mustard

½ teaspoon dried basil leaves

½ teaspoon dried oregano leaves

¼ teaspoon fine sea salt

SALAD:

1 medium cucumber, diced

1 medium tomato, diced

1 cup sliced black olives

¼ cup diced red onions

2 tablespoons capers, rinsed and drained

1. Set a steamer basket in a 6-quart Instant Pot and pour in 1½ cups of cold water.

2. Season the fish on all sides with the salt and pepper. Take four 12-inch square sheets of parchment paper and place 3 lemon slices on each sheet. Place a piece of fish on top of the lemon slices. Wrap the fish in the parchment by folding in the edges and folding the top down like an envelope to close tightly.

3. Stack the packets in the steamer basket with the seam sides down. Seal the lid, press Pressure Cook or Manual, and set the timer for 6 minutes. Once finished, let the pressure release naturally.

4. Meanwhile, make the vinaigrette and salad. To make the vinaigrette, place all the ingredients in a blender and purée until smooth. (See the Tip below.) To make the salad, place the cucumber, tomato, olives, onions, and capers in a medium-sized bowl. Add half of the vinaigrette and stir well to coat. Set aside.

5. Remove the fish packets from the pot. Serve the fish right out of the packets for a no-mess dinner: Open the packets and garnish with the salad. Or place the fish on plates and top with the salad. Serve with the remaining vinaigrette.

 Complete Step 2, then place the packets in a 6-quart slow cooker with the seam sides down. Cover and cook on high for 45 minutes or on low for 1½ hours. Proceed to Step 4.

STORE the fish and salad in separate airtight containers in the fridge for up to 5 days. The vinaigrette will keep in an airtight container in the fridge for up to 2 weeks. The fish can be frozen for up to a month. To reheat the fish, place in a lightly greased skillet over medium-high heat for 5 minutes, or until heated through.

TIP: This vinaigrette also tastes great with Greek Chicken (page 220) or over salad greens.

NUTRITIONAL INFO (per serving)				
calories	fat	protein	carbs	fiber
595	55g	20g	8g	2g

gumbo

   yield: 8 servings *prep time:* 7 minutes *cook time:* 15 minutes

5 tablespoons unsalted butter (or coconut oil for dairy-free)

⅓ cup chopped yellow onions

Cloves squeezed from 2 heads Roasted Garlic (page 324), or 6 cloves garlic, minced

1 green bell pepper, seeded and chopped

3 stalks celery, chopped

8 ounces medium shrimp, peeled and deveined

6 boneless, skinless chicken thighs, cut into 1-inch cubes

1 teaspoon fine sea salt

1 teaspoon mustard powder

1 teaspoon dried oregano leaves

¼ teaspoon cayenne pepper

1 pound smoked sausage, cut into ¼-inch-thick slices

4 cups beef broth, homemade (page 320) or store-bought

2 cups frozen sliced okra

1 (14½-ounce) can stewed tomatoes, with juices

1 cup tomato sauce

2 tablespoons lime juice

2 bay leaves

Finely chopped fresh flat-leaf parsley, for garnish

1. Place the butter in a 6-quart Instant Pot and press Sauté. Once melted, add the onions, garlic, bell pepper, and celery and cook, stirring often, for 4 minutes, or until the onions are soft.

2. Add the shrimp and sauté for 4 minutes, or until the shrimp have just turned pink. Remove the shrimp and set aside. Press Cancel to stop the Sauté.

3. While the shrimp is cooking, place the salt, mustard powder, oregano, and cayenne in a small bowl and stir to combine. Season the chicken on all sides with the mixture. Add the seasoned chicken, sausage, broth, okra, tomatoes, tomato sauce, lime juice, and bay leaves to the Instant Pot.

4. Seal the lid, press Pressure Cook or Manual, and set the timer for 7 minutes. Once finished, turn the valve to venting for a quick release.

5. Remove the lid and discard the bay leaves. Return the shrimp to the pot and stir well.

6. Serve in bowls and garnish with fresh parsley.

Complete Steps 1 and 2 using a large skillet over medium-high heat. Follow Step 3 and place the seasoned chicken, sausage, broth, okra, tomatoes, tomato sauce, lime juice, and bay leaves in a 6-quart slow cooker. Cover and cook on high for 3 to 4 hours or on low for 6 to 8 hours, until the chicken is cooked through and no longer pink inside. Proceed to Step 5.

STORE in an airtight container in the fridge for up to 5 days or in the freezer for up to a month. To reheat, place in a lightly greased skillet over medium-high heat for 5 minutes, or until heated through.

NUTRITIONAL INFO (per serving)				
calories	fat	protein	carbs	fiber
538	38g	37g	10g	3g

shrimp scampi

  yield: 4 servings   *prep time:* 10 minutes   *cook time:* 16 minutes

½ cup unsalted butter (or butter-flavored coconut oil for dairy-free)

2 tablespoons lemon juice

1 tablespoon Dijon mustard

Cloves squeezed from 1 head Roasted Garlic (page 324), or 2 cloves garlic, minced

4 cups very thinly sliced cabbage, for "noodles"

1 pound medium shrimp, peeled and deveined

1 tablespoon chopped fresh flat-leaf parsley

1. Place the butter, lemon juice, mustard, and garlic in a 6-quart Instant Pot and press Sauté. Cook for 3 minutes, or until the garlic is fragrant.

2. Scoop out half of the garlic butter mixture with a measuring cup and set aside.

3. Add the cabbage to the pot and stir to coat. Press Cancel to stop the Sauté.

4. Seal the lid, press Pressure Cook or Manual, and set the timer for 8 minutes. Once finished, turn the valve to venting for a quick release.

5. Remove the cabbage from the pot and set aside on a serving platter.

6. Add the reserved garlic butter and the shrimp to the pot and press Sauté. Cook for 5 minutes, or until the shrimp have just turned pink.

7. Add the shrimp and sauce from the pot to the cabbage "noodles" on the serving platter. Garnish with freshly ground pepper and parsley.

Complete Steps 1 and 2 using a large skillet over medium-high heat, scooping half of the garlic butter mixture into a 6-quart slow cooker. Add the cabbage to the slow cooker and stir to coat. Cover and cook on high for 2 hours or on low for 4 hours, or until the cabbage is very soft. About 10 minutes before the cabbage is done, heat the reserved garlic butter in the skillet over medium-high heat. Add the shrimp and cook for 5 minutes, or until the shrimp have just turned pink. Proceed to Step 7.

STORE in an airtight container in the fridge for up to 5 days or in the freezer for up to a month. To reheat, place in a saucepan over medium heat, stirring occasionally, for 5 minutes, or until heated through.

NUTRITIONAL INFO (per serving)				
calories	fat	protein	carbs	fiber
393	26g	33g	8g	2g

garlicky tuna casserole

  yield: 4 servings *prep time:* 7 minutes *cook time:* 9 minutes

1 (8-ounce) package cream cheese (1 cup), softened

1 cup grated Parmesan or shredded cheddar cheese (about 4 ounces), plus more for topping

½ cup chicken broth, homemade (page 320) or store-bought

1 tablespoon unsalted butter

1 cup diced onions

½ small head cauliflower, cut into 1-inch pieces

2 cloves garlic, minced, or more to taste

2 (4-ounce) cans chunk tuna packed in water, drained

FOR GARNISH:

Cherry tomatoes, halved

Chopped fresh flat-leaf parsley

Sliced green onions

Ground black pepper

1. Place the cream cheese, Parmesan cheese, and broth in a blender and purée until smooth. Set aside.

2. Put the butter in a 6-quart Instant Pot and press Sauté. Once melted, add the onions and cauliflower and cook for 4 minutes, or until the onions are soft. Add the garlic and sauté for another minute. Press Cancel to stop the Sauté.

3. Place the tuna and the cheese sauce from the blender in a large bowl. Add the cauliflower mixture and stir to combine. Transfer the tuna and cauliflower mixture to a 1-quart casserole dish.

4. Set a trivet in the Instant Pot and pour in 1½ cups of cold water. Use a foil sling (see page 19) to lower the casserole dish onto the trivet. Tuck in the sides of the sling.

5. Seal the lid, press Pressure Cook or Manual, and set the timer for 5 minutes for al dente cauliflower or 8 minutes for softer cauliflower. Once finished, turn the valve to venting for a quick release.

6. Serve warm, topped with more cheese and garnished with cherry tomatoes, parsley, green onions, and freshly ground pepper.

 Complete Step 1. Pour the broth mixture into a 6-quart slow cooker. Add the remaining ingredients, cover, and cook on low for 4 hours or until the cauliflower is tender. Proceed to Step 6.

STORE in an airtight container in the fridge for up to a week or in the freezer for up to a month. To reheat, place in a baking dish in a preheated 350°F oven for 5 minutes, or until heated through.

NUTRITIONAL INFO (per serving)				
calories	fat	protein	carbs	fiber
429	27g	29g	12g	2g

lemony fish with asparagus

   yield: 4 servings *prep time:* 6 minutes *cook time:* 3 minutes

This recipe may seem simple; however, it was tested again and again, and we got some very unappetizing results before we perfected it. Be sure to follow the directions as written, which includes having a cover for the steamer pans. We tested this recipe with the asparagus placed in the steamer pans first; I thought the fish would have something to sit on for a nice steam, like in a slow cooker. Nope! That asparagus was so overcooked that it went directly into the compost pile.

2 lemons

2 tablespoons extra-virgin olive oil

4 (4-ounce) white fish fillets, such as cod or haddock

1 teaspoon fine sea salt

1 teaspoon ground black pepper

1 bundle asparagus, ends trimmed

2 tablespoons lemon juice

Fresh dill, for garnish

1. Grate the zest off the lemons until you have about 1 tablespoon; set the zest aside. Then cut the lemons into ⅛-inch slices.

2. Pour 2 cups of cold water into a 6-quart Instant Pot. Pour 1 tablespoon of the olive oil into each of two stackable steamer pans or 7-inch soufflé dishes.

3. Season the fish on all sides with the lemon zest, salt, and pepper. Place two fillets in each steamer pan and top each with the lemon slices and then the asparagus. Season the asparagus with a touch of salt and drizzle with the lemon juice. Stack the steamer pans in the Instant Pot. (Or, if using soufflé dishes, use a foil sling [see page 19] to lower and stack the dishes into the pot; tuck in the sides of the sling.) Cover the top steamer pan with its lid (or cover the top soufflé dish with aluminum foil).

4. Seal the lid, press Pressure Cook or Manual, and set the timer for 3 minutes. Once finished, let the pressure release naturally for 7 minutes, then turn the valve to venting to release any remaining pressure. Lift the steamer pans or soufflé dishes out of the Instant Pot.

5. Transfer the asparagus and fish to a serving platter. Garnish with the lemon slices and dill.

 *Complete Step 1. Place the asparagus in a 6-quart slow cooker. Sprinkle the fish with the lemon zest, salt, and pepper. Place the lemon slices on the asparagus, then set the fish on top of the lemons. Drizzle the lemon juice into the slow cooker. Cover and cook on low for 1 hour, or until the fish is cooked through and opaque and the asparagus is tender.*

STORE in an airtight container in the fridge for up to 5 days or in the freezer for up to a month. To reheat, place in a lightly greased skillet over medium-high heat for 5 minutes, or until heated through.

NUTRITIONAL INFO (per serving)				
calories	fat	protein	carbs	fiber
158	5g	23g	7g	3g

simple salmon packets

   yield: 4 servings *prep time:* 8 minutes *cook time:* 6 minutes

4 (5-ounce) salmon fillets

½ teaspoon fine sea salt

¼ teaspoon ground black pepper

1 lime, thinly sliced

4 teaspoons extra-virgin olive oil, divided

Fresh thyme leaves

1. Set a steamer basket in a 6-quart Instant Pot and pour in 1½ cups of cold water.

2. Season the fish on all sides with the salt and pepper. Take four 12-inch square sheets of parchment paper and place 3 lime slices on each sheet. Cover the lime slices with a piece of fish. Drizzle with 1 teaspoon of olive oil and top with a few thyme leaves. Wrap each fillet in the parchment by folding in the edges and folding the top down like an envelope to enclose the salmon.

3. Stack the packets in the steamer basket with the seam sides down. Seal the lid, press Pressure Cook or Manual, and set the timer for 6 minutes. Once finished, let the pressure release naturally.

4. Remove the fish packets from the pot. Serve the fish right out of the packets for a no-mess dinner: Open the packets and garnish with more fresh thyme.

Complete Step 2, then place the packets in a 6-quart slow cooker with the seam sides down. Cover and cook on high for 45 minutes or on low for 1½ hours, or until the fish is cooked through and opaque.

STORE in an airtight container in the fridge for up to 5 days or in the freezer for up to a month. To reheat, place in a lightly greased skillet over medium-high heat for 5 minutes, or until heated through.

NUTRITIONAL INFO (per serving)				
calories	fat	protein	carbs	fiber
207	10g	28g	2g	1g

bbq shri

option

...mp

yield: 8 servings prep time: 5 minutes cook time: 1 minute

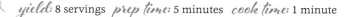

2 pounds medium shrimp, peeled and deveined

½ cup (1 stick) unsalted butter (or butter-flavored coconut oil for dairy-free), melted

½ cup tomato sauce

1 tablespoon Swerve confectioners'-style sweetener or equivalent amount of liquid or powdered sweetener (see page 39)

1 teaspoon hot sauce, or more to taste

1 teaspoon liquid smoke

1 teaspoon fine sea salt

½ teaspoon ground black pepper

Place all of the ingredients in a 3-quart or larger Instant Pot. Seal the lid, press Pressure Cook or Manual, and set the timer for 1 minute. Once finished, turn the valve to venting for a quick release. Serve immediately.

Place all of the ingredients in a 3-quart or larger slow cooker. Cover and cook on high for 1 hour or on low for 2 hours, or until the shrimp have just turned pink. Serve immediately.

STORE in an airtight container in the fridge for up to a week or in the freezer for up to a month. To reheat, place in a baking dish in a preheated 350°F oven for 5 minutes, or until heated through.

NUTRITIONAL INFO (per serving)				
calories	fat	protein	carbs	fiber
266	14g	31g	2g	0.2g

pesto fish packets

 yield: 4 servings   *prep time:* 8 minutes   *cook time:* 6 minutes

4 (4-ounce) white fish fillets, such as cod or haddock

1 teaspoon fine sea salt

½ teaspoon ground black pepper

1 (4-ounce) jar pesto (soybean oil–free)

½ cup shredded Parmesan cheese (about 2 ounces)

Halved cherry tomatoes, for garnish

1. Set a steamer basket in a 6-quart Instant Pot and pour in 1½ cups of cold water.

2. Season the fish on all sides with the salt and pepper. Take four 12-inch square sheets of parchment paper and place a fillet in the middle of each sheet. Dollop 2 tablespoons of the pesto on top of each fillet, then sprinkle with 2 tablespoons of the Parmesan cheese. Wrap the fish in the parchment by folding in the edges and folding down the top like an envelope to close tightly.

3. Stack the packets in the steamer basket with the seam sides down. Seal the lid, press Pressure Cook or Manual, and set the timer for 6 minutes. Once finished, let the pressure release naturally.

4. Remove the fish packets from the pot. Transfer to a serving platter and garnish with cherry tomatoes, or serve the fish right out of the packets for a no-mess dinner.

Complete Step 2, then place the packets in a 6-quart slow cooker with the seam sides down. Cover and cook on high for 45 minutes or on low for 1½ hours, or until the fish is cooked through and opaque. Proceed to Step 4.

STORE in an airtight container in the fridge for up to 5 days or in the freezer for up to a month. To reheat, place in a lightly greased skillet over medium-high heat for 5 minutes, or until heated through.

NUTRITIONAL INFO (per serving)				
calories	fat	protein	carbs	fiber
254	17g	23g	2g	1g

classic tuna hotdish

 yield: 8 servings *prep time:* 6 minutes *cook time:* 12 minutes

If you have never had heart of palm, you are in for a real treat! It comes from the heart of a palm tree, and it makes a perfect noodle substitute in this tuna casserole. If you can't find it, you can use cauliflower instead. This casserole can be served warm or cold.

1 (8-ounce) package cream cheese (1 cup), softened

1 cup shredded sharp cheddar cheese (4 ounces), plus more for garnish

1 cup chicken broth, homemade (page 320) or store-bought

1 tablespoon coconut oil or unsalted butter (Instant Pot only)

¼ cup diced onions

¼ cup chopped celery

4 (5-ounce) cans chunk tuna packed in water, drained

2 cups halved hearts of palm

Fine sea salt and ground black pepper

1 cup diced mini dill pickles

Fresh dill, for garnish

1. Place the cream cheese, cheddar cheese, and broth in a blender and purée until smooth.

2. Place the coconut oil in a 6-quart Instant Pot and press Sauté. When hot, add the onions and celery and cook, stirring often, for 4 minutes, or until soft. Add the cheesy broth mixture, tuna, and hearts of palm and gently stir to combine. Press Cancel to stop the Sauté.

3. Seal the lid, press Pressure Cook or Manual, and set the timer for 5 minutes. Once finished, turn the valve to venting for a quick release.

4. Preheat the oven to broil.

5. Remove the lid and season the tuna mixture with salt and pepper to taste. Stir in the pickles.

6. Transfer the tuna and pickle mixture to a serving dish and top with additional cheddar cheese. Place under the broiler for a few minutes to melt the cheese topping. Garnish with dill.

Complete Step 1, then pour the cheesy broth mixture into a 6-quart slow cooker. Add the onions, celery, tuna, and hearts of palm and stir gently to combine. Cover and cook on high for 1 hour or on low for 2 hours. Proceed to Step 4.

STORE in an airtight container in the fridge for up to a week or in the freezer for up to a month. To reheat, place in a baking dish in a preheated 350°F oven for 5 minutes, or until heated through.

NUTRITIONAL INFO (per serving)				
calories	fat	protein	carbs	fiber
276	16g	25g	5g	1g

white fish poached in garlic cream sauce

  yield: 2 servings *prep time:* 5 minutes *cook time:* 3 minutes

¼ cup heavy cream (or full-fat coconut milk for dairy-free)

Cloves squeezed from 1 head Roasted Garlic (page 324), or 2 cloves garlic, minced

1 pound walleye or cod fillets, cut into 2 by 1-inch pieces

1 teaspoon fine sea salt

¼ teaspoon ground black pepper

Extra-virgin olive oil, for drizzling (optional)

Chopped fresh Italian parsley leaves, for garnish

1 lemon, thinly sliced, for garnish

1. Place the cream and garlic in a food processor or blender and purée until very smooth.

2. Set a trivet in a 6-quart Instant Pot and pour in 1½ cups of cold water.

3. Season the fish on both sides with the salt and pepper, then put the fillets in a 7-inch soufflé or casserole dish. Pour the garlic cream over the fish.

4. Set the dish on the trivet in the Instant Pot. Seal the lid, press Pressure Cook or Manual, and set the timer for 3 minutes. Once finished, let the pressure release naturally.

5. Place the fish on a serving platter and cover with the cream sauce. Drizzle with olive oil, if desired, and garnish with parsley and lemon slices.

Complete Step 1. Season the fish on both sides with the salt and pepper and put in a 6-quart slow cooker. Pour the garlic cream over the fish. Cover and cook on high for 30 minutes, or until the fillets are cooked through and starting to flake.

STORE: This dish is best served fresh, but extras can be stored in an airtight container in the fridge for up to 3 days. To reheat, place in a skillet over medium heat for 3 minutes, or until heated through.

TIP: If you prefer a thicker cream sauce, remove the fish from the cooker, transfer the sauce to a saucepan, and boil over high heat, stirring often, for 10 minutes, or until thickened to your liking.

NUTRITIONAL INFO (per serving)				
calories	fat	protein	carbs	fiber
314	14g	44g	2g	0.2g

alaya

2 cups roughly chopped cauliflower (about 1 inch in size)

2 tablespoons unsalted butter (or coconut oil for dairy-free)

½ medium onion, chopped

1 green bell pepper, seeded and chopped

1 stalk celery, chopped

1 pound boneless, skinless chicken breasts, cut into 1-inch cubes

2 teaspoons Cajun or Creole seasoning

2 teaspoons dried oregano leaves

1 teaspoon fine sea salt

½ teaspoon ground black pepper

½ teaspoon dried thyme leaves

8 ounces andouille sausage, sliced

1 (28-ounce) can diced tomatoes, drained

1 (5½-ounce) jar tomato paste

1 cup chicken broth, homemade (page 320) or store-bought

1 teaspoon hot sauce

2 bay leaves

Pinch of saffron (optional)

1 pound frozen peeled and cooked shrimp, thawed

8 ounces fully cooked and thawed mussels (optional)

Chopped fresh flat-leaf parsley, for garnish

1. Place the cauliflower in a food processor and pulse until it resembles grains of rice. Set aside.

2. Place the butter in a 6-quart Instant Pot and press Sauté. Once melted, add the onion, bell pepper, and celery and cook, stirring often, for 4 minutes, or until the onion is soft.

3. Meanwhile, season the chicken on all sides with the Cajun seasoning, oregano, salt, pepper, and thyme. Add the seasoned chicken, sausage, tomatoes, tomato paste, broth, hot sauce, bay leaves, and saffron, if using, to the Instant Pot.

4. Seal the lid, press Pressure Cook or Manual, and set the timer for 7 minutes. Once finished, turn the valve to venting for a quick release.

5. Just before serving, stir in the shrimp and mussels, if using, and press Sauté. Cook until the shrimp are heated through, about 5 minutes. Discard the bay leaves.

6. Transfer the jambalaya mixture to a serving dish, leaving 3 tablespoons of sauce in the pot.

7. Place the riced cauliflower in the pot, press Sauté, and cook for 3 minutes, or until tender.

8. Place the cauliflower rice in bowls, top with the jambalaya, and garnish with parsley.

Complete Step 1. Season the chicken on all sides with the Cajun seasoning, oregano, salt, pepper, and thyme. Place the seasoned chicken, sausage, onion, bell pepper, celery, tomatoes, tomato paste, broth, hot sauce, bay leaves, and saffron (if using) in a 6-quart slow cooker. Cover and cook on high for 3 hours or on low for 6 hours, or until the chicken is cooked through. Just before serving, stir in the shrimp, mussels (if using), and riced cauliflower. Cover and cook on high for 10 minutes, or until the cauliflower is tender. Proceed to Step 8.

STORE in an airtight container in the fridge for up to 5 days or in the freezer for up to a month. To reheat, place in a lightly greased skillet over medium-high heat for 5 minutes, or until heated through.

NUTRITIONAL INFO (per serving)				
calories	fat	protein	carbs	fiber
535	29g	44g	23g	6g

sweet endings
& drinks

crème brûlée

option

yield: 4 servings *prep time:* 7 minutes, plus time to chill *cook time:* 9 minutes

Craig's birthday is on Christmas Day, and his favorite dessert is crème brûlée. Because the holidays can be quite busy and desserts are everywhere, I decided to make this simple dessert for him a few days early. It's best served chilled, so making it ahead is a great way to enjoy it!

1 cup heavy cream (or full-fat coconut milk for dairy-free)

2 tablespoons Swerve confectioners'-style sweetener or equivalent amount of powdered sweetener (see page 39), or more to taste

2 large egg yolks

Seeds scraped from ½ vanilla bean (about 8 inches long), or 1 teaspoon vanilla extract

4 teaspoons Swerve confectioners'-style sweetener, for topping

1. Heat the cream in a saucepan over medium-high heat until very hot but not boiling, about 2 minutes (or microwave in 20-second increments).

2. Place the sweetener, egg yolks, and vanilla seeds in a blender or food processor and purée until smooth. While the blender is running, slowly pour in the hot cream. Taste and adjust the sweetness to your liking. Use a spatula to scoop the mixture into four 2-ounce ramekins. Cover the ramekins with aluminum foil.

3. Set a trivet in a 6-quart Instant Pot and pour in 1 cup of cold water. Place the ramekins on the trivet. Seal the lid, press Pressure Cook or Manual, and set the timer for 7 minutes. Once finished, turn the valve to venting for a quick release.

4. Keep the ramekins covered with the foil and place in the refrigerator to chill completely, about 2 hours.

5. Once chilled, sprinkle 1 teaspoon of confectioners'-style Swerve on top of each crème brûlée. Use a kitchen torch or the oven broiler to melt the sweetener. (If using the broiler, watch carefully so the sweetener doesn't burn.) Place in the fridge to chill the topping for a few minutes before serving; it will harden as it cools.

Complete Steps 1 and 2. Place the ramekins in a 6-quart slow cooker and add water to go about halfway up the sides of the ramekins; this ensures even baking and a creamy texture. Cover and cook on high for 2 hours, or until just set and a little jiggly in the middle. Proceed to Step 4.

STORE in an airtight container in the fridge for up to 5 days.

NUTRITIONAL INFO (per serving)				
calories	fat	protein	carbs	fiber
234	25g	4g	2g	0g

lemon ricotta torte

 yield: one 7-inch round torte (12 servings) *prep time:* 15 minutes, plus time to chill *cook time:* 35 minutes

TORTE:

1⅓ cups Swerve confectioners'-style sweetener or equivalent amount of liquid or powdered sweetener (see page 39)

½ cup (1 stick) unsalted butter, softened

2 teaspoons lemon or vanilla extract

5 large eggs, separated

2½ cups blanched almond flour

1¼ cups whole-milk ricotta cheese (10 ounces), homemade (page 322) or store-bought

¼ cup lemon juice

2 tablespoons lemon zest (optional, for more lemon flavor)

LEMON GLAZE:

½ cup (1 stick) unsalted butter

¼ cup Swerve confectioners'-style sweetener or equivalent amount of powdered sweetener (see page 39)

2 ounces cream cheese (¼ cup)

2 tablespoons lemon juice

1 teaspoon lemon extract, or a few drops of food-grade lemon oil (optional)

Grated lemon zest and lemon slices, for garnish

1. Line the bottom and sides of a 7-inch round cake pan with parchment paper and grease the parchment well; set aside.

2. Make the torte: Place the sweetener, butter, and extract in the bowl of a stand mixer and beat for 8 to 10 minutes, until the mixture is pale in color and well combined. Scrape down the sides of the bowl as needed.

3. Add the egg yolks and continue to beat until fully combined. Add the almond flour and mix until smooth, then fold in the ricotta, lemon juice, and lemon zest, if using.

4. In a separate medium-sized bowl, beat the egg whites until stiff peaks form. Gently fold the whites into the batter. Pour the batter into the prepared pan and smooth the top.

5. Set a trivet in a 6-quart Instant Pot and pour in 1 cup of cold water. Make a foil sling (see page 19) and use it to lower the cake pan onto the trivet. Tuck in the sides of the sling.

6. Seal the lid, press Pressure Cook or Manual, and set the timer for 30 minutes. Once finished, let the pressure release naturally.

7. Use the foil sling to lift the pan out of the Instant Pot. Place the torte in the fridge for 40 minutes or in the freezer for 20 minutes to chill before glazing. Having a very cold torte will help the glaze harden faster.

8. While the torte is cooling, make the glaze: If using butter, place the butter in a large saucepan over high heat. Cook, whisking occasionally, for about 5 minutes. The butter will start to sizzle and fluff up. Watch for brown (not black!) flecks. Once the butter is brown, remove from the heat. If using butter-flavored coconut oil, place the oil in a bowl. While whisking the browned butter or coconut oil vigorously, add the sweetener.

9. Carefully add the cream cheese, lemon juice, and lemon extract, if using, to the browned butter mixture; if you're not careful, the mixture might froth over. Let the glaze cool slightly so it thickens a little (or it will leak off the torte).

10. Transfer the chilled torte to a serving platter. Pour the glaze over the torte and place back in the fridge to chill for another 30 minutes. Before serving, sprinkle the lemon zest on top of the torte and arrange the lemon slices on the platter around the torte.

NUTRITIONAL INFO (per serving)				
calories	fat	protein	carbs	fiber
362	34g	10g	6g	3g

Line a 6-quart slow cooker with parchment paper and grease the parchment well. Complete Steps 2, 3, and 4, pouring the batter directly into the prepared slow cooker. Cover and cook on low for 4 to 5 hours, until a knife inserted in the center of the torte comes out clean. Turn off the slow cooker and allow the torte to cool before removing, using the parchment to lift the torte out of the slow cooker. Place the torte in the fridge for 40 minutes or in the freezer for 20 minutes to chill before glazing. Proceed to Step 8.

STORE in an airtight container in the fridge for up to 5 days or in the freezer for up to a month.

chocolate fondue

   yield: 4 servings   *prep time:* 5 minutes   *cook time:* 2 minutes

1 cup heavy cream, divided

⅓ cup Swerve confectioners'-style sweetener or equivalent amount of liquid or powdered sweetener (see page 39), divided

2 ounces unsweetened baking chocolate, finely chopped, divided

Fine sea salt

SERVING SUGGESTIONS:

Glazed Pumpkin Bundt Cake (page 302), unglazed, cut into cubes (omit for egg- and nut-free)

Maple-Glazed Zucchini Bundt Cake (page 308), unglazed, cut into cubes (omit for egg-free)

Fresh strawberries

SPECIAL EQUIPMENT:

Set of fondue forks or wooden skewers

1. Divide the cream, sweetener, and chocolate evenly among four 4-ounce ramekins. Add a pinch of salt to each one and stir well. Cover the ramekins with aluminum foil.

2. Set a trivet in an 8-quart Instant Pot and pour in 1 cup of cold water. Place the ramekins on the trivet. Seal the lid, press Pressure Cook or Manual, and set the timer for 2 minutes. Once finished, let the pressure release naturally. Tilt the lid to open the Instant Pot so that condensation doesn't drip into the ramekins.

3. Use tongs to remove the ramekins from the pot. Use a fork to stir the fondue until smooth. It may look like the chocolate has broken, but keep stirring and it will combine with the other ingredients.

4. To serve, use fondue forks to dip cake cubes and/or strawberries into the fondue.

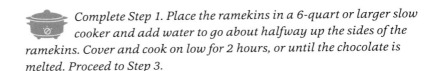 *Complete Step 1. Place the ramekins in a 6-quart or larger slow cooker and add water to go about halfway up the sides of the ramekins. Cover and cook on low for 2 hours, or until the chocolate is melted. Proceed to Step 3.*

STORE in an airtight container in the fridge for up to 5 days. To reheat, place the ramekins in a hot water bath to gently warm the fondue.

NUTRITIONAL INFO (per serving)				
calories	fat	protein	carbs	fiber
297	30g	3g	6g	2g

deconstructed tiramisu

option

yield: 4 servings   *prep time:* 5 minutes, plus time to chill   *cook time:* 9 minutes

1 cup heavy cream (or full-fat coconut milk for dairy-free)

2 large egg yolks

2 tablespoons Swerve confectioners'-style sweetener, or ¼ teaspoon liquid stevia, or more to taste

2 tablespoons brewed decaf espresso or strong brewed coffee

1 teaspoon unsweetened cocoa powder, or more to taste

1 teaspoon rum extract

Pinch of fine sea salt

4 teaspoons Swerve confectioners'-style sweetener, for topping

1. Heat the cream in a saucepan over medium-high heat until very hot but not boiling, about 2 minutes (or microwave in 20-second increments).

2. Place the egg yolks, sweetener, coffee, cocoa powder, rum extract, and salt in a blender or food processor and purée until smooth. While the blender is running, slowly pour in the hot cream. Taste and adjust the sweetness to your liking, and add more cocoa powder, if desired. Use a spatula to scoop the mixture into four 2-ounce ramekins. Cover the ramekins with aluminum foil.

3. Set a trivet in a 6-quart Instant Pot and pour in 1 cup of cold water. Place the ramekins on the trivet. Seal the lid, press Pressure Cook or Manual, and set the timer for 7 minutes. Once finished, turn the valve to venting for a quick release.

4. Keep the ramekins covered with the foil and place in the refrigerator to chill completely, about 2 hours.

5. Once chilled, sprinkle 1 teaspoon of confectioners'-style Swerve on top of each tiramisu. Use a kitchen torch or the oven broiler to melt the sweetener. (If using the broiler, watch carefully so the sweetener doesn't burn.) Place in the fridge to chill the topping for about 20 minutes before serving; it will harden as it cools.

Complete Steps 1 and 2. Place the ramekins in a 6-quart slow cooker and add water to go about halfway up the sides of the ramekins; this ensures even baking and a creamy texture. Cover and cook on high for 2 hours, or until just set and a little jiggly in the middle. Proceed to Step 4.

STORE in an airtight container in the fridge for up to 5 days.

NUTRITIONAL INFO (per serving)				
calories	fat	protein	carbs	fiber
243	25g	5g	2g	0.2g

cinnamon roll cheesecake

 yield: one 7-inch round cake (12 servings) *prep time:* 15 minutes, plus time to chill *cook time:* 35 minutes

CRUST:

3½ tablespoons unsalted butter or coconut oil

1½ ounces unsweetened baking chocolate, chopped

⅓ cup Swerve confectioners'-style sweetener or equivalent amount of liquid or powdered sweetener (see page 39)

1 large egg, beaten

2 teaspoons ground cinnamon

1 teaspoon vanilla extract

¼ teaspoon fine sea salt

FILLING:

4 (8-ounce) packages cream cheese, softened

¾ cup Swerve confectioners'-style sweetener or equivalent amount of liquid or powdered sweetener (see page 39)

½ cup unsweetened almond milk (or hemp milk for nut-free)

1 teaspoon vanilla extract

¼ teaspoon almond extract (omit for nut-free)

¼ teaspoon fine sea salt

3 large eggs

CINNAMON SWIRL:

6 tablespoons (¾ stick) unsalted butter (or butter flavored coconut oil for dairy-free)

½ cup Swerve confectioners'-style sweetener or equivalent amount of liquid or powdered sweetener (see page 39)

Seeds scraped from ½ vanilla bean (about 8 inches long), or 1 teaspoon vanilla extract

1 tablespoon ground cinnamon

¼ teaspoon fine sea salt

1. Line the bottom and sides of a 7-inch springform pan with two layers of aluminum foil.

2. Make the crust: Melt the butter in a saucepan over medium-low heat. Slowly add the chocolate, stirring constantly so it doesn't burn. When the chocolate is melted, add the sweetener, egg, cinnamon, vanilla extract, and salt and stir to combine.

3. Transfer the crust mixture to the prepared pan, spreading it with your hands to cover the bottom completely.

4. Make the filling: Place the cream cheese, sweetener, milk, extracts, and salt in a large bowl or the bowl of a stand mixer and beat with a hand mixer or stand mixer until well blended. Add the eggs, one at a time, mixing on low speed after each addition just until blended. Then beat until the filling is very smooth. Pour half of the filling over the crust.

5. Make the cinnamon swirl: In a saucepan, heat the butter over high heat, stirring often, until the butter froths and brown (not black!) flecks appear. Whisk in the sweetener, vanilla seeds, cinnamon, and salt. Remove from the heat and let cool slightly.

6. Spoon half of the cinnamon swirl on top of the cheesecake filling in the springform pan. Using a knife, cut the cinnamon swirl through the filling several times for a marbled effect. Top with the rest of the cheesecake filling and cinnamon swirl. Cut the cinnamon swirl through the cheesecake filling again several times.

7. Set a trivet in a 6-quart Instant Pot and pour in 1 cup of cold water. Make a foil sling (see page 19) and use it to lower the springform pan onto the trivet. Cover the cheesecake with 3 large sheets of paper towel to ensure that condensation doesn't leak onto it. Tuck in the sides of the sling.

NUTRITIONAL INFO (per serving)				
calories	fat	protein	carbs	fiber
401	37g	8g	4g	1g

8. Seal the lid, press Pressure Cook or Manual, and set the timer for 26 minutes. Once finished, let the pressure release naturally. Gently open the lid and use the foil sling to lift the pan out of the Instant Pot.

9. Allow the cheesecake to cool, then place in the refrigerator for 4 hours to chill and set completely before slicing and serving.

Complete Steps 1 through 6. Pour 1 cup of hot water into a 6-quart or larger slow cooker. Make sure the foil is wrapped tightly around the springform pan so that the water can't leak in. Place the pan in the slow cooker. Lay 3 large sheets of paper towel on top of the cheesecake so that condensation doesn't leak onto it. Cover and cook on high for 2 hours. Turn off the slow cooker and leave the cheesecake in the slow cooker for 1 more hour. Proceed to Step 9.

STORE in an airtight container in the fridge for up to 5 days.

custard

ps heavy cream (or full-fat
conut milk for dairy-free)

4 large egg yolks

**¼ cup Swerve confectioners'-style
sweetener or equivalent amount
of liquid or powdered sweetener
(see page 39), or more to taste**

**1 tablespoon plus 1 teaspoon
unsweetened cocoa powder, or
more to taste**

½ teaspoon almond extract

Pinch of fine sea salt

1. Heat the cream in a saucepan over medium-high heat until very hot but not boiling, about 2 minutes (or microwave in 20-second increments).

2. Place the remaining ingredients in a blender or food processor and purée until smooth. While the blender is running, slowly pour in the hot cream. Taste and adjust the sweetness to your liking, and add more cocoa powder, if desired. Use a spatula to scoop the custard mixture into four 4-ounce ramekins. Cover the ramekins with aluminum foil.

3. Set a trivet in an 8-quart Instant Pot and pour in 1 cup of cold water. Place the ramekins on the trivet. Seal the lid, press Pressure Cook or Manual, and set the timer for 5 minutes. Once finished, turn the valve to venting for a quick release.

4. Remove the foil and set the foil aside; allow the custard to cool for 15 minutes. Cover the ramekins with the foil again and place in the refrigerator to chill completely, about 2 hours.

Complete Steps 1 and 2. Place the ramekins in a 6-quart or larger slow cooker and add water to go about halfway up the sides of the ramekins; this ensures even baking and a creamy texture. Cover and cook on high for 2 hours, or until just set and a little jiggly in the middle. Proceed to Step 4.

STORE in an airtight container in the fridge for up to 5 days.

TIPS: Don't let the ramekins cool with the foil on—then all the condensation will drip onto the custard. Take the foil off, let cool, and then put the foil back on.

I highly suggest scooping the custard mixture into ice pop molds and freezing for a few hours or until set. It makes delicious fudge pops!

NUTRITIONAL INFO (per serving)				
calories	fat	protein	carbs	fiber
239	25g	5g	5g	0.2g

...in pie spiced pots de crème

 yield: 4 servings   *prep time:* 5 minutes, plus time to chill   *cook time:* 7 minutes

2 cups heavy cream (or full-fat coconut milk for dairy-free)

4 large egg yolks

¼ cup Swerve confectioners'-style sweetener or equivalent amount of liquid or powdered sweetener (see page 39), or more to taste

2 teaspoons pumpkin pie spice

1 teaspoon vanilla or maple extract

Pinch of fine sea salt

1. Heat the cream in a saucepan over medium-high heat until very hot but not boiling, about 2 minutes (or microwave in 20-second increments).

2. Place the remaining ingredients in a medium-sized bowl and whisk until smooth. (*Note:* You can use a stick blender or hand mixer for this task, but if you do, you will end up with air bubbles on the tops of your baked pots de crème.)

3. Slowly pour in the hot cream while whisking. Taste and adjust the sweetness to your liking. Use a spatula to scoop the mixture into four 4-ounce ramekins. Cover the ramekins with aluminum foil.

4. Set a trivet in an 8-quart Instant Pot and pour in 1 cup of cold water. Place the ramekins on the trivet. Seal the lid, press Pressure Cook or Manual, and set the timer for 5 minutes. Once finished, turn the valve to venting for a quick release.

5. Remove the foil and set the foil aside; allow the pots de crème to cool for 15 minutes. Cover the ramekins with the foil again and place in the refrigerator to chill completely, about 2 hours.

Complete Steps 1 through 3. Place the ramekins in a 6-quart or larger slow cooker and add water to go about halfway up the sides of the ramekins; this ensures even baking and a creamy texture. Cover and cook on high for 2 hours, or until just set and a little jiggly in the middle. Proceed to Step 5.

STORE *in an airtight container in the fridge for up to 5 days.*

TIPS: *Don't let the ramekins cool with the foil on—then all the condensation will drip onto the dessert. Take the foil off, let cool, and then put the foil back on.*

I highly suggest scooping the mixture into ice pop molds and freezing for a few hours or until set. It makes delicious ice pops!

NUTRITIONAL INFO (per serving)				
calories	fat	protein	carbs	fiber
242	25g	4g	3g	0.4g

yield: 18 servings   *prep time:* 5 minutes   *cook time:* 10 minutes

1 Glazed Pumpkin Bundt Cake (page 302) or Maple-Glazed Zucchini Bundt Cake (page 308), unglazed, cut into cubes (use zucchini cake for nut-free)

1 cup unsweetened almond milk (or full-fat coconut milk for nut-free)

½ cup heavy cream (or full-fat coconut milk for dairy-free)

3 large eggs

⅔ cup Swerve confectioners'-style sweetener or equivalent amount of liquid or powdered sweetener (see page 39)

1 teaspoon ground cinnamon

Seeds scraped from 1 vanilla bean (about 8 inches long), or 2 teaspoons vanilla extract

½ teaspoon fine sea salt

FROSTING:

½ cup unsalted butter (or butter-flavored coconut oil for dairy-free), softened

¼ cup Swerve confectioners'-style sweetener or equivalent amount of powdered sweetener (see page 39), or more to taste

1 teaspoon ground cinnamon

1. Put the cake cubes in a large bowl and pour the milk and cream over them; set aside.

2. Place the eggs, sweetener, cinnamon, and vanilla seeds in another large bowl and mix well. Pour the egg mixture over the soaked cake cubes and gently stir to combine.

3. Grease a 2-quart round casserole dish. Pour the cake mixture into the greased dish.

4. Set a trivet in a 6-quart Instant Pot and pour in 1 cup of cold water. Make a foil sling (see page 19) and use it to lower the casserole dish onto the trivet. Tuck in the sides of the sling.

5. Seal the lid, press Pressure Cook or Manual, and set the timer for 10 minutes. Once finished, let the pressure release naturally. Use the foil sling to lift the dish out of the Instant Pot.

6. Let the bread pudding cool for 10 minutes before slicing. Meanwhile, make the frosting: Place the softened butter, sweetener, and cinnamon in a small bowl and stir to combine. Taste and adjust the sweetness to your liking.

7. Serve warm or chilled. Dollop the frosting over the bread pudding slices.

Complete Steps 1 and 2, then pour the mixture into a greased 4-quart slow cooker. Cover and cook on low for 3 hours, or until the pudding is cooked through and set. Proceed to Step 6.

STORE in an airtight container in the fridge for up to 5 days.

NUTRITIONAL INFO (per serving)				
calories	fat	protein	carbs	fiber
248	22g	8g	7g	3g

flourless chocolate tortes

option

yield: 8 small tortes (1 per serving)   *prep time:* 7 minutes   *cook time:* 10 minutes

In this recipe, I fill eight ramekins and cook four at a time. I store the other four in the freezer for easy desserts later! These tasty tortes are best served warm, right from the ramekins.

7 ounces unsweetened baking chocolate, finely chopped

¾ cup plus 2 tablespoons unsalted butter (or butter-flavored coconut oil for dairy-free)

1¼ cups Swerve confectioners'-style sweetener or equivalent amount of liquid or powdered sweetener (see page 39), or more to taste

5 large eggs

1 tablespoon coconut flour

2 teaspoons ground cinnamon

Seeds scraped from 1 vanilla bean (about 8 inches long), or 2 teaspoons vanilla extract

Pinch of fine sea salt

1. Grease eight 4-ounce ramekins or mason jars. Place the chocolate and butter in a heavy saucepan over medium heat and stir until the chocolate is completely melted, about 3 minutes.

2. Remove the pan from the heat, then add the remaining ingredients and stir until smooth. If you're not concerned about consuming raw eggs, taste and adjust the sweetness to your liking. Pour the batter into the greased ramekins.

3. Set a trivet in a 6-quart Instant Pot and pour in 1 cup of cold water. Place four of the ramekins on the trivet. Seal the lid, press Pressure Cook or Manual, and set the timer for 7 minutes. Once finished, turn the valve to venting for a quick release.

4. Remove the ramekins with tongs. Repeat with the remaining ramekins or cover and store in the freezer for up to a month before cooking.

5. Serve the tortes either warm or chilled.

Complete Steps 1 and 2. Place four of the ramekins in a 6-quart or larger slow cooker and add water to go about halfway up the sides of the ramekins; this ensures even baking and a creamy texture. Cover and cook on high for 2 hours, or until just set and a little jiggly in the middle. Proceed to Step 4.

STORE in an airtight container in the fridge for up to 5 days or in the freezer for up to a month. To reheat in an Instant Pot, pour 1 cup of cold water into the Instant Pot. Cover the ramekins with foil and place in the pot. Seal the lid, press Pressure Cook or Manual, and set the timer for 2 minutes. Once finished, turn the valve to venting for a quick release. Or place in a 350°F oven for 3 minutes, or until warmed to your liking. You can also serve the tortes at room temperature.

NUTRITIONAL INFO (per serving)				
calories	fat	protein	carbs	fiber
407	37g	8g	9g	5g

glazed pumpkin bundt cake

  yield: 12 servings   *prep time:* 7 minutes   *cook time:* 35 minutes

CAKE:

3 cups blanched almond flour

1 teaspoon baking soda

½ teaspoon fine sea salt

2 teaspoons ground cinnamon

1 teaspoon ginger powder

1 teaspoon ground nutmeg

¼ teaspoon ground cloves

6 large eggs

2 cups pumpkin puree

1 cup Swerve confectioners'-style sweetener or equivalent amount of liquid or powdered sweetener (see page 39)

¼ cup (½ stick) unsalted butter (or coconut oil for dairy-free), softened

GLAZE:

1 cup (2 sticks) unsalted butter (or coconut oil for dairy-free), melted

½ cup Swerve confectioners'-style sweetener or equivalent amount of liquid or powdered sweetener (see page 39)

1. Place the almond flour, baking soda, salt, and spices in a large bowl and whisk to combine. Put the eggs, pumpkin, sweetener, and butter in another large bowl and mix until smooth. Stir the wet ingredients into the dry ingredients.

2. Grease a 6-cup Bundt pan (see Note below). Pour the batter into the prepared pan and cover with a paper towel and then with aluminum foil.

3. Set a trivet in an 8-quart Instant Pot and pour in 2 cups of cold water. Place the Bundt pan on the trivet. Seal the lid, press Pressure Cook or Manual, and set the timer for 35 minutes. Once finished, let the pressure release naturally. Allow the cake to cool in the pot for 10 minutes before removing.

4. While the cake is cooling, make the glaze: Mix the butter and sweetener together in a small bowl. Spoon the glaze over the warm cake. Allow to cool before slicing and serving.

 Complete Steps 1 and 2. Pour 2 cups of hot water into an 8-quart slow cooker. Place the Bundt pan in the slow cooker, making sure that the water goes halfway up the side of the pan. Cover and cook on high for 2 hours, or until a toothpick inserted in the middle of the cake comes out clean. Allow to cool in the slow cooker for 10 minutes before removing. Proceed to Step 4.

STORE in an airtight container in the fridge for up to 5 days or in the freezer for up to a month.

NOTE: If you don't have a 6-cup Bundt pan, you can use a 7-inch springform pan and place a 2-inch jar in the center to make a Bundt-shaped cake.

NUTRITIONAL INFO (per serving)				
calories	fat	protein	carbs	fiber
382	35g	10g	10g	4g

almond fudge

2½ cups Swerve confectioners'-style sweetener or equivalent amount of liquid or powdered sweetener (see page 39)

1¾ cups unsweetened almond milk

1½ cups almond butter

8 ounces unsweetened baking chocolate, finely chopped

1 teaspoon almond or vanilla extract

¼ teaspoon fine sea salt

1. Line a 9 by 11-inch baking dish with greased parchment paper, or have on hand chocolate molds with at least 30 cavities. (I used a butterfly-shaped mold.)

2. Place the sweetener, almond milk, almond butter, and chocolate in a 3-quart or larger Instant Pot and stir well. Press Sauté and cook for 2 minutes, stirring occasionally.

3. Turn the Instant Pot to Keep Warm mode for 3 minutes, or until the fudge mixture is completely melted and well combined. Stir in the extract and salt.

4. Pour the fudge mixture into the prepared baking dish (or into the chocolate molds), cover, and refrigerate for 4 hours or until firm. If you used a baking dish, cut the fudge into 30 equal-sized pieces.

Place the sweetener, almond milk, almond butter, and chocolate in a 2-quart or larger slow cooker. Cover and cook on low for 30 minutes, or until the mixture is completely melted when you stir it. Add the extract and salt and use a hand mixer to combine well. Proceed to Step 4.

STORE in an airtight container in the fridge for up to 5 days.

NUTRITIONAL INFO (per serving)				
calories	fat	protein	carbs	fiber
131	11g	4g	5g	2g

upside-down maple bacon mini cheesecakes

option

yield: 8 mini cheesecakes (1 per serving)   *prep time*: 15 minutes, plus time to chill
cook time: 10 minutes

Erin, one of my recipe testers, is a thoughtful and generous woman who lives in Canada. She tests so many recipes that she brought a crustless cheesecake to the local police department for them to taste-test. They laughed and said, "If this is a keto cheesecake, where's the bacon and whipped cream?" I had to add one more recipe to this book in honor of her generosity! I call it Upside-Down because the bacon crumbles act as a textured "crust" on the top instead of a crust on the bottom.

3 (8-ounce) packages cream cheese, softened

⅔ cup Swerve confectioners'-style sweetener or equivalent amount of liquid or powdered sweetener (see page 39)

½ cup unsweetened almond milk (or hemp milk for nut-free)

2 teaspoons maple extract

¼ teaspoon fine sea salt

1 large egg

4 slices bacon, chopped, for topping

SWEETENED WHIPPED CREAM:

½ cup heavy cream

2 tablespoons Swerve confectioners'-style sweetener or equivalent amount of liquid or powdered sweetener (see page 39), or more to taste

½ teaspoon maple extract

1. Place the cream cheese, sweetener, milk, maple extract, and salt in a large bowl or the bowl of a stand mixer. Using a hand mixer or the stand mixer, beat until well blended. Add the egg and mix on low speed until very smooth. Pour the batter into eight 4-ounce ramekins or mason jars. Gently tap the ramekins against the counter to bring the air bubbles to the surface.

2. Set a trivet in a 6-quart Instant Pot and pour in 1 cup of cold water. Stack the ramekins in two layers on top of the trivet. Cover the top layer of ramekins with 3 large pieces of paper towel to ensure that condensation doesn't leak onto the cheesecakes.

3. Seal the lid, press Pressure Cook or Manual, and set the timer for 6 minutes. Once finished, let the pressure release naturally. Gently open the lid and remove the ramekins with tongs.

4. Place the cheesecakes in the fridge to chill for about 4 hours. Meanwhile, make the topping: In a medium-sized skillet over medium-high heat, cook the bacon for 4 minutes, or until it is crisp and cooked through. Place the cooked bacon on a paper towel–lined plate to drain.

5. Place the cream in a medium-sized bowl and use a hand mixer on high speed to whip until soft peaks form. Add the sweetener and maple extract and whip until well combined. Taste and adjust the sweetness to your liking.

6. To serve, top the cheesecakes with the sweetened whipped cream and sprinkle the bacon on top.

NUTRITIONAL INFO (per serving)				
calories	fat	protein	carbs	fiber
395	36g	9g	2g	0g

 *Complete Step 1, then place four of the ramekins in a 6-quart or larger slow cooker. Add hot water to go about halfway up the sides of the ramekins; this ensures even baking and a creamy texture. Lay 3 large sheets of paper towel over the ramekins so that condensation doesn't leak onto the cheesecakes. Cover and cook on high for 1 hour. Turn off the slow cooker and leave the cheesecakes in the slow cooker for 30 more minutes, then use tongs to remove the ramekins and place them in the fridge to chill. Repeat with the remaining ramekins, then proceed to Step 4.*

STORE *in an airtight container in the fridge for up to 5 days.*

maple-glazed zucchini bundt cake

 yield: 8 servings *prep time:* 7 minutes, plus time to chill *cook time:* 40 minutes

CAKE:

6 large eggs

1 cup full-fat coconut milk

¾ cup (1½ sticks) unsalted butter (or butter-flavored coconut oil for dairy-free), melted

½ cup Swerve confectioners'-style sweetener or equivalent amount of liquid or powdered sweetener (see page 39)

2 teaspoons ground cinnamon

1 cup coconut flour

1 teaspoon baking powder

1 teaspoon fine sea salt

1 cup shredded zucchini

3 teaspoons vanilla or maple extract

MAPLE GLAZE:

½ cup (1 stick) unsalted butter (or butter-flavored coconut oil for dairy-free)

¼ cup Swerve confectioners'-style sweetener or equivalent amount of powdered sweetener (see page 39)

2 ounces cream cheese (¼ cup) (or Kite Hill brand cream cheese style spread for dairy-free)

2 teaspoons maple extract

Chopped raw walnuts, for garnish (omit for nut-free)

1. In large bowl, beat the eggs with a hand mixer until light and foamy. Add the coconut milk, melted butter, sweetener, and cinnamon and combine well.

2. Put the coconut flour, baking powder, and salt in another large bowl and whisk to combine. Add the dry ingredients to the wet ingredients and stir with a large spoon, then stir in the grated zucchini and extract.

3. Grease a 6-cup Bundt pan (see Note, page 302). Pour the batter into the prepared pan and cover the pan with a paper towel and then with aluminum foil.

4. Set a trivet in an 8-quart Instant Pot and pour in 2 cups of cold water. Place the Bundt pan on the trivet. Seal the lid, press Pressure Cook or Manual, and set the timer for 35 minutes. Once finished, let the pressure release naturally. Allow the cake to cool in the pot for 10 minutes before removing.

5. Chill the cake in the fridge or freezer for 1 hour before removing from the Bundt pan. Having a very cold cake will help the glaze harden faster.

6. While the cake is cooling, make the glaze: If using butter, place the butter in a large saucepan over high heat. Cook for about 5 minutes, whisking occasionally. The butter will start to sizzle and fluff up. Watch for brown (not black!) flecks. Once the butter is brown, remove from the heat. If using butter-flavored coconut oil, place the oil in a bowl. While whisking the browned butter or coconut oil vigorously, add the sweetener.

7. Carefully add the cream cheese and maple extract to the browned butter mixture; if you're not careful, the mixture might froth over. Let the glaze cool slightly so it thickens a little (or it will leak off the cake).

8. Transfer the chilled cake to a serving platter and drizzle the glaze over the cake. Sprinkle on the walnuts while the glaze is still wet. Place the cake in the fridge to chill for another 30 minutes before serving.

NUTRITIONAL INFO (per serving)				
calories	fat	protein	carbs	fiber
507	45g	9g	12g	6g

Complete Steps 1 through 3. Pour 2 cups of hot water into a 6-quart or larger slow cooker. Place the Bundt pan in the slow cooker, making sure that the water goes halfway up the side of the pan. Cover and cook on high for 2 hours, or until a toothpick inserted into the middle of the cake comes out clean. Allow to cool in the slow cooker for 10 minutes before removing. Proceed to Step 5.

STORE in an airtight container in the fridge for up to 5 days or in the freezer for up to a month.

gingerbread café au lait

   yield: 4 (8-ounce) servings *prep time:* 5 minutes *cook time:* 5 minutes

option

4 cups unsweetened almond milk (or hemp milk for nut-free)

½ cup Swerve confectioners'-style sweetener or equivalent amount of liquid or powdered sweetener (see page 39)

Seeds scraped from 2 vanilla beans (about 8 inches long), or 4 teaspoons vanilla extract

2 teaspoons ginger powder

1 teaspoon ground cinnamon

4 whole cloves, or ¼ teaspoon ground cloves

¼ teaspoon ground nutmeg, plus more for garnish

2 cups freshly brewed coffee or espresso

1. Place the milk, sweetener, vanilla seeds, ginger, cinnamon, cloves, and nutmeg in a 3-quart Instant Pot.

2. Seal the lid, press Pressure Cook or Manual, and set the timer for 5 minutes. Once finished, turn the valve to venting for a quick release.

3. Pour the mixture through a fine-mesh strainer into a 2-quart heat-safe jar or pitcher.

4. Divide the hot coffee equally among four 8-ounce coffee cups or glass mugs.

5. Top off the coffee with the milk mixture, dividing it equally among the cups. Garnish with a sprinkle of nutmeg, if desired.

 Complete Step 1 using a 3-quart slow cooker. Cover and cook on low for 2 hours, then proceed to Step 3.

STORE *the milk mixture in an airtight container in the fridge for up to 5 days. To reheat, place in a saucepan over medium-high heat for 2 minutes, then top off with freshly brewed coffee or espresso.*

NUTRITIONAL INFO (per serving)				
calories	fat	protein	carbs	fiber
42	3g	1g	3g	1g

hot chocolate

4 cups unsweetened almond milk (or full-fat coconut milk for nut-free)

2 ounces unsweetened baking chocolate

⅓ cup Swerve confectioners'-style sweetener or equivalent amount of liquid or powdered sweetener (see page 39)

½ teaspoon fine sea salt

½ teaspoon vanilla extract

Sweetened whipped cream (page 306), for serving (optional; omit for dairy-free)

1. Place the milk, chocolate, sweetener, salt, and vanilla extract in a 3-quart Instant Pot. Seal the lid, press Pressure Cook or Manual, and set the timer for 1 minute. Once finished, let the pressure release naturally. Stir well until the chocolate is fully melted.

2. Pour the hot chocolate into two 8-ounce glass or ceramic mugs and top with sweetened whipped cream, if desired.

Place the milk, chocolate, sweetener, and salt in a 3-quart slow cooker. Cover and cook on low for 1 to 2 hours, stirring occasionally, until the chocolate is melted and the ingredients are well blended. Just before serving, stir in the vanilla extract. Proceed to Step 2.

STORE in an airtight container in the fridge for up to a week. To reheat, place in a saucepan over medium heat for 3 minutes, or until warmed to your liking.

NUTRITIONAL INFO (per serving)				
calories	fat	protein	carbs	fiber
263	21g	6g	9g	5g

homemade chai

option   *yield:* 2 (8-ounce) servings   *prep time:* 3 minutes   *cook time:* 5 minutes

3 bags black tea

1 cup filtered water

1 cup unsweetened almond milk (or hemp milk for nut-free)

½ teaspoon vanilla-flavored liquid stevia

4 cinnamon sticks

4 green cardamom pods

4 thin slices fresh ginger

2 whole cloves

½ teaspoon fennel seeds

1. Place all of the ingredients in a 3-quart Instant Pot. Seal the lid, press Pressure Cook or Manual, and set the timer for 5 minutes. Once finished, turn the valve to venting for a quick release.

2. Pour the tea mixture through a fine-mesh strainer into teacups and serve.

Place all of the ingredients in a 3-quart slow cooker. Cover and cook on high for 2 hours. Proceed to Step 2.

STORE *in an airtight container in the fridge for 5 days. To reheat, place in a saucepan over medium-high heat for 2 minutes, or until warmed to your liking.*

NUTRITIONAL INFO (per serving)				
calories	fat	protein	carbs	fiber
28	2g	1g	3g	1g

ginger ale

  yield: 4 (8-ounce) servings *prep time:* 3 minutes *cook time:* 1 minute

1 pound fresh ginger, unpeeled, cut into small dice

Peels and juice of 2 lemons

1½ cups Swerve confectioners'-style sweetener or equivalent amount of liquid or powdered sweetener (see page 39)

1 quart carbonated water, plus more for serving

Lemon slices, for garnish

1. Combine the ginger and lemon juice in a food processor and process until minced, stopping the machine periodically to scrape down the sides as needed.

2. Place the ginger puree, lemon peels, sweetener, and carbonated water in a 3-quart Instant Pot. Seal the lid, press Pressure Cook or Manual, and set the timer for 1 minute. Once finished, let the pressure release naturally, about 15 minutes.

3. Stir the ginger syrup well. Pour through a strainer into a container with a lid.

4. To serve, place about 2 tablespoons of the ginger syrup in a glass full of ice. Fill the glass with carbonated water; taste and add more ginger syrup if you like. Garnish with a lime wedge, then serve.

Complete Step 1, then place the ginger puree, lemon peels, sweetener, and water in a 3-quart slow cooker. Cover and cook on high for 4 to 8 hours—the longer the better. Turn off the slow cooker and allow to cool in the fridge for 1 hour. Stir the ginger syrup well, then pour through a strainer into a container with a lid. Proceed to Step 4.

STORE *the ginger syrup in an airtight container in the fridge for up to a week or in the freezer for up to a month.*

NUTRITIONAL INFO (per serving)				
calories	fat	protein	carbs	fiber
19	0.2g	1g	5g	1g

The Benefits of Ginger

- *Problems with mineral absorption? This is a common problem with people who have gluten sensitivities and celiac disease. Ginger improves the absorption and assimilation of essential nutrients in the body.*

- *Indigestion? Ginger increases the production of digestive juices.*

- *Sinus issues? Ginger clears the sinuses' microcirculatory channels in the body that flare up from time to time.*

- *Nausea and tummy cramps after surgery? Chewing ginger post-operation can help overcome nausea, which can occur after a surgical procedure.*

- *Gas? Ginger helps reduce flatulence.*

- *Joint pain? Ginger has anti-inflammatory properties. Rub ginger essential oil onto aching muscles and joints.*

- *Congestion? Stir up some ginger tea to get rid of throat and nose congestion.*

- *Low libido? Ginger has aphrodisiac properties.*

homemade root beer

 *yield:* 16 (8-ounce) servings (about 3 quarts of syrup) *prep time:* 5 minutes *cook time:* 10 minutes

This homemade root beer was a hit with my little boys! I'm sure they would have enjoyed it even more if we lived in an area where sassafras grows, allowing us to forage for our own sassafras roots, but I found sassafras root bark on Amazon. Of course, you are welcome to forage for sassafras roots if you live in an area where it grows!

20 pieces sassafras root bark, about ½ inch in diameter (see Tip)

4 allspice berries

2 whole cloves

1 cinnamon stick

½ teaspoon anise seed

¼ teaspoon fine sea salt

4 cups filtered water

1 cup Swerve confectioners'-style sweetener or equivalent amount of liquid or powdered sweetener (see page 39)

2 quarts sparkling water, for serving

1. Rinse the sassafras root bark under cold water for 3 minutes, pat dry, and cut into ½-inch-long pieces.

2. Place the root bark, allspice berries, cloves, cinnamon stick, anise seed, salt, and water in a 6-quart Instant Pot. Seal the lid, press Pressure Cook or Manual, and set the timer for 10 minutes. Once finished, turn the valve to venting for a quick release.

3. Pour the mixture through a fine-mesh strainer into a medium-sized bowl.

4. Add the sweetener, stir well, and allow to cool. Store the root beer syrup in containers (such as large mason jars) in the fridge until ready to drink.

5. To serve, fill a glass with ice cubes. Start with a 1:2 ratio of root beer syrup to sparkling water: Pour in ⅓ cup of the syrup and ⅔ cup of sparkling water. Stir well and taste. If you like it stronger, add more syrup; if it's too strong, add more sparkling water.

Place the sassafras root bark, allspice berries, cloves, cinnamon stick, anise seed, salt, and water in a 6-quart slow cooker. Cover and cook on high for 2 hours. Proceed to Step 3.

STORE the root beer syrup in airtight containers in the fridge for up to 2 weeks or in the freezer for up to 2 months.

TIP: You can store extra sassafras root bark in an airtight container in a dry pantry for up to a year.

NUTRITIONAL INFO (per serving)				
calories	fat	protein	carbs	fiber
3	0.1g	0.1g	1g	0.3g

basics

healing bone broth

  yield: 4 quarts (1 cup per serving)   *prep time:* 12 minutes   *cook time:* 30 minutes

3½ pounds beef, chicken, ham, or fish bones

2 stalks celery, chopped

1 medium onion, chopped

7 cloves garlic, whacked with the side of a knife and peeled

2 bay leaves

2 teaspoons fine sea salt

¼ cup apple cider vinegar or coconut vinegar

¼ cup fresh herbs of choice, or 1 teaspoon dried herbs (optional)

1. Place the bones, celery, onion, garlic, bay leaves, salt, and vinegar in an 8-quart Instant Pot, then add enough cold filtered water to cover everything. Add the herbs, if using.

2. Seal the lid, press Pressure Cook or Manual, choose low pressure, and set the timer for 30 minutes. (Cooking on low pressure allows more gelatin and minerals to be extracted from the bones.) Once finished, let the pressure release naturally.

3. Pour the broth through a strainer and discard the solids.

Complete Step 1 using an 8-quart slow cooker, then turn the heat to high. Bring to a simmer, uncovered, then reduce the heat to low. Cover and cook for a minimum of 8 hours or up to 48 hours. The longer the broth cooks, the more nutrients and minerals it will have in it! Proceed to Step 3.

STORE in an airtight container in the fridge for up to 5 days or in the freezer for up to a month. To reheat, place in a saucepan over medium heat, stirring occasionally, for 5 minutes, or until heated through.

NUTRITIONAL INFO (per serving)				
calories	fat	protein	carbs	fiber
21	1g	2g	1g	0.2g

homemade ricotta

 yield: about 4½ cups (8 servings)   *prep time:* 5 minutes, plus 10 minutes to rest   *cook time:* 5 minutes

To lower the carbs and boost the flavor in this ricotta, I substituted heavy cream for 1 cup of the milk. You will never buy ricotta at the store again after tasting this one!

3 cups whole milk

1 cup heavy cream

½ teaspoon fine sea salt

3 tablespoons lemon juice

1. Place the milk, cream, and salt in a 3-quart Instant Pot that has a Yogurt function. (A 6-quart will work, too.) Seal the lid, press Yogurt, and then press Adjust until the display reads Boil.

2. Once finished, remove the lid and use a candy thermometer to check the temperature of the ricotta to make sure it is between 170°F and 180°F. If necessary, continue to heat it until it reaches that range.

3. Slowly add the lemon juice and gently stir to combine. Press Cancel to stop the cooking. Let the ricotta rest with the lid on the pot for at least 10 minutes.

4. Place the ricotta in a fine-mesh strainer or several layers of cheesecloth laid over a medium-sized bowl for 5 minutes to allow the liquid (known as whey) to drain; discard the whey. Taste the ricotta and add more salt, if desired.

Place the milk, cream, and salt in a 2-quart or larger slow cooker and stir. Cover and cook on low until the temperature of the ricotta reaches 180°F, about 30 minutes. (At elevations of 7,000 feet or above, bring it to 172°F.) Once the ricotta has reached temperature, turn off the heat, stir in the lemon juice, cover, and set aside in a warm (80°F to 100°F) place, such as a warm oven (with the oven off) for 6 hours. The ricotta is ready to strain when a solid curd has formed. Proceed to Step 4.

STORE in an airtight container in the fridge for up to 5 days.

NUTRITIONAL INFO (per serving)				
calories	fat	protein	carbs	fiber
154	14g	4g	5g	0g

roasted garlic

 *yield:* 10 servings *prep time:* 5 minutes *cook time:* 5 minutes

I always keep roasted garlic in the fridge or freezer for easy additions to soups, entrees, side dishes, sauces, and salad dressings. Roasted garlic takes the flavors of other foods to a whole new level!

10 heads garlic

2 tablespoons extra-virgin olive oil

Fine sea salt

1. Set a trivet in a 3-quart or larger Instant Pot and pour in 1 cup of cold water.

2. Remove the papery outer layers from the heads of garlic. With a sharp knife, cut ⅛ inch off the top of each head to expose the tops of the cloves. Rub the olive oil over the cloves and sprinkle with salt.

3. Place the garlic heads cut side up on the trivet in the Instant Pot. Seal the lid, press Pressure Cook or Manual, and set the timer for 5 minutes. Once finished, turn the valve to venting for a quick release.

4. Allow the garlic to cool enough that it is safe to handle, then remove from the pot and squeeze the bulbs to extract the roasted garlic as needed.

Complete Step 2, then wrap each head of garlic in foil. Place the wrapped garlic in a 3-quart or larger slow cooker and cook on low for 4 hours. Unwrap one head and squeeze it. If garlic squirts out (like toothpaste or frosting coming out of a tube), it is done. If not, wrap it up again and cook for another hour. Proceed to Step 4.

STORE the roasted garlic inside the bulbs for easy removal by squeezing. It will keep in an airtight container in the fridge for up to 5 days or in the freezer for up to a month.

NUTRITIONAL INFO (per serving)				
calories	fat	protein	carbs	fiber
30	3g	0.2g	1g	0.1g

low-carb loaf bread

 yield: one 6-inch round loaf (12 servings) *prep time:* 6 minutes, plus 10 minutes to rest
cook time: 30 minutes

2 cups blanched almond flour

2 tablespoons coconut flour

1 tablespoon plus 1 teaspoon baking powder

1 tablespoon Swerve confectioners'-style sweetener or equivalent amount of liquid or powdered sweetener (see page 39)

1½ teaspoons garlic powder

½ teaspoon fine sea salt

6 ounces sharp cheddar cheese, shredded (1½ cups)

1 cup unsweetened almond milk

2 tablespoons unsalted butter, melted but not hot

1 large egg, beaten

1. Set a trivet in a 6-quart Instant Pot and pour in ½ cup of cold water. Line a 6-inch round cake pan with parchment paper and grease the parchment.

2. Place the almond flour, coconut flour, baking powder, sweetener, garlic powder, and salt in a medium-sized bowl and whisk to combine well. Stir in the shredded cheese.

3. In another medium-sized bowl, stir together the almond milk, melted butter, and egg. Add the wet ingredients to the dry ingredients and mix until well combined. Spoon the dough into the prepared pan.

4. Use a foil sling (see page 19) to lower the pan onto the trivet in the Instant Pot. Tuck in the sides of the sling.

5. Seal the lid, press Pressure Cook or Manual, and set the timer for 30 minutes. Once finished, let the pressure release naturally. Lift the cake pan out of the Instant Pot using the foil sling.

6. Let the bread rest for 10 minutes, then invert onto a plate and peel off the parchment paper. Invert again onto a serving platter and let cool completely.

7. Once the bread is cool, cut into 1-inch-thick slices and serve.

Place a piece of greased parchment paper in a 4-quart slow cooker, covering the bottom and sides. Complete Steps 2 and 3, scooping the dough directly into the prepared slow cooker. Cover and cook on low for 4 hours, or until a toothpick inserted in the middle of the loaf comes out clean. Use the parchment to lift the bread out of the slow cooker, then proceed to Step 6.

STORE in an airtight container in the fridge for up to a week or in the freezer for up to a month.

NUTRITIONAL INFO (per serving)				
calories	fat	protein	carbs	fiber
199	17g	9g	6g	3g

keto "rice"

   yield: 4 servings   *prep time:* 5 minutes   *cook time:* 5 minutes

8 large eggs

½ cup full-fat coconut milk

2 tablespoons beef broth, homemade (page 320) or store-bought, or vegetable broth

1 teaspoon fine sea salt

½ teaspoon ground black pepper

Chopped fresh cilantro, rosemary, or thyme, for garnish (optional)

1. Place the eggs, coconut milk, broth, salt, and pepper in a medium-sized bowl and whisk until well combined.

2. Pour the egg mixture into a 6-quart Instant Pot and press Sauté. Cook until the mixture thickens and small curds form, continuously whisking and scraping the bottom of the pot to keep larger curds from forming, about 5 minutes. Press Cancel to stop the Sauté.

3. Place the "rice" on a platter. If it has released excess liquid, soak up the liquid with a paper towel before serving. Garnish the "rice" with fresh herbs, if desired.

To make the "rice" on the stovetop, complete Step 1. Pour the egg mixture into a medium-sized saucepan and cook over medium-high heat until the mixture thickens and small curds form, continuously whisking and scraping the bottom of the pan to keep larger curds from forming, about 5 minutes. Proceed to Step 3.

STORE in an airtight container in the fridge for up to 4 days. To reheat, place in a lightly greased skillet over medium heat for 3 minutes, or until heated through.

NUTRITIONAL INFO (per serving)				
calories	fat	protein	carbs	fiber
194	14g	13g	1g	0.1g

mashed cauliflower

 yield: 6 servings *prep time:* 5 minutes *cook time:* 5 minutes

4 cups chicken broth, homemade (page 320) or store-bought, or vegetable broth

1 head cauliflower, cut into florets

Fine sea salt and ground black pepper

Unsalted butter, sour cream, or cream cheese, for serving (optional; omit for dairy-free)

Fresh thyme leaves, for garnish

1. Set a steamer basket in a 6-quart Instant Pot and pour in the broth. Place the cauliflower florets in the basket.

2. Seal the lid, press Pressure Cook or Manual, and set the timer for 5 minutes. Once finished, turn the valve to venting for a quick release.

3. Drain the liquid. Transfer the steamed cauliflower to a food processor or blender and purée until smooth. Season with salt and pepper to taste.

4. Place in a serving dish and top with butter, cream cheese, and/or sour cream, if desired. Garnish with thyme and freshly ground pepper.

STORE in an airtight container in the fridge for up to a week or in the freezer for up to a month. To reheat, place in a saucepan over medium heat for 3 minutes, or until heated through.

Place the cauliflower in a 6-quart slow cooker and pour in enough broth to completely cover the cauliflower. Cover and cook on high for 2 to 3 hours, until the cauliflower is tender. Proceed to Step 3.

NUTRITIONAL INFO (per serving)				
calories	fat	protein	carbs	fiber
57	1g	9g	5g	2g

hard-boiled eggs

   yield: 12 servings *prep time:* 3 minutes *cook time:* 5 minutes

12 large eggs

1. Place the eggs in a 6-quart Instant Pot and pour in 1½ cups of hot water. Seal the lid, press Pressure Cook or Manual, and set the timer for 5 minutes. Once finished, turn the valve to venting for a quick release, then remove the lid.

2. Remove the eggs from the Instant Pot and rinse under cold running water until chilled. Peel and eat, or use as desired.

STORE in the fridge, unpeeled, for up to a week. Peel just before using.

 *Place the eggs in a 6-quart slow cooker. Pour enough water into the slow cooker to cover the eggs. Cover with the lid and cook on low for 3½ hours, then remove the eggs from the slow cooker and rinse under cold running water until chilled. Peel and eat, or use as desired.*

NUTRITIONAL INFO (per serving)				
calories	fat	protein	carbs	fiber
77	5g	6g	0.5g	0g

mama maria's marinara sauce

option

yield: 8 cups (10 servings) *prep time:* 4 minutes *cook time:* 15 minutes

I have many versions of this sauce; I'm always tweaking it. This version, developed for the Instant Pot, is my new favorite! It is simple and packed with delicious flavor.

2 tablespoons unsalted butter (or coconut oil for dairy-free)

1 medium onion, diced

1½ teaspoons minced garlic

6 cups crushed tomatoes

1 (6-ounce) can tomato paste

1 tablespoon Swerve confectioners'-style sweetener or equivalent amount of liquid or powdered sweetener (see page 39)

1 tablespoon coconut vinegar or balsamic vinegar

2 bay leaves

1 tablespoon dried basil leaves

1½ teaspoons dried oregano leaves

1 teaspoon fine sea salt

½ teaspoon ground black pepper

1. Place the butter in a 6-quart Instant Pot and press Sauté. Once melted, add the onion and garlic and cook, stirring, until the onion is soft, about 5 minutes. Press Cancel to stop the Sauté.

2. Add the tomatoes, tomato paste, sweetener, vinegar, herbs, salt, and pepper to the Instant Pot. Stir well to combine.

3. Seal the lid, press Pressure Cook or Manual, and set the timer for 10 minutes. Once finished, turn the valve to venting for a quick release.

4. Remove the lid, stir the sauce, and discard the bay leaves. Season with additional salt to taste. Enjoy the marinara over your favorite keto pasta, or use it in one of my recipes!

Complete Step 1 using a large skillet over medium-high heat to sauté the onion and garlic. Transfer the mixture to a 4-quart or larger slow cooker. Add the tomatoes, tomato paste, sweetener, vinegar, herbs, salt, and pepper and stir well to combine. Cover and cook on low for 8 hours. Proceed to Step 4.

STORE in an airtight container in the fridge for up to 5 days or in the freezer for up to a month. To reheat, place the sauce (defrosted first, if frozen) in a saucepan over medium heat for 5 minutes, or until heated through.

NUTRITIONAL INFO (per serving)				
calories	fat	protein	carbs	fiber
75	3g	2g	10g	3g

allergen index

recipe index

Breakfast

Pumpkin Coffee Cake
44

Blueberry Cereal
46

Crustless Quiche Lorraine
48

Granola
50

Easy Baked Eggs
52

Pumpkin Pie Breakfast Pudding
54

Appetizers & Side Dishes

Buffalo Wings with Blue Cheese Dressing
58

Crab Rangoon Dip
60

Pizza Hit Breadsticks
62

Pizza Dip
64

Tender Mexican Spice Wings
66

Crab-Stuffed Mushrooms
68

Mexican Meatballs
70

Gyro Mushrooms
72

Ham & Cauliflower au Gratin
74

French Onion Casserole
76

Sesame Broccoli
78

Buttery Mushrooms
79

Alfredo Veggies
80

Sweet 'n' Sour Eggplant
82

Nutty "Noodles"
84

Soups & Stews

Reuben Soup
88

Cream of Asparagus Soup
90

Chicken "Noodle" Soup
92

New England Clam Chowder
94

Pumpkin Chili
96

Italian Chicken Chili
98

Tomato Basil Parmesan Soup
100

102
Provolone
Chicken Soup

104
Cioppino

106
Seafood Chowder

108
Broccoli & Brie
Soup

110
Curry Beef Stew

112
Spicy Chicken
Stew

114
African "Nut"
Stew

116
Venison Stew

118
French Onion
Soup

120
Creamy Chicken &
Tomato Soup

122
Belgian Booyah

124
Supreme Pizza
Soup

126
Green Borscht

128
Egg Roll Soup

130
Chicken Cordon
Bleu Soup

132
Immune-Boosting
Soup

134
Mexican Beef
Soup

136
Broccoli Cheddar
Soup

138
Cheesy Bacon
Noodle Soup

140
Chicken &
Asparagus Red
Curry Soup

142
Lasagna Soup

Beef & Lamb

146
Santa Fe Meatloaf

148
Mocha Pot Roast

150
Lamb Vindaloo

152
Mushroom
& Swiss Mini
Meatloaves

154
Mama Maria's
Italian Meatballs

156
Swedish Meatballs

158
Ranch Mini
Meatloaves

160
BBQ Short Ribs

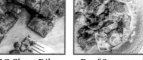

162
Beef Stroganoff

164
Corned Beef &
Cabbage

166
Smoky BBQ
Brisket

168
Blue Cheese Steak
Roll-Ups

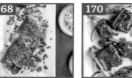
170
Asian Orange
Short Ribs

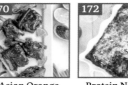
172
Protein Noodle
Lasagnas

174
Korean Rib Wraps

176
Spaghetti
Bolognese

178
Barbacoa

180
Chili Cheese Dog
Casserole

182
Unagi Ribs

Pork

186
Pork Lettuce Cups

188
Smoky Baby Back Ribs

190
Perfect BBQ Pulled Pork

192
Melt-in-Your-Mouth Pork Belly

194
Sweet 'n' Sour Pork

196
Five-Ingredient Pork Roast

198
Stuffed Pork Tenderloin

200
Pot Roast Pork

202
Sausage Fajita Bowls

204
Sweet 'n' Sour Ribs

206
Pot Sticker Bowls

208
Toscana Paglia e Fieno

210
Brats with Onion Gravy

212
Amazing Asian-Inspired Pulled Pork

Poultry

216
Chicken Adobo

218
Mama Maria's Italian Chicken Cupcakes

220
Greek Chicken

222
Roast Chicken

224
Buffalo Chicken Lettuce Wraps

226
Sesame Chicken

228
BBQ Chicken & "Cornbread" Casserole

230
Hot Chicken Caesar Sandwiches

232
Easy Reuben Chicken

234
Chicken Asparagus Rolls

236
Cornish Game Hens

238
Chicken Broccoli Casserole

240
Chicken with Mushroom Cream Sauce

242
Chicken Piccata

244
Chicken & Bacon Lasagna Roll-Ups

246
Chicken Cacciatore

248
Chicken Cordon Bleu

250
Chicken Fajita Bowls

252
Chicken Parmigiana

Fish & Seafood

256
Crab-Stuffed Avocados

258
Italian Salmon

260
Easy Greek Fish

262
Gumbo

264
Shrimp Scampi

266
Garlicky Tuna Casserole

268
Lemony Fish with Asparagus

270

Simple Salmon
Packets

272

BBQ Shrimp

274

Pesto Fish Packets

276

Classic Tuna
Hotdish

278

White Fish
Poached in Garlic
Cream Sauce

280

Jambalaya

Sweet Endings & Drinks

284

Crème Brûlée

286

Lemon Ricotta
Torte

288

Chocolate Fondue

290

Deconstructed
Tiramisu

292

Cinnamon Roll
Cheesecake

294

Chocolate Custard

296

Pumpkin Pie
Spiced Pots
de Crème

298

Bread Pudding

300

Flourless
Chocolate Tortes

302

Glazed Pumpkin
Bundt Cake

304

Chocolate Almond
Fudge

306

Upside-Down
Maple Bacon
Mini Cheesecakes

308

Maple-Glazed
Zucchini
Bundt Cake

310

Gingerbread
Café au Lait

312

Hot Chocolate

313

Homemade Chai

314

Ginger Ale

316

Homemade
Root Beer

Basics

320

Healing
Bone Broth

322

Homemade
Ricotta

324

Roasted Garlic

326

Low-Carb
Loaf Bread

328

Keto "Rice"

330

Mashed
Cauliflower

331

Hard-Boiled Eggs

332

Mama Maria's
Marinara Sauce

general index